MINISTERS' WIVES

Ministers' Wives

WILLIAM DOUGLAS

HARPER & ROW, PUBLISHERS

New York

Contents

Preface

Authors often end a preface with words like these: "Finally, may I express appreciation to my wife. . . ." May I *begin* with expression of gratitude to Alice, with whom I have conducted research of the most basic type for more than twelve years on what it is like to be a minister's wife. She has been "a mate who not only will grace your parsonage but be a co-worker in, and an ornament to your holy calling," but has fortunately *not* fitted the rest of Charles Smith's description of the ideal clergy wife: "a good, plain-looking wife whom you like, and about whom you can think with affection but without passion."[1] (No plainness, but much passion, here!) She has supplied critical judgment, as well as support and encouragement, throughout the extended six-and-a-half-year gestation period of this manuscript. And when emergency help of a secretarial, research, or administrative assistant type has been called for, she has been the irreplaceable pinch-hitter able and willing to fill in at any position—often quite unrelated to her own training as schoolteacher and librarian. Most basic, she has been a good wife, and mother to our children, now six and five years of age.

Experience provides the context for interpretation. I have learned about the covenant relationship between a congregation and a minister and his family through a series of rewarding pastorates. Immediately after graduation from Yale Divinity School, I was welcomed to Solon, Ohio by the twenty people who had organized the Pioneer Memorial Church (Presbyterian and Disciples of Christ). For four years we discovered together the

meaning of Christian discipleship, witness, and service in our time
and place. They taught me what the Church was like, in an inter-
racial fellowship in which men outnumbered women, youth
outnumbered oldsters, and all had a meaningful part. In the
manner of the Iona Community, we rebuilt an abandoned his-
toric structure with our own hands, and a community of faith with
our lives.

Since coming to the Boston area for doctoral study at Harvard
University (1955-57), I have served as interim minister of a suc-
cession of parishes, in inner-city Union Square, Somerville; suburban Natick; mill-town Westerly, Rhode Island; blue-collar Hyde
Park; and Back Bay Boston. In all of these interim pastorates,
Alice was the minister's wife, and we both benefited from the
love and support extended to us during our period of work and
worship together. We now feel a real part of many church families.
In recent summers, we have had the rare privilege of being part
of the community of Cuttyhunk Island, Mass., a sport fishing
center near Martha's Vineyard. As the pastor of the only church
on an island with a winter population of about twenty and summer population of about three hundred there have been many interesting experiences. Serving as the Presbyterian pastor of the
Union Methodist Church, which covers all denominations including Roman Catholic, Christian Science, and Unitarian in its active
constituency, has been an experiment in ecumenical Christianity—
as has the regular 8 A.M. service of Holy Communion according to
the Book of Common Prayer, with Episcopal clergy as celebrants.

It is out of such a background that I have conducted research
on ministers' wives. Certainly my status and experience as an
ordained minister of the United Presbyterian Church in the
U. S. A. affects the way in which I understand and interpret
issues. I hope, however, that I write not as a Presbyterian, but
as an ecumenical Christian. One of the great rewards of this research has been that of coming to know and respect groups within
Evangelical and Pentecostal Protestantism with which I had
previously had limited contact, as well as other groups such as
the Southern Baptist Convention and the Lutheran Church-

Missouri Synod, which are not members of the National Council of Churches. In all instances, I found that the stereotypes I had developed, on the basis of differentness and separatism, were shattered. This, in fact, is the logical point at which to express gratitude for the beyond-the-line-of-duty co-operation of the executives of all the 37 denominations which participated in this study. Without their support, as well as that of the approximately 6,000 ministers' wives who completed questionnaires, research would not have been possible.

This book is written, then, by a married minister. But it is also written by a psychologist, whose professional orientation is that of the psychology of personality and social psychology. In fact, my personal interest in research on ministers' wives was a result of my doctoral dissertation with Gordon W. Allport, Professor of Psychology at Harvard University, on *Predicting Ministerial Effectiveness.* For, as I explored the relationship of the results of psychological tests such as the Rorschach to the ministerial effectiveness of seventy Episcopal clergy (as judged by their superiors, their laity, and themselves) it became increasingly clear that effectiveness was both compound and relational, as well as developing over time. (These studies continue, with the collection of longitudinal case material, and will be published in book form at a later date, under the tentative title of *Patterns of Ministry.*) Part of the mix of ministerial effectiveness is a man's marriage, and therefore a recommendation of my 1957 dissertation was that research such as that reported on in this book be conducted.

Research depends on a community of shared values. In this case, two communities and two value systems are involved: the Christian faith and social science. My own judgment on the interaction of these communities has been presented in other contexts.[2] In essence, I believe that truth is unitary, but perspectives on truth diverge and often conflict. Therefore, to seek pure objectivity, naked fact stripped of interpretation, is both illusory and dangerous. What is required, rather, is calibrated subjectivity, which involves discovering how you "read" under varying circum-

stances, and how your assumptions influence your conclusions—
and even your perceptions. Because of selective assumptions and
distorting biases, as well as limited competence, adequate research demands the collaboration of those with varying perspectives. In this regard, I have been fortunate, so much so that
selecting names for acknowledgment is a matter of real anxiety
and potential guilt. So many have assisted in this research, in so
many ways at so many points, that any list of people is necessarily incomplete.

Without the Lilly Endowment, and its late Director for Religion, G. Harold Duling, this project could never have been
undertaken. Whenever needed, the Endowment and Mr. Duling
provided support and guidance, but at no point was there any
attempt to control research or influence its results. Therefore,
when I state that I alone am responsible for positions taken,
which do not necessarily reflect the views of the Lilly Endowment, its staff or directors, this is an expression of gratitude for
freedom and trust, as well as a definition of accountability. Likewise, Dean Walter Muelder and my other colleagues and friends
in the Boston University School of Theology, Professors Paul
Johnson, Donald Maynard, and Herbert Stotts, assisted at many
points. It was in Professor Johnson's Hyannis, Massachusetts home
that the initial research proposal was developed. Professor Stotts,
as associate director during the first year of the project, established sampling and data analysis procedures. And throughout
research, Professors John Alman and Sylvia Fleisch, and their
associates in the Boston University Computation Center, provided
wisdom and equipment to make machine data analysis both possible and effective.

Key people throughout have been the members of the Interdenominational Advisory Committee to the project. Present at all
four meetings of the committee—Boston, Mass. (1960, amidst
Boston's record March blizzard), Berkeley, Cal. (1961), Louisville, Ky. (1962), and Boston, Mass. (1963)—were Mr. Duling
of the Lilly Endowment; Martha (Mrs. Hugh) Miller, Baptist
minister's wife; Dr. William Oglesby of Union Theological Semi-

nary, Richmond, Va.; and Dr. Jesse Ziegler, associate director of
the American Association of Theological Schools. Attending two
or three meetings were: Dr. Wallace Denton (Southern Baptist,
then in a Christian Counseling Center, now at Purdue University);
Virginia (Mrs. David) Held, a United Church of Christ minister's
wife; Virginia (Mrs. Daniel) Walker, a Methodist minister's wife;
and Dr. Louise Foreman Blount, Director of Women's Activities
in the Southern Baptist Theological Seminary, Louisville, Ky.
Also serving on the Advisory Committee were: Betty (Mrs.
Evans) Crawford, wife of the Dean of the Chapel of Howard
University; Dr. Margaret Mead, anthropologist, of the American
Museum of Natural History; Gladys (Mrs. Stanley) Sandberg,
wife of a pastor in the Lutheran Church in America; Cynthia
(Mrs. Theodore) Wedel, Episcopal clergyman's wife, psycholo-
gist, and officer of the National Council of Churches; and Susie
(Mrs. R. V.) Umphenour, wife of an Assemblies of God pastor.
Dr. Blount, Professor Russell Becker of Yale Divinity School, and
Professor John Vayhinger (then of Garrett Biblical Institute) as-
sisted in the 1962-63 Pilot Program for Theology Couples, an experiment in role orientation of seminarians' wives.

At the Berkeley, Cal., meeting in which preliminary drafts of
the MW-5 questionnaire were reviewed and decisions on necessary revisions made, Dr. Charles Glock of the Survey Research
Center of the University of California and Dr. Roy Fairchild of
the San Francisco Theological Seminary provided just the type of
critical appraisal necessary. Esther (Mrs. James) Pike, wife of the
Episcopal Bishop of California, raised basic questions of wording
and content. Similarly, in establishment of procedures of data
analysis and interpretation, Dr. Urie Bronfonbrenner, Dr. Isidor
Chein, Dr. John Harding, Dr. Martin Hoffman, and Dr. Earl
Loomis made key suggestions, during a consultation on research
design at Cornell University in the summer of 1961. Throughout
the project, Dr. Margaret Mead, Professors Gordon Allport and
Talcott Parsons of Harvard University, and Dr. Samuel Klausner
(then of the Bureau of Applied Social Research of Columbia University) provided theoretical criticism of the type which was most

useful. Research assistants and associates at various stages of the project included: Ray Martin, Gene McMahon, Albert Sherring, Ruth Aisenberg, Teresita Tiansay, Michal Frank, Waller Wiser, Robert Ayling, and Jane Anne Moore. Functioning as co-ordinator of research assistants, as well as office manager and personal secretary, during the most critical phases of data collection was Lou (Mrs. Jerry) Fix, without whom the project could never have been completed. I am grateful, too, to my other secretaries over the course of the past six and a half years: Harlene Swanson, Jane Carter, Marie Treese, Noreen Oleksak, and Sarah Stamey.

My deepest indebtedness, however, is to the thousands of ministers' wives who supplied the information of which I am basically the recording and transmitting agent. In particular, the members of the Boston Panel, which met at various points of the project when issues were being defined or questionnaires constructed, deserve recognition. Members of group interviews held in Cleveland, Topeka, Denver, San Francisco, Portland, and Seattle also contributed in many ways. I am grateful, too, to authors of books, articles, dissertations, etc., who gave me permission to quote from their writings. But, most of all, my thanks go to "Martha Bond" and the other ministers' wives whose case material, from questionnaires, interviews, letters, and diaries provide the major substance of this book. Though their names were changed, everyone who was asked gave permission to be quoted, and no one requested that her statements be changed in any way. This is honesty, trust, and the desire to help others of the highest order.

Now the book is done, and ready for its readers. As an author, I feel toward this manuscript as a parent feels when his child is ready to leave home: he is not adequate for all he must face, and you wish you could take time to develop him further. But the time has come, and you must let him go. I turn now to work on the sequel to this book, *Memo to a Young Minister's Wife: Guidelines for Effective Decision-Making.* Gestation of this second book should not take as long as for this one. Nor should development occur under as varied circumstances; for the bulk of this manuscript was written during summers on Cuttyhunk Island, Massachusetts and on sabbatical leave in Kyoto, Japan in 1963-64, but portions were composed in Honolulu, Hong Kong, New Delhi, Jerusalem, Beirut, Rome, and London. Environmentalists may speculate, too, on the influence of Stokowski's interpretation of Beethoven's nine symphonies, the background music during much of the writing, with interludes of Bach, Mozart, and Copland.

Now the drama begins. Ministers' wives—in their flesh and blood humanity and rich variety—will appear. Masks will be dropped, and stereotypes challenged.

WILLIAM DOUGLAS

Cuttyhunk, Massachusetts
Summer, 1965

MINISTERS' WIVES

CHAPTER 1

Introduction

NOTHING IS MORE disturbing to most young ministers' wives than
the stereotypes of them presented in popular literature and maintained in the minds of so much of the general population. As
William James imagined a crab might feel when called a crus-
tacean, they too want to assert: "I am not a member of a class or
category. I am myself—myself alone!" Before presenting research
data indicating something of the *individuality* of ministers' wives,
it is necessary, however, to consider the *stereotypes.* For these
cultural role models, with specific variations related to particular
church and community settings, form the expectations to which
women must respond. Predominant among the influences that
shape and preserve existing stereotypes is the literature produced
for the guidance of ministers' wives.

Some Historical Perspectives

As early as 1832, a book was published in England by an
anonymous author entitled *Hints for a Clergyman's Wife; or,
Female Parochial Duties.*[1] As the writer indicated, her

only object in publishing this volume is the hope that it may, under
God's blessing, prove of some little utility to those Christian females
who are anxious to become true yoke-fellows to their husbands, in the
faithful discharge of the high office of the Christian Ministry.[2]

After discussion of "the duties incumbent upon a clergyman's
wife," "her personal character," "the right employment of influence," "consistency in her daily conduct," "habitual self-

examination," and "her active exertions among the poor," the
author concludes that the goal of a minister's wife (hereafter
referred to as MW) should always be

the advancement of her husband's ministry, the salvation of the souls
committed to her pastoral charge, and the alleviation of their temporal
wants. Let her feel, that on becoming a clergyman's wife she has, as
it were, wedded herself to her husband's parish, and to the best interests of his flock. . . . Happy, thrice happy, the Christian female,
who is permitted to consecrate her life, her time, and her talents to
the service of her God and Saviour! He will not forget her work and
labor of love. She shall receive a crown of glory.

In this 1832 portrait, therefore, to be a MW necessarily meant
to "renounce the world, and the things of the world, its fashions,
its amusements, its pursuits. . . ." It meant calling "but a very
small portion of her time her own . . ." since "every moment of
the day must have its appropriate employment." Motivating such
active service was the conviction of "her Saviour's love . . . in having intrusted to her care some portion of the lambs of his flock,
to train and nurture for His heavenly fold," and the realization
that her "peculiar situation gives her much influence over the
parish in which she resides," due both to her husband's position
and to "her own individual character and exertions."

For this anonymous author stresses not only the MW's *performance*, but also the *quality* of her life—the two basic dimensions
of any role definition.[3] Realizing that "the minister's family will
ever be regarded as the model upon which the families of the
parish are to be framed," the MW will "converse with her own
heart, and inquire into the state of her individual progress
heavenward." She will investigate her own acceptance of the
truths she is seeking to communicate to others, her motives, the
employment of her time, and her "feelings connected with the
success of her work."

But even good character is not enough, if a MW fails to "adopt
every method to open [the hearts of her husband's people] for the
reception of those divine truths which he is . . . delivering from
the pulpit." If they reject her ministries, then she must "mildly
but firmly represent to them the awful guilt and folly of their

conduct as ungrateful to their Heavenly Father . . . destroying every hope of present happiness and bringing eternal ruin upon their immortal souls." The focus of her "yoke-fellowship" is, therefore, *evangelistic*, but it has important *educational* and *social service* dimensions as well.

To be a MW in 1832 England involved being a parish visitor, with particular concern for the poor and the sick. Guidance is given regarding forms on which she may record her calls systematically, and a type of zone plan by which she may plan her visitation according to geographic regions. To assist the poor in self-improvement, with purchase of a Bible as the first step, a parsonage savings bank may be established. In addition, the MW should develop a used clothing salesroom, an employment agency (especially for servant girls), and a program of vocational education for those lacking in adequate skills.

Moreover, in her visits the nineteenth-century MW may have to act as the equivalent of the modern visiting nurse. This will involve determining the nature of the illness, so that she may "advise the parish doctor to be sent for in emergencies; while in ordinary cases a little experience and observation will enable her to prescribe simple and effectual remedies." If the patient does not recover, then the time of death can be used as an occasion for "seasons of profitable instruction to all parties." (Whether or not this includes the deceased is not made clear.)

Since being co-pastor, social worker, employment agent, and visiting nurse may not occupy all her time, the 1832 MW is also reminded of her responsibilities in education, both general and religious, especially of "the females among her husband's flock." Here, as in her parish visitation, the main goal is

to make them sensible of their lost condition as "children of wrath," their need of a Saviour to cleanse them from their sins and of the Holy Spirit to renew their nature, instruct their hearts, and fit them for heaven.

If possible, the MW should be Sunday-School superintendent, but in any case she must meet regularly with the young people to examine and encourage them, and have responsibility for the "weekly schools," the parish nursery, and the "adult school." If she feels "discouraged . . . by the apparent difficulty of giving *individual* instruction to all who have a claim upon her attention and interest," then she can organize neighborhood study groups or "cottage meetings." To assist these groups, she should establish a parish library, with proper catalog and circulation procedures. Thus the evangelist–social worker–nurse–educator reminds herself that "diligent and regular employment of time tends much to the encouragement of religion and good order. Where idleness is once allowed to creep in, every vice and evil follows in its train."

Such were the all-inclusive duties and Puritan ethic[4] urged on the English MW in 1832. No wonder, perhaps, that the "happy, thrice happy" authoress chose to remain anonymous! Catherine L. Adams showed somewhat more sympathy for American MWs in 1835, as she discussed *Daily Duties—Inculcated in a Series of Letters Addressed to the Wife of a Clergyman.* Though concerned with the "duties devolving upon the wife of a minister" and "the individual traits of character requisite," she also kept in mind

the inexperienced female who is introduced, from a circle of confiding friends, to a broad and extended field of labor, where it is utterly impossible, in the nature of things, that any one course of conduct, however judicious, should be acceptable to all.[5]

Thus it is probably significant that the first letter concerns meekness and humility ("at the head of requisites for usefulness in a minister's wife"), while the last two letters discuss quiet endurance and prayer.

For, as Mrs. Adams recognized and made quite clear, there is the problem of not sacrificing independence in the desire to gratify a congregation, knowing that

it is a hopeless task to meet in all things the approbation of a people, who feel themselves at liberty to dictate as to the course which a minister's wife shall pursue. The only way in which a woman will succeed in being useful is by following the dictates of conscience.

Moreover, when one faces the nature of the task there comes the realization that no one is sufficient for these duties, and that resources beyond oneself are necessary, through prayer. With this Margaret Blackburn, writing in 1898 on *Things a Pastor's Wife Can Do, by One of Them*, agreed, adding: "It sometimes occurs that the very best thing a pastor's wife can do is to say 'No.' Always refuse to be pressed into the mold of some former pastor's wife."[6]

Not all MWs reported themselves as "thrice happy" in the life, either—even in the nineteenth century. Thus H. M. Eaton, writing in 1851 on *The Itinerant's Wife*,[7] spoke of the trials connected with the frequent moves of the American Methodist minister, of the poor housing, the faultfinders, and the generally impossible combination of expectations. Harriet Angell Anthony, writing to her parents about what it meant to her to be "The Parson's Wife" in nineteenth-century Maine, said she loved the life, but:

It is drive, drive, drive, with callers and meetings and a vain attempt to sandwich in reading, letter writing, or anything else. A stormy day which let me finish cleaning out a closet seemed a real blessing. . . . I sometimes long for a desert isle; I get so tired of seeing people and talking to people.[8]

There was a constant financial struggle, too, with the salary from the church three months behind at one point, and family finances often down to a few cents due to this sort of delay.

Mrs. Henry Ward Beecher in 1859 also described how the combination of financial hardships and an impossible combination of duties could make the life of a nineteenth-century MW very difficult. Her book, published at first anonymously, had the goal of helping

leading laymen to perceive how easily, by kindness, considerateness, and prompt payments they could strengthen their Pastor's hands, or, on the contrary, paralyze all his efforts and energy by negligence, thoughtlessness, and selfishness.[9]

In a similar vein, though almost a century later, Margaret Watt concluded *The History of the Parson's Wife* ("the child of the Reformation") with these observations:

She has had very little thanks for all the unpaid work she has done through the course of five centuries. . . . There was a time . . . when life flowed smoothly in spacious rectories where there were plenty of servants. . . . But those days are long past and gone. . . . The parson's wife may not expect an atmosphere of peace and leisure but . . . she may continue in the ways of unselfconscious goodness.[10]

Sometimes, indeed, the life of the MW has been a desperate struggle. Harriot Boynton Thompson's "Letters 1842-1844" make this, as well as the high spirit of dedication and the great abilities of MWs, abundantly clear. Writing on July 11, 1844, from a missionary home in the Iowa Territory, this educated young woman from Boston described her life as follows:

We live in a cabin 18 feet square on the outside . . . have for all household purposes a room between 16 and 17 feet square. There is a loft above with a ladder of 4 steps to get up to it. . . . It has rained almost constantly for 10 weeks, and as our roof is so loose that hogsheads of water come in when the wind blows hard, I have been fully employed, when I could be, in trying to keep our clothing dry, and Mr. Thompson's library from being utterly spoiled. . . . We have been obliged to "endure hardness" of many kinds, which I hope will work for our spiritual good, though I have doubted sometimes. . . . I have thought we were exposing ourselves more than is consistent with prudence. We have comparatively few comforts and almost no conveniences, and I think I have done harder and dirtier work than much of the hired help in Boston. . . . I have often thought it would do all complaining Christians good to live a few months in our cabin and to be situated in all respects as we are. Still we hope it will not be in vain. . . . Common coarse clothing is all that is needed. . . . We need something of the kind to change our water so that we can get it down.[11]

Such quotations from nineteenth-century sources indicate that the situation of MWs has changed in many ways during the past century, but that the basic expectations held concerning them by church and society have remained remarkably consistent. Certainly few modern MWs have a housing situation quite as bad as Mrs. Thompson's or a financial struggle as severe as that of Mrs. Anthony or the Methodist itinerant preacher's wife. Objective circumstances have greatly improved, despite the minority of MWs who still must cope with most difficult conditions and for whom (like the poor in America) the general improvement may make little difference.

Changes have taken place, too, with regard to making parishioners "sensible of their lost condition as 'children of wrath'" in the form recommended by the anonymous authoress in 1832. Also, not many contemporary MWs would accept such a tremendous range of duties—with the assumption that one should possess all the requisite abilities, and the almost compulsive activism required to perform them. In any case, increased professional specialization over the past century now makes it unnecessary for most MWs (except perhaps in isolated rural areas, or inner-city areas lacking in social services) to serve as social worker, nurse, and educator. And, as professional specialization affects even the ministry, MWs are increasingly content to leave even the task of the evangelist to their husbands, or to other ministers "specializing in evangelism."

Much that is presented in the nineteenth-century literature for MWs appears, therefore, irrelevant and out of date. Yet in feeling tone and the dynamics of seeking to adjust ideals to realities (and vice versa) many sections of these books appear surprisingly contemporary. For like the anonymous authoress of 1832, many modern MWs feel called by God to be "true yoke-fellows to their husbands, in the faithful discharge of the high office of the Christian Ministry." But on a number of occasions they are forced to realize, with Mrs. Adams, that "it is utterly impossible, in the nature of things, that any one course of conduct, however judicious, should be acceptable to all," and to do their best through "following the dictates of conscience." With Mrs. Blackburn, they have had to learn to "say No" and to "refuse to be pressed into the mold of some former pastor's wife." With Mrs. Anthony, they often long to "get away from it all," at the same time as they yearn for real friends, with whom they can be themselves.

Contemporary Portraits of "the Ideal MW"

Comparison of the 1832 volume with those published in the last twenty years for the guidance of MWs reveals interesting similarities and differences.[12] As already mentioned, contemporary MWs do not generally have to assume such diffuse responsibilities as did nineteenth-century MWs in communities lacking social services and with few educated people. They are not "mothers" of extended families (parishes) in quite the same sense as in pre-industrial England or America. As the clergyman has ceased to be really "the Parson" (the outstanding person of the community) so has his wife declined in general social status and leadership.[13] Yet despite all these differences, despite the whole process of historical and cultural change, the general role conception transmitted and reinforced by the literature remains much the same.

First of all, contemporary portraits agree, "the ideal MW" must be a *good wife* to her husband. This involves accepting him as a person, with all his weaknesses as well as strengths. But it also means accepting his *career*, realizing that she has married not only a man, but in a sense, the Church. She has chosen, whether she realized it or not, a way of life as well as a marriage-mate. This way of life involves her husband's belonging to the congregation as well as to her and the children. If she fails to accept and respect her husband's complete dedication to his ministry, then jealousy and resentment will inevitably arise.

But—the authors of the guidebooks continue—acceptance of him and of his career is not enough. She must actively encourage and support him, praising him in his triumphs, comforting him in his failures and sorrows. On occasion, constructive criticism ("the truth in love") may be necessary. But most important, she will demonstrate that she believes in him, trusts in him, and confides in him. She will make their home a refuge to which he may retreat for renewal and refreshment. She will respect and protect his need for solitude and defend him against distractions and interruptions. Through regular personal and family devotions, as well as study and service, she will seek to grow with her husband in spiritual usefulness and power.

Consistent emphasis is laid, too, on her responsibilities as hostess of a parsonage with doors open to all, where she is able to make everyone feel at ease. As she must come to accept that her husband is shared property, so must she adjust to this element of parsonage living, with patience, charity, and forbearance. Authors stress the necessity of being an efficient and resourceful home executive, who can make the most of the least, proportion time and finances among many competing demands, and train and care for her children—often without her husband's assistance. She will need to serve as buffer between the children and the demands on them of church and community, and on occasion she may have to put home responsibilities before church activities. For her first duty is to be a good wife and mother.

Yet, as all her guides make clear, a MW is expected to be more than just her husband's helpmate and gracious hostess. She is also urged to be a dedicated Christian woman who feels a call to service, loving the Church and becoming an instrument of service in it. She is to set an example for others in church attendance and participation, in spiritual discernment, and in radiant, contagious faith. Though an educated and competent leader in her own right, she will concentrate on training others for leadership, pinch-hitting in emergencies and serving as a general resource person. She may, if local tradition encourages it, call on the bereaved, the sick, and newcomers to the community. She joins few nonchurch community activities, so that she does not neglect her basic duties in home and church. However, she is aware of her representative role in the community, since others will judge her husband's church and indeed the Christian faith itself in terms of what they see in her.

For, as her mentors emphasize, what a MW *is* as a person is at least as important as what she *does* as homemaker and church worker. In general, this "uncrowned queen of the parish" is urged to follow the golden mean. She is to be attractive but not over-dressed, poised but not oversophisticated. She is to be educated and well-informed, but not lacking in common sense or the common touch; sympathetic and concerned, but not overly sentimental; radiating peace and serenity, but brimming with contagious energy and enthusiasm.

These personal qualities, it is indicated, make a MW a valued counselor of others; her own maturity and faith make it unnecessary for her to tell others her own troubles. She loves people and

gets along well with them because of her friendliness, gracious-
ness, sincerity, and adaptability. She knows how to handle criticism with her tact and keen sense of humor. She is not jealous of
others, or ever shocked, but always wise and humble. In all these
ways she becomes more and more of a "central pivot, guiding,
advising, encouraging, and tirelessly laboring."

Confronted with such an overpowering multiple ideal, it is
scant wonder that many young women who have just married
ministers wonder what they have got into. Within the last few
years, however, significant changes in the literature directed to
MWs have occurred, indicating that there may indeed be a "New
Look in Preachers' Wives" as Halford Luccock (alias Simeon
Stylites) prophesied in 1955.[14] For the old models described by
Luccock—"the solemn saint . . . whose greatest thrill was to play
the piano in prayer meeting," "the wifely pastor's assistant . . .
Giant Economy Size, getting two workers for one salary," and
"the protecting mother model . . . keeping her beloved from taking any risk, sheltering him from all danger and undue exertion"
—do appear to be "passing out of production and becoming, by
the grace of God, obsolete." No longer is a MW "shown one
model and told that she had better conform—or else. Lincoln
freed the slaves, and time and good sense are bringing freedom
to the preacher's wife to be herself."

This, indeed, has been one difficulty with much of the literature produced by and for MWs—that it fails to take account of
the *specificity* of woman, husband, and situation. There is seldom
the realization that what is appropriate for a 57-year-old MW in
a Baptist church of 120 members in a rural area of Mississippi
will probably be most inappropriate for a 32-year-old MW in
an Episcopal church of 600 members in a suburban section of
Connecticut. Though many helpful suggestions are presented in
the literature, summarizing the lore of years of experience by
many women, the attempt to move beyond basic principles to
specific rules usually means the negating of individuality, and
indeed of selfhood. As Denton has observed:

She appears to be playing a character in which the script for the role
has been written by tradition. Some variations on the theme are per-

missible, but they are to be minor ones. She is forced to follow a pre-
determined path of action as a train does, and does not have even the
freedom of being an "automobile."[15]

Recent publications by Denton, Nyberg, and others therefore
give more attention to individual variation, rather than seeking
to construct a "cooky cutter" role model.[16] Further, they attempt
a more reality-grounded approach, which accepts our humanity
and finiteness rather than setting up the MW as a sort of superwoman who can do and be all things—and without strain, always
radiantly! And in recent years there is the increasing realization
that MWs have *rights* as well as duties, joys as well as frustrations, opportunities as well as limitations. In general, then, there
is now a more balanced and discriminating picture of MWs and
—especially in books written by Lutheran and Episcopal MWs—
more emphasis on self-fulfilling opportunities and less on self-
constricting obligations.

However, the very real improvement in the adequacy of
guidance-type literature for young MWs does not necessarily
make the situation easier for the women themselves. For all evidence—including popular periodical articles[17]—would indicate
that the cultural image of a MW tends to remain that of a "poor
thing" with little zip, sparkle, or attractiveness, condemned to a
hard life with few elements of fun or comfort. To be oneself, for
many young MWs (and often older ones as well), frequently
seems to imply rejection of being a MW.[18] For they just don't
want to be dumpy, dowdy, and "holier than thou."

Persistence of a negative cultural image of the MW means,
then, that it is difficult for many young women to co-ordinate
their mental conception of "me" with their mental conception of
"an MW." In the extreme case, this inconsistency can lead to
rebellious, acting-out behavior in the effort to demonstrate,
through cocktail glass, cigarette holder, and low-cut dress, that
"I'm not what you think I am!" More typically, the mental conflict between a nineteenth-century missionary-type role image
and a twentieth-century model-type self-image leads to uncertainty and confusion as to what is appropriate.

Even more basically, however, young MWs appear to experience conflict between the "calm Corinne" ideal presented by much of the literature and the "harried Hannah" reality experienced, especially by young mothers of small children whose husbands serve small churches on low salaries. They believe that they *should* be radiant and serene, riding above the storms of life with a perfectly arranged home and well-behaved children. But they judge themselves as *actually* driven and distraught, in the midst of competing responsibilities, none of which they feel able to perform adequately.

Therefore, even though the *external* pressure of the cultural role model may have lessened, the *internal* pressure and resulting guilt from nonconformity to the self-accepted ideal remain great. In fact, potential conflict and frustration may be greater for MWs today than in earlier periods, since expectations are less consistent and more in flux, often deriving from earlier historical and cultural epochs and therefore quite unrelated to present realities. In particular, there are the effects of the shift of the meaning of the ministry for many engaged in it away from a set-apart calling toward a profession-among-other-professions. With this shift, the specific nature of the ordained (as distinguished from the lay) ministry has become less clear, and there has been increasing criticism of the machinery and self-maintenance preoccupation of the institutional church. These changes affect the expectations and self-concepts of MWs.

MWs are not unique, of course, in having a sense of inability to cope with competing multiple responsibilities; rather, they appear to represent a particular variation on the general theme of the middle-class mother of young children who feels like a trapped housewife, with no meaningful escape. Many of the role conflicts of MWs seem similar, also, to those of wives of other business and professional men—only more so, in terms of the all-inclusiveness of the role, the emphasis on personal example, and the expectation of something like semiprofessional knowledge and competence. For wives of executives or even physicians have much more freedom to be plain Mary Jones (by contrast with "our MW") and are seldom expected to give last-minute talks on business trends or the newest technique in appendectomies.

Research Goals

Considered in terms of cultural history, the ancestry of this research project might be discerned in William Whyte's articles in *Fortune* for October and November 1951, on "Wives of Management" and "Corporation and the Wife."[19] While there had been little or nothing published in periodical form between 1941 and 1950 (or, indeed, in any earlier decade) on wives of business and professional men, Whyte's articles literally opened the floodgates of interest in and discussion of this topic. Thus, between 1951 and 1960, at least twenty-five articles appeared in major American periodicals on the "Wife Problem," "Corporate Cupid," "Wives . . . Net Quick Assets," "Help Your Husband Get Ahead" (and "[ditto] Stay Alive"), etc.[20] There was discussion, too, of wives of artists, doctors, teachers, and politicians as well as ministers.

While these articles were, in one sense, merely another manifestation of the American preoccupation with navel-gazing, especially in the form of catch-phrase self-criticism ("the lonely crowd," "the organization man," "the status seekers," and so on—but never a positive title!), they represented a cultural conflict as well. On the one hand, men in executive positions in business and the professions found it increasingly difficult to separate business from home life; a man was never really away from his work, and everything else must be subordinated to it. But on the other hand, as Pearl Buck observed, "Marriage Is Different Today," in that men now expect from their wives "the kind of companionship which heretofore men have usually expected only from other men." Modern man demands, she says,

a different kind of woman . . . whose mind matches his own in intelligence, curiosity, capacity for growth, interest in life at home and in the world at large . . . he demands that she be herself at full growth, his mate in every sense and perception.[21]

On the surface, there may seem to be no conflict between marital companionship and a woman's fulfilling the corporation's blueprint of an ideal executive's wife: highly adaptable, highly gregarious, accepting that her husband belongs to the corporation. (As will be noted, this might be translated into some congregations' blueprint of an ideal MW.) However, the danger with the "different kind of woman" that Pearl Buck describes is that she does not tend to be content with merely being a means to corporate ends. To be "a good listener, sounding board, refueling station, social operator, and good, low-key stabilizer—attractive, but not too good or outstanding" somehow doesn't challenge the best in a person, or give a motive for living. And the "new kind of woman" is concerned with challenge and motive, not with being an auxiliary carburetor to her husband's motor—to be adjusted so that *he* will run better.

As women, marriage, and the nature of business and professional life changed there was, then, an increased interest in the wives of business and professional men, including clergymen. In addition, in social science the post-World-War-II period had seen increased attention to role theory and analysis. For these reasons, the time was ripe for study of the role of the MW in terms of both public interest and scientific "tool kit." Moreover, denominational and seminary executives were interested, as were MWs themselves—"We'd like to know what the facts really are." Public interest—scientific tool kit—institutional support—co-operative potential respondents: the only missing ingredient was research funds, and they were supplied in the fall of 1958 by the Lilly Endowment of Indianapolis, Indiana. For out of Lilly-supported research on "The Selection of Clergy" at the Educational Testing Service had come the conviction that MWs represented an important element in the "mix" of ministerial effectiveness.

On January 1, 1959, the Lilly research project "The Minister's Wife" came into formal existence with headquarters at the Boston University School of Theology. As proposed in the fall of 1958, this was to be a three-year pilot project of exploratory research concerning

the status and condition of the wife of the Protestant parish minister in America, with two foci of consideration: (1) effects of husband's vocation on marriage and family life, and (2) effects of marriage and family life on husband's vocational performance.[22]

It soon became clear, however, that to trace such interactions required measures of marriage, family life, and vocational performance not readily obtainable, and that the original purpose—"the determination of the value and possibility of a future full-scale study"—was not realistic. If basic investigation were to be done, it had to be done now.

For these reasons, by the spring of 1959 the goal of research had shifted to more adequate study of a more limited and accessible set of topics.

1. What American Protestantism expects a minister's wife to be and do, including the possible structuring of these expectations in a defined role;

2. The ambiguities and contradictions which exist in this constellation of expectations from a variety of sources, and the resulting conflicts for the woman who must respond to them; and

3. The factors which affect expectations and the response of the minister's wife to them—including a "typology" of ministers' wives, if such exists.

In other words, the study had moved from attempted prediction of outcomes to role analysis. Yet in four successive pretest questionnaires (MW-1, MW-2, MW-3, and MW-4) it became increasingly clear that, at the level of a *mailed* questionnaire, it was difficult to get deeper than a test of the individual's knowledge of *cultural* (vs. personal) role conception, as long as one dealt with *expectations* as such. By the spring of 1960, therefore, the goals of research were redefined once more.

1. A composite portrait of "the wife of the Protestant parish minister in America";

2. Variables which affect expectancy and operational patterns—e.g., denomination, geographic region, age, education, etc.—possibly involving subgroups or "types"; and

3. Predictive indicators, in woman and situation, of "happiness and effectiveness as a minister's wife."

What had been proposed in the fall of 1958 as a foundation-laying pilot project became by spring 1960 a complete-in-itself descriptive study. Concern for prediction of outcomes reappeared, but now in terms of the *interaction* of predictor variables such as denomination and age with criterion variables such as

"happiness and effectiveness as a minister's wife." The main goal
was a composite portrait—which inevitably meant generalizing
from a carefully selected sample. But in addition there was the
hope that knowledge might be gained concerning factors contributing to the "happiness" and "effectiveness" of MWs. By now
it had become clear that there was no such creature as "the MW"
who had "the role." Yet the hope was that *individualized* guidance might be possible if one could trace the influence of background and situational variables.

When the final progress bulletin of the project appeared in the
spring of 1962, as basic data analysis neared completion, there
was therefore this reformulation of the purpose of the project:

. . . to learn more concerning the varying psychosocial situations of
the many different kinds of women married to many different kinds
of minister-husbands, in varying geographic regions, religious traditions, and church-community settings . . . to explore individual differences, and determine those variables which, singly or in interaction,
produce those differences . . . [especially] those factors affecting (1)
wives' involvement in their husbands' vocation, and (2) their own
personal satisfaction and fulfillment as women, wives, and mothers.

In other words, from the fall of 1958 (when the project application was submitted to the Lilly Endowment) to the spring of
1962, there was increasing realization of an irreducible individuality of people and relationships which made it impossible to
discuss meaningfully "the status and condition of the wife of the
Protestant parish minister in America." There were almost as
many statuses and conditions as there were MWs. Moreover, such
global variables as "marriage and family versus vocational performance" or "what American Protestantism expects" did not
prove particularly fruitful. In both cases the area of consideration
was too broad and ambiguous. Rather, the focus—at least in this
study, in the hope that future studies might supplement it—was
on how MWs (not the MW) perceived their own involvements
in their husbands' ministry, and their satisfactions and frustrations in these involvements.

Such a focus leaves many basic questions unanswered. There
was some check on wives' reports through parallel reports by a

subsample of husbands (in intensive interviews and the MMW-1 and MW-7 questionnaires) and through evaluating the "internal consistency" of questionnaires in terms of responses to related items.[23] Nevertheless, the interpretation of research results rests on trust of the respondents' *accuracy* of perceptions as well as their *honesty* in reporting them. We have, in the data from this study, a portrait of the perceptions of a quite representative cross-section of MWs from the major Protestant denominations. But without other parallel research projects we cannot know with any certainty how their perceptions match, or deviate from, those of their husbands, their congregations, and the culture at large. Nor, without other studies, can we establish just how MWs are similar to, or differ from, wives of other business and professional men.

In addition, many of the practical questions to which denominational and seminary executives, as well as MWs themselves, seek answers are precisely those which an exploratory, descriptive study cannot answer. Quite naturally, denominational leaders would like to know "what makes a good MW," with the definition of "good" primarily in terms of high interest and involvement in her husband's work, and keeping him contented so that he doesn't "run around with other women" or otherwise tip the institutional applecart. While this study provides certain leads or clues with regard to possible influence of such variables as education, employment, religious background, and time of marriage on involvement and satisfaction, we are still far from any IBM-atic prediction of "probable success as a MW."

Nor can research results, from this or any study, answer the *should, ought,* or *must* type of question that MWs often raise. It might provide security for a young, inexperienced woman to have a blueprint of correct, acceptable behavior, a kind of combined Emily Post and Dr. Spock which she might consult for a wide range of possible circumstances. Under *O,* she might learn whether or not she "should be officer of a women's group." Under *F* would come guidance regarding "Can I have friends in the local church?" Turning to *P, W,* and *S* she might discover the

answers to "What's the best way to get the parsonage improved?";
"What will people say if I work?"; and "Can I wear shorts to the
supermarket?" Yet no statistical summary of what *most MWs* do
or think with regard to a given issue will ever settle what *I*, as a
particular person in a particular situation, should do or think.
Statistics are not ethics, nor can even the most reliable summary
of the general *is* yield the individual *ought*.

To state such limitations is not, however, to conclude that this
project has been without value (and what director or author
would conclude that?). At the present preliminary state of
knowledge, with the present scientific tool kit, and with the personnel, financial, and time resources available it was necessary to
settle for rough survey rather than detailed mapping. At many
points, quantitative exactitude had to be sacrificed for meaningfulness. Nevertheless, through the co-operation of almost 6,000
MWs, significant advances in understanding have taken place.
Dependable data are now available for the first time on a variety
of significant issues. Landmarks have been established and preliminary measurements made in a previously quite uncharted
area. Perhaps most significant, ranges of variation on defined
variables have been established, so that some advance can be
made beyond stereotypes to individuality—of person, situation,
relationship, and growth process.

Future research concerning MWs and their guidance should
be able to proceed, then, with clearer understanding of the relevant variables and issues. Hopefully, there will be more tolerance
for variation, rather than an effort to establish norms through
tradition, literature, or consensus. General principles will be
sought, rather than rules enforced. In succeeding chapters of this
research report, data regarding MWs will be presented under
such headings as "Involvement and Activity Patterns," "Motivations and Meanings," "Fulfillments and Frustrations," "Ages and
Stages," and "Backgrounds and Situations." The material presented depends on the tabulation and analysis of data by IBM
equipment, with accuracy checks at all stages of the process from
coding to factor analysis, and no results reported unless they

reach at least the .05 level of statistical significance.[24] (If adjectives such as "very," "much," or "great" are used with regard to group differences, these differences would occur less than one time out of a thousand on the basis of chance.)

To make results more accessible to the general reader, however, statistics and other technical considerations have been kept to a minimum, and this may be the first report of large-scale research without a single table in the body of the text. Social scientists should consult first the Technical Appendix and the discussion of predictor variables found in Chapter 6. Even these materials will be too limited, however, for the scholar, who must await future journal articles presenting more detail on methods and findings. The young MW, likewise, who wonders "What do I do about it?" must await the principle-oriented guidance volume being prepared as a sequel to this research report. For the general reader, it is time now to move to consideration of various types of involvement and activity patterns of MWs explored in Chapter 2. The following discussion of research methods may be omitted by those not concerned with the technical aspects of the study.

Research Methods

As in all research, decisions were made in this project regarding (1) the significant questions which need to be asked, (2) of whom, and (3) in what form, so that answers may be valid and reliable. That is, there was a sampling of *issues*—with some included and others omitted, some emphasized and others minimized—as well as a sampling of the total *population* of MWs and *data collection procedures*: in this instance, a broad sampling since both group and personal interviews, both precoded and open-ended questionnaires, both scales and projective techniques, both case-study and multivariate statistical techniques were employed. As in all research on complex social problems, there were many false starts and wrong directions; decisions were sometimes made without being aware of them, or of the underlying bases for judgment. And like all research reports, this one will of necessity oversimplify and rationalize backward the tortuous process by which conclusions were finally reached.

As difficult as any problem was that of deciding which issues were to be explored in the study and which could not be—even though they might be of importance. In the process of making this selection, four major sources were consulted: (1) literature by, for, and/or about MWs, with approximately 125 books and 110 articles annotated and more than 100 other references listed, for a total of close to 350 items consulted; (2) social science literature and scholars, in terms of role theory, marriage and family, business and the professions, church women, personality theory and development, and so on; (3) denominational and seminary executives, with regard to issues of greatest practical concern and current programs oriented toward those issues; and (4) MWs in local churches, through solicited letters, group and personal interviews, and analysis of existing program materials for MWs' groups, conferences, and retreats.

In the process of identifying issues to be surveyed, an annotated bibliography was prepared in tentative form in the summer of 1960 and distributed to seminary and Bible college libraries, for their corrections and additions. All major books and articles were summarized in outline form, and ten major "self-help" books were subjected to "theme analysis" with regard to the "image of the ideal MW" presented. Themes and emphases of the literature were related, then, to those of nineteen denominational executives who had indicated their conceptions of "good" and "problem" MWs, and of about one hundred letters from local MWs on what it "meant to them to be a MW." These letters came in response to requests placed in various denominational pastors' journals (e.g., *Christian Advocate* and *Monday Morning*) and gave the parsonage-porch rather than the headquarters-desk perspective. After a theme analysis of the letters, a summary was prepared of points of agreement and disagreement among literature, executives, and local MWs.

Issues defined in this way were then explored in group inter-

views (each of fifteen to thirty MWs chosen to represent different ages, denominations, and church-community settings) in
Boston, Cleveland, Topeka, Denver, San Francisco, Portland, and
Seattle. In addition, personal "depth" interviews were conducted
with fifteen of these women. And during the process of developing and revising research instruments, the project director spoke
to forty-two groups of MWs and seminarians' wives, in all sections of the United States except the Southwest. Conferences
with social scientists with particular competence regarding issues
under investigation or relevant data collection and analysis procedures, as well as annual meetings of the Interdenominational
Advisory Committee, tested developing theories and methods.

Issues are not items, however. To be researchable, issues such
as "Is the wife behind her husband in his work?" had to be translated into variables such as: degree and kind of involvement,
motivation to take part, scope of responsibility, activities, attitudes toward these activities, felt deprivation as a MW, etc.
These represent some of the dependent or criterion variables
built into Section B of the MW-5 questionnaire. Furthermore,
concepts (what we were "getting at") and indicators (that taken
as evidence of the concepts) were involved in each of these variables, and the nature of the relationship between concept and
indicator is often a tricky business, especially in the reporting of
research results.

For example, when a MW circled no. 3 ("Involved, but no
more than if he were in another vocation") in response to Item
40 on the MW-5 questionnaire ("How would you describe your
degree of involvement?") this was considered as indicating lower
involvement in her husband's ministry than if she circled no. 1
("as a teamworker") or no. 2 ("in a background, supportive
way"). But in order to evaluate what a 1, 2, or 3 response means,
one must be clear as to what such phrases as "no more than,"
"teamworker," and "background, supportive" mean to particular
respondents. Without careful relating of item responses to questionnaire response patterns as a whole, it is easy to misinterpret
specific findings. Also, it is necessary to remember throughout

that many variables (including desire to maintain and enhance a positive self-image) influence what is reported on even an anonymous mailed questionnaire, and that report-reality relationships pose as many problems for the researcher as concept-indicator relationships.

Sampling of issues implies the setting of limits on the potential *range* of results at the point of construction of the research instruments—in this case, the MW-5 questionnaire. Similarly, sampling of people means that the generalizability of results is limited by the respondents' representativeness of the total population from which they were selected. In this study, it was clear from the beginning that limitations of time, finances, and personnel, as well as the nature of church records from which lists of MWs had to be prepared, made a strict probability sample virtually impossible. Rather than attempt a theoretically preferable stratified random sample, the decision was made to construct a 5 per cent systematic sample, with about 8,000 MWs chosen (on an every-twentieth-name basis, after a random start in the denominational list) to represent the total population of about 160,000 wives of Protestant parish ministers.[25]

But the issue immediately arose as to how "Protestant" was to be defined: that is, how wide a group of denominations would be included in the study. And here the decision was made to include as wide a spectrum of Protestantism as possible, and not just the "main-line" denominations, provided that the denomination met these conditions: (1) at least 100,000 members—since these groups would be most apt to have accurate listings of ministers and personnel through whom respondents might be contacted, (2) national in distribution, and (3) an ordained and married clergy, with the majority in full-time church work. (The major source of data on groups was the 1960 edition of the *Yearbook of American Churches*, supplemented by *Religious Bodies in the U. S. A.* and other references on denominational organization and membership.)

On these bases, forty-three Protestant religious groups were contacted, enlisting their co-operation in the study, only six of which declined to participate: the National Baptist Convention of America; Church of God (Queens); Church of God in Christ; Church of Our Lord Jesus Christ of the Apostolic Faith, Inc.; Wesleyan Methodist Church of America; and the United Pentecostal Church, Inc. The thirty-seven participating denominations are listed in the Technical Appendix, with totals of questionnaires mailed and respondents. One group (Advent Christian Church) was included in the study even though its membership was below 100,000, while another (the Reformed Church in America) was omitted by error. Of the thirty-seven participating groups, eighteen (on the whole, the largest ones) sent advance covering letters to MWs selected to represent their denominations, indicating their support of the study and encouraging participation in it.

Constructing lists of MWs from each of these thirty-seven denominations, from which to select every twentieth name, involved many problems. Of necessity, lists of *ministers* had to be used, and these were not always comparable. Indeed, eleven of the thirty-seven participating groups (and most of the nonparticipating groups) had no regular annual or biennial listing of clergy at all. When journals existed, they were not always compiled as of the same year—most journals consulted used data for 1959, but some were for 1957 or 1958. When there was no journal, a listing of ministers had to be prepared from denominational office files. Furthermore, some groups (such as the United Lutheran or Protestant Episcopal churches) had 40 per cent or more of their clergy in nonparochial ministries (such as administrative, educational, or institutional positions) while others (such as the Church of the Brethren or the Southern Baptist Convention) had a high percentage of part-time ministers, and still others (such as the Methodist Church) included many student pastors.

For these reasons, it was necessary to verify address labels through denominational pension boards or other record-keeping agencies, to see if a given minister was alive (journals are not always kept up to date!), married, in active full-time service of one or more local churches, and at the address listed. New names, to replace those eliminated, were randomly selected from the original list, and these names were in turn verified. Furthermore, to adjust for varying percentages of nonparochial clergy, 5 per cent of the "ordained clergy with charges" figure in the 1960 *Yearbook* was made the maximum sample size for each denomination, and excess names eliminated through random selection. Overall, about 20 per cent of those selected required address changes.

As a result of these stages of selection and verification, 7,975 MW-5 questionnaires were mailed to a one-in-twenty cross-section of MWs from thirty-seven Protestant religious groups in the spring of 1961. But before these questionnaires were mailed, considerable pretesting had occurred with regard to questionnaire construction, distribution, data analysis, and summary. After defining issues and exploring concept-indicator and report-reality relationships, there was still the task of translating questionnaire items into terms as meaningful as possible to a wide range of MWs. For example, "residence" seemed to communicate better than "parsonage," "manse," or "rectory" (cf. MW-5, items 18 and 19, in the Technical Appendix). "Ministerial income" was less offensive to groups where ministers depended on free-will offerings than was "salary" (cf. item 25).

In order to pretest and progressively refine the precoded mailed questionnaire (MW-5), five other forms were developed and the results from them analyzed. The MW-1 and MW-2 questionnaires were used as the basis for guided group interviews with both students' wives and MWs. The MMW-1 form was used in group meetings of ministers and their wives of several denominations, with 76 couples completing questionnaires, which were tabulated and analyzed. By the late spring of 1959 the MW-3 questionnaire, revised for clarity and conciseness, was ready for mailing to MWs who had written to the project in response to notices in denominational journals. Of 103 MW-3s mailed, 85 were returned and tabulated.

The final pretest for the MW-5 questionnaire came in the spring of 1960, when 286 MW-4s were distributed to an interdenominational cross-section of MWs in Indiana, with 142 returned 90 per cent or more complete. With MW-4, there was pretest not only of questionnaire contents and structure, but also of various methods of mailing and "anonymity controls," of coding and IBM data processing, and of the summarizing of results.[26] A selected subsample of nonrespondents was interviewed to determine bases for nonresponse. To further evaluate regional and denominational differences, 110 MW-4s were distributed (with 99 completed) to West Virginia Methodist MWs and 300 (with 189 completed) to Massachusetts Congregational MWs. In all, data from 430 MW-4 questionnaires were tabulated and analyzed. In addition to study of each item, with regard to deciding which should be included, omitted, or revised in form with regard to the MW-5 questionnaire, cross-tabulations were carried out to test inter-item relationships, as the basis for hypotheses to be tested through MW-5 data.

Data from the MW-1, MW-2, MW-3, MW-4, and MMW-1 questionnaires have been used to supplement and confirm results from the major data collection instrument (MW-5). The approximately 650 MWs who shared their insights, feelings, and concerns on these questionnaires made important contributions to the issues under consideration. Indeed, some topics, particularly within the area of role analysis (degree of reported obligation to do and be certain things) are discussed only in the MW-3 and MW-4 questionnaires, and not in MW-5. This is true, too, of sections of the preliminary draft of the MW-5 questionnaire—with open-ended questions on "Personal and Family Religious Life," "Marriage and Family," "Church and Community," etc.—which about 100 MWs in various sections of the country completed.

Of the total of 7,975 MW-5 questionnaires mailed in April, 1961, 4,777 usable questionnaires (90 per cent or more complete) had been returned by that September, for a response rate of about 60 per cent. However, the response rate increases to about 75 per cent (5,331/7,062) when one adds 554 questionnaires returned less than 90 per cent complete, and adjusts "expected returns" to take account of 913 questionnaires returned for insufficient or incomplete address or because inapplicable to the

persons to whom they were sent. For, despite all attempts at
verification, at least 15 questionnaires were sent to bachelors and
45 to MWs whose husbands had retired, died, or were no longer
in the *parish* ministry, and so on, while for more than 850 others
the address provided through denominational headquarters did
not satisfy the Post Office. For a mailed questionnaire, with no
second mailing to nonrespondents except for a reminder letter to
those from low-response-rate denominations, 60-75 per cent is an
extremely high return.[27]

That response rate is not a factor of theological position is indicated by the four groups from which there was 100 per cent
response: Augustana Lutheran, General Conference Mennonite,
International Church of the Four-Square Gospel, and Universalist. Eight other groups had more than 90 per cent response
rate: "Northern" and "Southern" Presbyterian; United, Missouri
Synod, American, and United Evangelical Lutheran; Christian
Reformed; and Evangelical United Brethren. Overall, 27 of the
37 groups had a response rate of over 70 per cent, with the highest response rates coming from Presbyterian and Lutheran bodies, and from small groups in which each MW felt personal
responsibility to participate. However, of the large denominations
only one had a response rate of less than 70 per cent—the
Southern Baptist Convention (48 per cent). From all available
evidence, including comparison of data on Southern Baptist respondents and nonrespondents with denominational records, the
response rate was about 75 per cent from wives of the better-
trained ministers, but only about 10 per cent from wives of less-
trained ministers in this denomination.

As nearly as can be determined, what limits response from
wives of less-trained Southern Baptist ministers, as well as from
other groups with less than a 40 per cent response rate—American
Baptist Association; Church of God (Cleveland, Tenn.); Free
Will Baptist; National Baptist, U.S.A.; African Methodist Episcopal; African Methodist Episcopal Zion; and Christian Methodist Episcopal—is the combination of loose denominational
organization with personal lack of interest in the problems being

investigated. Interviews with Negro MWs, for whom response rates are particularly low, revealed that nonresponse on their part was not due primarily to the questionnaire's being too difficult a task in relation to their level of education. Rather, even those who had a college education (and less than 40 per cent of all respondents to MW-5 are college graduates) were not trained in, or used to, an analytic-interpretive approach. They couldn't see "what all the fuss is about; just love God, and do your best—that's all it takes!" They failed to fill out and return the questionnaire because they were uninterested in the task it represented—not because they found it too difficult or offensive. (Of about 250 nonrespondents from whom data were secured, only eight considered it too difficult or time-consuming, and four "objectionable or too personal.")

Research results, then, are most applicable to wives of better-trained ministers in the larger denominations—who are also those most likely to read this book. Even within some denominations for which there are high response rates, there appears to be underrepresentation of pastors of small churches with low salaries. This is particularly true for the Disciples of Christ, where husbands of only 26 per cent of the respondents served churches of less than 200 members, versus a 1961 denominational figure of 80.6 per cent of all churches having under 250 members.[28] Even when one considers only churches with full-time ministers (only about 60 per cent of the total), 36 per cent of the husbands of Disciple *respondents* are serving churches of 500 members or more, versus 20.3 per cent of *all* full-time Disciple ministers. Since the response rate for the Disciples of Christ is about 83 per cent, these discrepancies are probably related to the composition of denominational journals—which may be the case for the Methodist Church as well, where wives of "approved supply" pastors are seriously underrepresented.

Because of these circumstances, data analysis and reporting for the MW-5 questionnaire focus on description and comparison of specific religious groups from which response rates run 70 per cent or higher, with the qualifications noted with regard

to Disciple and Methodist MWs, and with the addition of Southern Baptist MWs. In cross-tabulations (testing inter-item relationships) a subsample of 2,000 wives of full-time ministers of
one church as *the* minister of that church (that is, not part-time,
or in a multiple charge or multiple staff) was used. These MWs
come from the following denominational groupings: "Evangelical" (Church of God, Anderson; Church of the Nazarene; and
Evangelical United Brethren), Baptist (American and Southern
Conventions), Lutheran (American, Augustana-United, and Missouri Synod), Methodist, Presbyterian (U.S. and U.P., U.S.A.),
Disciples of Christ, and United Church of Christ.[29] On some data
analyses, two other groupings are included: Episcopal and
Pentecostal.

As a precoded questionnaire ("circle the number of the answer
closest to your situation, experience, or opinion, even though
none may fit exactly . . . and circle *one* answer only for each
question") the MW-5 inventory permitted machine data tabulation and analysis. But it meant that the respondent was limited
in what she could express by the specific questions included, as
well as the answers provided—unless she added other sheets, as
many did. This was inevitably frustrating, since she might want
to choose more than one response, or to qualify it in some
way. It is encouraging, therefore, that of the 70 MW-5 items, for
only two did the total of "no answer" and "other" responses exceed 10 per cent. For all items, the average was only 3 per cent.
Nevertheless, it seemed desirable to supplement MW-5 with a
questionnaire which, through using open-ended questions, would
give greater opportunity for the sharing of feelings, experiences,
and insights. This questionnaire (MW-6) has the following sections: "Feelings," "Home and Family," "Personal Growth and
Fulfillment," "Critical Incidents," "Values and Theology," "Mental
Picture of a MW and Me," and "Employment and Its Effects."

In June and July, 1961 (not a good time to mail questionnaires!), 879 MW-6 questionnaires were mailed, to a random
10 per cent sample of MW-5 respondents, supplemented by
about 200 each of "frustrated" and "employed" MWs—two sub-

groups of special interest. Despite ministerial vacations and changes of pastorate, 623 MW-6s had been returned by the time content analysis coding began in the winter of 1961-62. This represents a response rate of 71 per cent, which is remarkably high considering the nature of the task and the time of year involved. Coding of the MW-6 questionnaire, especially at the point of getting intercoder reliability, proved a most difficult task, and the development of coding categories took five research assistants almost a year.

There was some control on coding bias through the varying perspectives represented by the different coders, four of whom were doctoral candidates and the fifth a Ph.D. For one was male and four were female; two were Protestant, one Roman Catholic, one Jewish, and one agnostic; they represented the academic disciplines of clinical psychology, counseling psychology, pastoral psychology, sociology, and anthropology. In the development and testing of coding categories, to ensure their exhaustiveness and lack of overlap as well as theoretical meaningfulness, weekly coding conferences were held to review agreements and disagreements on particular questionnaires. At this stage, each questionnaire was coded by at least two persons and the coding reviewed by a third. Final coding, however, was done by two coders on a subsample of 300 MW-6s chosen to give equal representation to the random, employed, and "frustrated" groups, and to nine denomination-region combinations.[30] Data for these 300 MWs, including information from both the MW-5 and MW-6 questionnaires, were key-punched onto IBM cards, and tabulations and cross-tabulations performed by an IBM 650 computer.

As a further check on some of the basic variables, particularly with regard to stability of response patterns over time, and to check wives' perspectives with husbands' perspectives, a final open-ended questionnaire (MW-7) was prepared. This "Roles and Relationships" questionnaire has parallel forms for husband and wife, the back of each form containing the same four sections: "Values and Goals," "Self and Mate Description," "Critical Incidents," and "Ages and Stages." On the wife's form, some of the same questions asked previously on the MW-5 and MW-6 questionnaires are asked again, and other areas—especially with regard to "pressure points" in a MW's life—are explored. A "husband's form" and "wife's form" were sent to each MW-6 respondent in the spring of 1962.

Data from the MW-7 questionnaires of 419 couples (a response rate of 67.3 per cent) are being analyzed and related to MW-5 and MW-6 data, as a basis for a future longitudinal study. While reported involvement and satisfaction of MW-7 respondents tended to be the same as reported a year earlier on the MW-5 questionnaire (about 70 per cent made exactly the same report), reported motivation and sense of "set-apartness" shifted quite frequently (about 50 per cent different from MW-5 reports) and significantly. Parallel data from MW-5 and MW-7 permit, then, some analysis of what factors may be situationally determined, versus those which are related to a particular point in the personal growth process or to basic long-range personality tendencies.

Further clarification of these issues will come, too, through the Lilly Pilot Program for Theology Couples, conducted at Boston University School of Theology in the academic year of 1962-63, with co-operating groups of seminarians' wives in Garrett, Southern Baptist (Louisville), and Yale Seminaries.[31] Data collected during this program, including a battery of five psychological instruments completed by 103 wives of theological students at the beginning and end of the academic year, require further analysis. At some points in this report, information gained from this study and from MW-7 is presented. However, major findings from those sources will be incorporated in the guidance volume for young MWs planned as a sequel to this volume. This report is based mainly on the data provided by almost 5,000 wives of Protestant parish ministers through the MW-5 inventory, supplemented by the interpretations provided by about 600 of them in their responses to the MW-6 questionnaire.

So far as the non-social-scientist is concerned, this book will have particular applicability if you are the wife of a seminary-trained minister in one of the denominations for which the response rate is 70 per cent or higher. It may also apply more if you are *under* 50 years of age, since this is one other area in which there may be "nonrespondent bias."[32] Most of all, the key is whether you seek fuller understanding of your situation and yourself, and seek to grow in personal effectiveness and fulfillment. If you do, then this book is for you.

CHAPTER 2

Involvement and Activity Patterns

WHEN LOCAL CHURCH officers and denominational executives judge ministers' wives, the emphasis tends to be on their involvement in their husbands' ministry and their activity in the church. Does a particular MW (minister's wife) believe in her husband and his work, and generally support and encourage him? Does she demonstrate her commitment in local, regional, and/or national church work? These are the questions used to separate the sheep from the goats. Thus, while questions of motivation and meaning, as they relate to fulfillment and frustration, will concern the wives themselves, involvement and activity usually form the standard of judgment for others.

But how can one judge, or even describe, a particular MW's involvement in her husband's ministry? There is no simple, unambiguous answer to this question, and certainly none that is definitive. Yet anyone who has listened to a large number of women describe the parts they take in their husbands' work soon recognizes different patterns. The task of this chapter is to describe the five patterns that most often occur among American MWs: the Teamworker (Martha), the Purpose-Motivated Background Supporter (Mary), the Useful Work–Motivated Background Supporter (Dorcas), the Detached-on-Principle (Jane), and the Detached-in-Rebellion (Kate).

In order to sharpen the analysis, these patterns will be presented in their most clear-cut, least-diluted form, in terms of "pure types." And, to give the patterns flesh-and-blood reality rather than theoretical abstraction, case material will be presented from eight particular MWs (including two Marthas and two Marys) selected by IBM computer as best matching the theoretically defined pure types.[1]

Though the names used are fictitious, all the data are factual, with verbatim quotations from questionnaires and interviews. Through this material, types come alive in such a way that other MWs may begin to understand their own involvement and activity patterns. Most individuals will discover that they fall between types, but that the types represent a first approximation which assists in understanding one's own unique selfhood—a first step beyond stereotypes to individuality.

The Teamworker

Martha Bond. Of the approximately 5,000 respondents to the MW-5 questionnaire, about 20 per cent described themselves as "very involved, as a *teamworker* sharing in his ministry." Of particular interest, as one who represents this pattern in its most unqualified form, with the highest degree of involvement and activity possible among MWs, is Martha Bond. For Martha, to be a MW is to be a minister. She and her husband form a team, with division of responsibilities at some points and shared responsibility at others. They are "yoke-fellows" for Christ. They are side by side on the firing line. She feels as much called to witness, to serve, to minister in the broadest sense of that term, as does her husband.

Martha Bond is the wife of a minister of a Southern Baptist church of about 200 members in a medium-sized town. She is in her thirties, with four children, two in school and two still at home. What is most important in life for her is "trying through the organizations and services of our church to win the lost to Christ." Always being an example causes her "to feel a real sense of responsibility and privilege which calls out the best in me." She expects her husband to "give first place to his service to God" and has "more faith in my husband's feelings for me than to be jealous of the ties the church has on him. Also we believe the

Scripture which says, 'He that loveth father or mother more than Me, is not worthy of Me.' "

Though troubled by questions of "Who needs me most? Where to first? How will I ever get it all done?" Martha has found the life of a MW richly satisfying and fulfilling.[2] Problems do arise, since her husband's ministerial income of less than $4,000 has meant that she has had to hold a full-time job as a public school-teacher, in addition to family and church responsibilities. But she finds real joy in showing people a better way of life, and for her this is dependent on her own deepening personal commitment to Christ and the Church. She feels set apart to witness for Christ, and her teamwork represents the fulfillment of a "call to full-time Christian service," that is, to a church service vocation.

Teamworker Martha performs thirteen activities in her local church, a congregation organized by her husband less than three years ago. She enjoys teaching a Sunday-School class and leading a church youth group, calling on sick and shut-ins and counseling people with problems, attending church women's groups and being an officer in one of them, conducting leadership training and leading devotional services, playing the piano for services and entertaining parishioners in her home. Some other jobs, such as church secretarial or office work, committee responsibilities, and "housekeeping" functions around the church, Martha does just "to get them done." Her present schedule leaves no time for nonchurch community activities, or to "use a hobby as it should be used, regularly and seriously. Mine are worked in just when I can steal a moment from something else and are purely for relaxation."

In Martha's value system, achieving personal immortality and doing God's will come first, with providing love and security for one's family next in priority.[3] Self-development rates high, as do peace of mind, contentment, and stillness of spirit, but under-standing yourself is of considerably less relative importance. Theologically, her emphasis falls on salvation through faith in Christ, as described in Ephesians 2:8-9. But, as she makes clear, this is "not a ground for laziness or unrighteous living, but an incentive to do the best that is in us." Purely on the basis of our faith, we are promised "immortality in Heaven with Him."

Here is a person, then, with a stable, organized value system expressed in a total integrated way of life. Yet even *she* feels conflict. Her self-image is that of a "harried Hannah" rushing about, but her mental picture of a minister's wife is of one who is "calm, helpful, composed, adequate," smilingly instructing children (themselves still and quiet!) from the Bible.[4] Despite her high degree of commitment and her satisfaction and fulfillment as a MW, she is bothered at times by inadequate finances, lack of time for self and family, and a relative lack of close personal friends.

She finds it easy, however, to adjust to new situations, and her work experience as a church secretary, librarian, and teacher has given her invaluable experience in interpersonal relationships. Moreover, her own somewhat impetuous, impatient, active personality acts as a complement to her more quiet, studious husband, who in turn is her "balance wheel." They enjoy a happy home and family life, with her husband sharing in decision-making and discipline and "deeply concerned with being a good husband and father as well as a good pastor to his congregation and a good citizen to his community."

In summary, this teamworker reports never having found it hard to "be yourself" as a MW, nor having found being an example a strain. Though she states that she has not found it wise to form close friendships within her husband's congregations, she feels that they "belong to us in a special intangible relationship brought about by our common union in Christ and the local church." Her closest friends are two other ministers' wives with whom she was associated in college and seminary, and they "live close enough and yet far enough that they are safe 'confidantes.' [But] God is my safest 'confidant.' This I try to remember."

Martha Bond's life is, on the whole, internally motivated, not externally driven. Though this judgment may be questioned, she honestly does not believe that her life would be any different if she were not a MW. She does not feel that her husband holds any special expectations of her because he is a minister, since "the Bible does not set forth a double standard. What it requires of the preacher and his wife and children, it also requires of any believer in Christ." There are, she states, no special moral or religious requirements for the MW, as distinguished from any other Christian believer. But she does believe that MWs should be trained for their special leadership responsibilities, which exceed those of other laywomen. In fact, her present situation "where the congregation is a new one and extremely young and leadership is a must, causes me to study, counsel and pray, which is good for personal growth and fulfillment."

Martha Green, like Martha Bond, has been a highly active teamworker with her husband in his ministry in Southern Baptist churches. She, too, feels set apart to witness for Christ, as the expression of her call to be a minister's wife. Like Martha Bond, her main joy is showing people a better way of life, and for her, too, this depends on deepening her own commitment to Christ and the Church. Though in general very satisfied and fulfilled as a MW, she, too, is bothered at times by inadequate finances and lack of time for self and family; in addition, "moving so often—with no real roots" is disturbing.

In other respects, however, these Marthas are quite different from each other—which simply illustrates once more the irreducible individuality of MWs, as of people in general. Martha Green is in her late forties, and her three children are all over 21 years of age. Though her husband serves a city church of more than 700 members, his ministerial income is only a few hundred dollars higher than that of Bill Bond, and their total family income is at least three thousand dollars less, since her part-time work does not produce much additional income. While Martha Bond's unfurnished parsonage is excellent on all counts, Martha Green's furnished parsonage is poor in most respects. Furthermore, the Green home is next door to the church and is often used for church meetings, while the Bonds live about a mile away, and their home is seldom used in this way.

Far more important than these differences in physical circumstances are differences in the possibilities for fulfillment. For Martha Green, being a MW has meant "the richest of blessings," but it has also brought "the deepest sorrows." Like Martha Bond, what is most important to her is "that Christ live through me to win the world to Him," and her husband and she have "labored closely in the Lord's work; our hearts have beat as one in His cause."

But Martha Green is agonized by the fact that, now that her husband is over 50, he finds it difficult to secure and retain a pastorate, because most congregations want a younger man. His past accomplishments in seven previous pastorates, in reviving dying congregations and carrying on extensive building programs, mean little. His advanced seminary training, rather than being an asset, often is a liability. For "jack-rabbit preachers" of high-school education or less are often willing to cater to the congregation's whims rather than fearlessly proclaiming the Gospel.

John and Martha Green find themselves, then, in what should be the prime of life, at the height of their abilities, in the midst of tremendous vocational and financial insecurity. Naturally, this is a most discouraging and disillusioning experience, made more difficult by the organizational structure of independent churches and the lack of denominational provision for professional or financial security, including retirement.

Teamwork, even when the wife has the dedication and motivation of a Martha Green, and even when the marital relationship is as good as the Greens', does not, therefore, automatically guarantee personal fulfillment. Satisfaction comes from "doing what I feel is right and God's will for my life," but external circumstances, including the response of congregations to her husband's age and training, can bring problems and conflicts.

Differences between Martha Bond and Martha Green are especially significant since they represent such a specific pattern of involvement and activity. They are the purest type of teamworker that survey research of this kind could identify.[5] While about 20 per cent of MWs describe themselves as teamworkers with their husbands in the ministry, only one in fifty Marthas also has the *very high* level of activity, satisfaction, and specific sense of call possessed by Martha Bond and Martha Green. Moreover, this is a pattern which is found most often in smaller Southern Baptist churches, in MWs who are daughters of farmers or laborers—now better off economically than their parents were—and in women who have more than a high-school education but seldom any graduate work beyond a B.A.[6]

The Marthas are alike in many ways, especially in the tone of their lives. But, as we discover with Martha Bond and Martha Green, beyond the group similarities are real personal differences. Not only can one not generalize regarding MWs in general (as most literature and discussion tends to do), but it is also important to realize that classification of MWs according to their particular patterns of involvement and activity does not give complete understanding. Beyond these patterns, one must also explore the meanings they express, the fulfillments and frustrations to which they contribute, the times of life and the stages through which they develop, and the backgrounds and situations that influence them. Chapters on these other aspects follow, and it is in those terms that this chapter must be understood.

To develop a typology of patterns of involvement and activity is, therefore, a beginning in the process of understanding, but not the end. To analyze a complex symphony of several movements, one must first discover the basic themes. But in human psychology as in music, the number of variations on the basic themes is almost infinite. And a theme is never static and fixed, but rather fluid and emergent—capable of many interpretations.

The Background Supporter

If about 20 per cent of MWs describe themselves as teamworkers with their husbands, 60 per cent describe themselves as "very involved, but in a *background supportive* way." Of the approximately 3,000 MWs who report their participation in this way on the MW-5 questionnaire, attention here will be focused on eleven "pure-type" background supporters who also report *moderate* satisfaction, activity, and semi-pro leadership.[7] They all describe themselves as motivated by "belief in the purposes of the Church," as considering themselves to be "a Christian, with the same responsibilities as any other church member," as finding their major joy in "learning more about the Christian faith," and as judging their "first responsibility to be a good wife and mother."

Mary Bernhardt. One of these purpose-motivated, not set apart, "homebody" background supporters is Mary Bernhardt. Mary's husband is a Lutheran pastor in the Far West, serving a church of about 200 members in a medium-sized community. They have been there a little over two years. In their early thirties, they have four children, all preschool, and a fifth on the way. Their unfurnished parsonage is next to the church, and Mary rates it good on all counts. Her husband's ministerial income of between $5,000 and $6,000—which is their total family income, since Mary does not work outside of the home—is sufficient for their family's needs, though it leaves no reserve for savings. Mary was the third child of a farmer, in a mixed marriage of Catholic and Baptist, and finished one year of education after high school. She married John when he was in seminary.

For Mary, being a MW has meant "personal Christian growth, Christian love, and consideration for others." As a child, she "had little knowledge of Christ's teachings. After instruction and confirmation into the Christian faith, I have hungered for His Word." What is most important to her is "to be a good Christian Shepherdess, wife, and mother," and she finds being an example a "God-given privilege, honor, and duty as a Christian." Her most satisfying experience is "getting through the daily routine . . . and having time to bake for, or visit, the sick and needy." She is proud of her husband as "a wonderful Christian Pastor, husband, and father," and "learns and benefits greatly" from his sermons.

As with Martha Bond, Mary Bernhardt sees conflict between her own self-image and her mental picture of "a minister's wife," by which she refers to the ideal. She feels that she ought to be "an angel—calm and cheerful," but she sometimes pictures herself as "a devil—tense, tired, cranky." She feels that "a minister's wife should be kind, understanding, patient, and able to adjust to many situations," but isn't sure how she measures up to this list. As she puts it, "Should I put down how others describe me? It would seem too vain. I am sure they exaggerated."

Despite such conflicts, Mary reports herself to have found being a MW in general "satisfying and fulfilling."[8] She has found her main joy in learning more about the Christian faith, and is glad also for the opportunity to share in her husband's work and to be of service to her fellow men. Problems and conflicts center in having few close personal friends, her husband's irregular work schedule, and the nature of a goldfish-bowl existence, with little privacy. To other young ministers' wives she would recommend that they realize that their first responsibility is to be good wives and mothers, but that they must also deepen their commitment to Christ and the Church, and have a genuine interest in people. If she were not a MW, she feels that she would have fewer opportunities for service and growth.

In contrast to Martha's thirteen local church activities, Mary's five activities represent moderate involvement, and with much less semi-pro or leadership emphasis. She greets parishioners, *informally* counsels people with problems, and attends church women's groups. She enjoys these activities, and unlike many other MWs also enjoys helping out on activities which others might consider unappreciated drudgery: church secretarial or office work and housekeeping functions around the church. When home circumstances permit, she would like to teach a Sunday-School class, sing in the choir, and/or call on sick and shut-ins. But she would not want to entertain church groups in her home, hold any church office or position, or direct musical activities. On principle, she will not take any role in church life which she or others might regard as overly dominant or aggressive. For her, teamwork would represent trespassing on the role of the pastor, undercutting her own role of good wife and mother, and violating the proper structure of church and ministry.

Mary Bernhardt's value system is much like that of Martha Bond; they agree on ends, though they may differ at many points on the best means to achieve those ends. Devotion to God and achieving personal immortality come first, closely followed by providing love and security for one's family and being genuinely concerned about other people. Mary assigns relatively low priority to *both* self-development and self-understanding, though like Martha she places "peace of mind, contentment, and stillness of spirit" in a relatively high position. Mary's faith is founded on Holy Scriptures, with her interpretation guided by official Lutheran exposition of Christian doctrine. Her total personal and family life is built on and organized around this faith and the value system deriving from it.

Within this framework, Mary has never found it hard to "be yourself" as a MW, nor has she found being an example a strain. She does agree, however, that though a MW has many acquaintances she usually has few close friends, and that she must be very careful about developing close friendships within her husband's congregation. Her own closest friends are her in-laws. She lacks any real confidante, though she can confide some things to her husband and "blow off some steam" with her children. Usually she "sobs silently" alone, then asks God for strength and forgiveness. She and her husband both enjoy the exercise, relaxation, and fellowship of a couples' bowling league.

Mary Bernhardt has worked out a satisfying and fulfilling way of life as a MW, due to a combination of circumstances, the foremost of which are probably her strong personal religious commitment and the dedication, love, and ability of her husband. She has been privileged to be in generally supportive congregational and community settings.

This has been the experience of *Mary Knowland* as well, for the almost thirty years she has been a Methodist MW in New England. Her husband now serves a church of about 500 members in a small city, with the furnished parsonage next to the church. Since his ministerial income is adequate for family needs, she does not work outside of the home. Her children are both

grown now, so her situation is quite different from that of Mary
Bernhardt. Despite these differences, in her motivation, her joys
and conflicts, and the over-all emphases of her life she is very
similar to the younger Mary. Though as a young wife she often
felt unworthy and unprepared, Mary Knowland has grown over
the years to the point where being a MW now means to her "the
completion of an early dedication and a very happy life." Always
being an example makes her "want to be the best possible person,
that I may not make our profession suffer" and what is most important to her is a "happy, hard-working congregation—then *I*
am happy and hard-working, too." The hardest thing for her is
moving. Her closest friends are her family; she has never, in her
husband's pastorates, moved far from her childhood home.

For Mary Knowland, "providing love and security for one's
family" comes first, with "devotion to God, doing God's will" a
close second in her value system. Self-understanding ranks high,
but self-development and peace of mind do not. More than the
Marthas, she is concerned with "serving the community of which
one is a part," which for her is one expression of "being genuinely
concerned about other people."

In contrast to the Marthas, she puts "achieving personal immortality in heaven" at the bottom of her ranking of values and
goals. Her theological position focuses on the *present* life:

> Believing that I am a child of God, and He has led me in these
> good paths for a purpose, I try to find the meaning and purpose for
> my life. I believe that it is my place to see that I encourage all I meet
> to try to find their purpose and meaning. As far as possible, I must
> help, heal, teach, learn, and express encouragement all along the way.
> Jesus Christ is my Lord, and with His Spirit to direct me, I feel that
> I can do all these things.

As a group, "pure-type" purpose-motivated background supporters are even more difficult to characterize than the pure-type
teamworkers. And again, influences of background and situation
will be reported more fully in Chapter 6. In basic summary, however, they tend to be in southern or midwestern Methodist
churches of more than 700 members, in communities of more

than 10,000 population.[9] In contrast to teamworkers, they are older, do not have preschool-age children, are from a higher social class background, and are better educated.[10] Also, their husbands' ministerial income (related to both denomination and church size) tends to be larger.

In general, they are more interpersonally oriented and less work-achievement-oriented than are teamworkers.[11] Their religious commitment takes the form more of the disciple than of the apostle: the emphasis is on *following* rather than *leading*, learning rather than witness, and in relation to their husbands there is greater deference than tends to be true for teamworkers. More often concerned about their own leadership abilities than teamworkers, they seldom take a direct leadership role, but rather prefer "hostess-type" activities such as calling, greeting, and entertaining.

In summary, purpose-motivated background supporters tend to have more interpersonal sensitivity and less available energy and competence than teamworkers. Their commitment is expressed in concern for personal growth rather than evangelistic witness. They are found most often in southern or midwestern Methodist churches, in larger churches and communities, in age groups over 35 years of age, and among those of higher social class background who yet feel inferior to their husbands in education, dedication, and ability.

Dorcas Patterson. Not all background supporters, however, are motivated by "belief in the purposes of the church." Others report their motivation as "desire to contribute through useful work." There are ten women whose response pattern to the basic MW-5 questionnaire items is exactly the same as that of the Marys, except for difference in reported motivation. Dorcas Patterson represents this orientation. In her middle forties and the mother of two grown children, she is married to a Disciples of Christ minister serving a church of about 200 members in a medium-sized town in the Midwest. They were married after her husband had completed ministerial training—he is a college graduate, but did not attend seminary—and she had finished business college. Her father was a Methodist minister, and she reports religion as very important in her childhood home.

For Dorcas, being a MW has meant "joy, heartaches, frustration, friends," and if she were not a MW she "would feel like a 'fish out of water' since my grandfather, father, mother, brother, and brother-in-law all were and are ministers." What is most important to her is "a sense of helpfulness," but the hardest thing is "feeling that I'm not qualified to be the kind of minister's wife I'd like to be." Always being an example "is no problem here because of the understanding congregation," but she does not feel able to have close friends, since "we feel we have to be impartial."

Her major concern at present is for her husband's health. The pressures of the parish ministry, especially preaching, often seem more than he is able to bear, though the congregation "can't be criticized because they are wonderful." She describes her husband as a person who is "kind and gentle, but lets people's problems get him down. He strives to do more for his family than he is financially able, thus creating financial problems that worry him and consequently undermine his ministry."

Dorcas is concerned, too, about her own somewhat withdrawn, worrying nature and the fact that she is not sufficiently educated. She gets "rather tired of having to conform my opinions to others. If I really said what I'm thinking . . . Ouch!" With her children leaving home and the problems of her husband's health, she is afraid of the future, in spite of her conviction that "we must have faith in God in order to really live—faith in spite of all the adverse conditions that arise. Without faith, trying to help others is an empty sham . . . words without meaning. Sometimes I admit I have to pray, Lord, Help my unbelief."

In her value system, devotion to God and achieving personal immortality come first, with providing love and security for one's family and peace of mind also rated high. Few things bother her more than contention or wrangling; when things bother her, her tendency is to keep her mouth shut about it and hope that it will improve.

In contrast to both teamworkers and purpose-motivated background supporters, Dorcas and other background supporters motivated by a desire to contribute through useful work tend to feel unsure of themselves. They feel inadequate for their responsibilities, and shy and timid in social situations. They dislike taking a firm stand and are overly sensitive to the judgments and responses of others. Rather slow and deliberate, they seek to avoid trouble whenever possible. More than the purpose motivated, they emphasize the need to deepen one's own personal commitment to Christ and the Church, perhaps in part due to the hope that faith will overcome other deficiencies.

What useful work means to these women is not exactly clear from examining their actual activity patterns in the local church. Here, as always, there is tremendous individual variation, but the activities most often performed and enjoyed are teaching a Sunday-School class and entertaining church groups in the home. Least often performed and least enjoyed are activities involving specific skills such as leadership training or counseling people with problems. Contrary to what one might expect, in terms of the self-deprecation associated with this orientation, church housekeeping and secretarial tasks are seldom performed, and in fact strongly disliked.

As Marthas tend to be found in small churches and Marys in large churches, Dorcases are most often in medium-sized (200-to-700-member) churches.[12] Other patterns (regional, denominational, etc.) are less clear-cut, perhaps since being a Dorcas is less a matter of situation or even background than it is of personality. Characteristically, however, their background has been a *stable* one. Religious influence in their childhood home tends to be judged as "very important," with both parents active in the church, and seldom has a Dorcas changed denominational affiliation since adolescence.

The possible influence of such a background will be discussed more fully in Chapter 6. It may be noted here, however, that Dorcases are seldom critical of the persons or program of the local congregation. They may feel put upon in terms of low ministerial salaries and the heavy demands of the ministry on their husbands' time. But in general they will "suffer silently," and on the whole they report themselves as in general satisfied with their lives as MWs.

It takes most Dorcases, nevertheless, considerable time to achieve relative contentment with their lot; seldom has satisfaction been achieved in less than ten years.[13] Apparently for those of the shy, retiring, trouble-avoiding personality common among the Dorcases, the process of "becoming a MW" is harder than for other MWs, except possibly for the "detached" described below.

The complex adjustments involved in the life of parish and parsonage tend to be overwhelming for those who feel unsure in both leadership (Martha-type) and social (Mary-type) situations, and who are constantly self-deprecating concerning their own abilities. Indeed, to be truly satisfied and fulfilled as a MW, a Dorcas will probably have to become a Mary, as she gains in self-confidence in social situations and becomes surer of her own beliefs.

The Detached

Of the almost 5,000 MWs who filled out questionnaires in this study, about one in five reported themselves to be teamworkers with their husbands, about three in five background supporters, and slightly less than one in five "no more involved than if he were in another vocation." (Actual percentages were 20.6 per cent, 63.9 per cent, and 15.1 per cent, with .4 per cent "other.")

For the "no-more-involved" (hereafter referred to as "the detached"), two orientations, as indicated by questionnaire response patterns, have particular interest: (1) Janes—motivated by "belief in the purposes of the Church," whose relatively low involvement represents their conception of the proper roles of laity and clergy,[14] and (2) Kates—motivated by either "the desire to be close to your husband" or because "it's expected of you," who rebel against the demands of local congregations on their time and energy.[15] While Janes are usually satisfied and fulfilled, Kates tend to be frustrated and confined, or at best to feel "so-so" about being MWs.

Jane Inman. Of the Janes, five are of particular interest in that they are like the Marys in reporting moderate satisfaction and activity, motivation through belief in the purposes of the Church, and major joy in learning more about the Christian faith. Like the purpose-motivated background supporters, they consider themselves to have the same responsibilities as any other church member, and place in highest priority being a good wife and mother.

Beyond this similarity in orientation (which differs from the Marys only in terms of judging themselves to be "no-more-involved than if [my husband] were in another vocation") these five "pure-type" detached-on-principle MWs share other characteristics. They all have three or more children, with at least one of them a preschooler. Thus, relatively low involvement is undoubtedly related to the demands of the home situation.

Janes are alike, too (and very different from the Dorcases), in tending *not* to have grown up as regular participants in the denomination in which their husband now serves. They are alike in wanting the freedom which a housing allowance, rather than a parsonage, would provide. And, more than other MWs, they are bothered by the demands of the parish on their husbands' time and interest to the point (they feel) of lack of consideration of the family's needs.

In all these ways, Janes are alike. Yet they differ at many other points, exhibiting more variation than the other orientations previously discussed. They represent a range of denominations, of sections of the country, of church size, of education, and of social class background. They are alike, though, in all being between 35 and 50 years of age, and in that four of the five are in city churches—perhaps indicating that low involvement on the part of the MW is more acceptable in an urban situation.

Like the Dorcases, the Janes have had a hard struggle to reach their present level of satisfaction and fulfillment. As Jane Inman reports it, "Life is good *now*! After fifteen years!" For her, as for many other Janes, the shift to the life of a MW was a radical one:

When I married, my husband was a Marine Corps pilot who wanted to be a football coach. However, after being married eighteen months, he knew he had received a call into the ministry. I was shocked and quite upset and it has taken me *all* these fifteen years to become adjusted. I now feel that I have matured enough to realize that God *can* use even *me*, just as I am, and so it is easy for me today to be myself and tell others of His love. It *does* become a difficult life at times—having to leave my housework undone, dressing and undressing, coming and going, but I can do it. My husband has encouraged me all the way, and has been a most patient, kind, and understanding person. I used to feel neglected, but not any more. Growing up has helped me, but most of all, my preacher-husband!

As this statement by Jane Inman indicates, the "happily detached-on-principle, and moderately active in the church" Janes have in no sense withdrawn from the Christian faith. Indeed, as a group, they place strong emphasis on "deepening personal commitment to Christ and the Church." Believing in the ideal purposes of the Universal, Biblical Church, they tend to be critical of the departure from this ideal of the realities of local congregational life. Holding a high conception of the ministry of the laity, as well as of the clerical profession, they do not consider a MW's responsibilities to be any different from those of any other laywoman.

They are no *more* involved in institutional *church* activities and leadership because their husbands are ministers, but they are no *less* involved in Christian *commitment* than are the teamworkers and background supporters. They regard themselves as disciples, not as church workers. If they were *not* MWs, they honestly do not believe that their lives would change in any significant respect. There would then be neither greater freedom nor fewer opportunities for service than now.

Janes, in general, prefer the hostess role, as in entertaining church groups in the home. But, they do not object to teaching a Sunday-School class, being program chairman of a woman's association, calling on sick and shut-ins, or any other activity that has *intrinsic purpose and worth.* (Curiously, and perhaps by chance, none of these five has any interest—to say nothing of activity—in the musical program of the church.) They have divided judgment on such issues as whether or not it is hard to be yourself as a MW and whether always being an example is a strain. Perhaps as another mark of their characteristic individualism and analytic approach, they interpret these terms in different ways. Indeed, generalizations regarding most of the issues discussed above with regard to Marthas, Marys, and Dorcases are impossible for Janes. They, more than other MWs, defy and vigorously resist generalizations.

Jean Wilson. Nevertheless, there is a certain "tone" to the detached theme. Jean Wilson, a Lutheran pastor's wife from the Northeast, is not a "pure-type" Jane, since she experiences considerable frustration as a MW. But she is like Jane Inman in not feeling " 'set apart' as far as the pastor's wife is concerned in our churches. They are naturally always honored and respected, . . . but we are just one of the congregation—and accepted as such, I believe." The detached often view this as in contrast to "the old-fashioned idea of a MW," and share Jean's judgment that "I don't have to be concerned whether I wear lipstick or nailpolish, or what kind of clothes or hats I want to wear. I can be myself. Very rarely do I have to watch out."

At times there are pressures, since "I do think that we as clergymen and their wives do take our work with us, no matter where we go. At times, to be perfectly honest, it is a drag." But, continues Jean,

. . . not in most cases. Because, in most cases, what we are doing, where we are going, what we are saying or how we are behaving, I feel is exactly like we would under any circumstances. We have had a marvelous experience here with our people. They know we enjoy a good time and enjoy it with them, no matter what we do—if it's playing baseball at a picnic, or jitterbugging at a dance. . . . We have never played a part, so that we have to be one type of person on Sunday and a different type on Saturday night. And I think this makes it easy. . . .

I have been treated like the rest of the women. . . . When they come to the parsonage and I'm in shorts, working around the house or the yard, I don't have to run and put on a black dress and high heels. This is *me*. And I feel that I can visit any of their homes and they don't have to quickly get out the dustcloth because *I* am coming and not just another friend.

Not all women who would like to be detached are able to be, however. It depends on the church situation and the husband, as well as their own orientation. For Jean Wilson, to be "no more involved" has been easier for the following reasons:

> The people who were here before us left under duress and the church was without a pastor for six months. So, we were welcomed with open arms. There was no difficulty whatsoever, and I didn't have to match someone else. And, I realize that it is because my husband is so well loved here that we are accepted as we are. He's very much loved, and very respected in the community as well as the church. . . . And, because of the sort of person he is, I've never felt that I had to put the church before the children. When they were younger and I had to be with them, I was. I haven't had the experience of the family having to take second place—as I guess some pastors' wives do. . . . I don't believe I could blame the church for taking up my time. I choose what I want to do—where I think I can be of help—and do it. It's not a matter of the church demanding it.

Unlike some MWs, Jean therefore feels freedom to be herself. Nevertheless, frustrations occur, largely because church and husband don't always measure up to her goal of "getting things done, *quickly* and *well*." On the MW-7 questionnaire, she and her husband agree on the "self and mate description" section that while Jean tends to be "too rigid and perfectionist" as well as "too sensitive for own good," Tom "procrastinates and puts off when possible." Since she enjoys organizational work, her husband's administrative weakness at times "gets on her nerves." She characterizes herself on the projective section of the MW-6 questionnaire as "hurry, scurry, get it done" in contrast to "a minister's wife," who is "sweet, calm, lovable."

Thus, while being a minister's wife "has meant for me being wife and mother, married to a busy, devoted man," at the same time she wishes she could "feel free to call necessary repairmen for our home. . . ." In recent years, this has been the hardest thing for her: the frustration of getting necessary repairs done to the parsonage. She dislikes "having always to go through channels" and the tendency of the congregation to save money through "do-it-yourself projects." Specifically, she has been disturbed by a flooded basement, an unfinished garage, and painting which has taken more than two years to complete. Through recognizing her own agitation and impatience, and through the help of professional counseling, she has become more able to "slow down and take things in stride." But it still isn't easy, even at age 35 after fifteen years of marriage!

Jean Wilson illustrates the point that being "detached-on-principle" does not necessarily lead to satisfaction and fulfillment, any more than other patterns of involvement and activity. Individual personality and the interaction of it with husband and church are also important. Another MW, confronted with a problem similar to Jean's in getting parsonage repairs done, commented:

> I painted the garage doors because it was easier for me to do it than to look at them unfinished and be patient until they got around to it. The same with parts of the porch, and the basement windows. I can't stand to brood. I'd sooner do something about it if I can. If I can't, why then, forget it. . . . This parsonage was new when we moved in, so we had a lot of work to do—cupboards in the basement, a front walk, a lawn. . . . It was my working that paid for the improvements, and we just felt it was money we were giving to the church. It made it nice for us, and it will be nice for the next family, too. It's a kind of stewardship.

After fifteen years as a MW, Jean Wilson is beginning to move toward such realism and flexibility. Jane Inman has likewise made a series of adjustments and matured in various ways, so that she is now able to find general satisfaction and fulfillment. Not all who share these two wives' commitments and ideals do as well, however. Tragically, some of the most frustrated MWs are those who have entered marriage and/or involvement in their husbands' ministry with the highest and most sincere beliefs and purposes. In their disillusionment, they have turned bitter and resentful. Jean Wilson is grateful for the general acceptance she finds among parishioners, and for her husband's dedication and ability. Jane Inman also bears testimony to her "preacher-husband." Others pay tribute to a series of understanding and supportive congregations. In any case, growth toward satisfaction and fulfillment can occur only when supporting "structures" of one sort or another exist.

Kate Moore. Thus the Kates, the rebellious individualists—who now report motivation to involvement and activity from either "the desire to be close to your husband" or because "it's expected of you"—are in essence Janes for whom these supporting structures have not been present. Rebellion and protection of individual rights against the demands of others have represented their response to the imbalance of demand over support, of pressure to produce over encouragement to grow.

Over-all, of almost 5,000 questionnaire respondents, less than 4 per cent reported themselves to have "in general found being a MW frustrating and confining." One of the less than 200 wives who made such a response is Kate Moore. Kate is in her late twenties, has four children, and is the wife of a Lutheran minister in the South. Her main joy as a MW has come in learning more about the Christian faith, and she stresses the importance for all MWs of deepening their commitment to Christ and the Church. She deeply admires her husband as a person and as a pastor, especially "his ability to really practice Christian principles even though people around him create situations which are completely unchristian."

Despite the best of intentions, however, Kate finds many frustrations and conflicts in her life as a MW. She finds it hard, in many congregational situations, to "be yourself," and considers always being an example "a headache." She recognizes that, in part at least, her problems may arise from having been the youngest child in a large family, and in "having been spoiled and given in to a lot. I have had to adjust to satisfying others besides myself."

Kate Moore's situation, as a young mother of preschool-age children in a small church and community, does place heavy demands on her. The combination of close social observation of the minister and his family, low salary and inadequate church staff, and poor housing next to the church can easily overpower a young woman who is probably still working through marital adjustments to her husband.

Why some women (such as Martha Bond or Mary Bernhardt) can cope with such situations more easily than does Kate Moore is a question to which we must seek answers. As Kate indicates, it is a matter of both background and situation. Moreover, a certain amount of just plain growing up, of learning to adjust to a variety of situations through a series of different stages of growth is called for. But perhaps most important are the motivations that contribute to particular fulfillment or frustration. These successive elements will be further explored in Chapters 3-6 (although in slightly different order).

Thus, full discussion of what leads to a MW feeling "frustrated and confined" must be deferred until the presentation of later material. At this point, however, something of the flavor of the rebellious individualist pattern can be given through quotations from questionnaire and interview material. (On the whole, there was very high consistency among responses to precoded questionnaires (MW-5), open-ended questionnaires (MW-6 and MW-7), and interviews. The material for a given individual hung together in a manner most encouraging to a researcher.)

What, then, can lead a woman to rebellious withdrawal from involvement in church and ministry? In part, at least, her *husband's* attitude is a factor.

My husband expects a great deal of me because he is a minister. He expects me to listen to him, day or night, to entertain for him, to always "be there" when he needs reassuring, to shoulder 80 per cent of the care of the house and children, in order to leave him completely free for his work. . . . It may be true that he would expect this of me no matter what his work might be, but because he is around so much, I notice it more.

In this connection, about one-third of MW-5 respondents indicated having on occasion experienced a lack of considerateness by their husbands concerning *their* needs as *persons*. ("Wish he would treat me as he does the congregation!") However, only 10 per cent reported this as a major problem, while 50 per cent reported it "not at all" a problem—ministers are better than other husbands if these reports are accurate!

In addition, the considerateness of the *congregation* is important, in terms of the demands made on the minister as well as his wife. Their demands, as well as the husband's manner of need-fulfillment, can lead to

the weeks on end which go by when my suggestions that we have an evening to ourselves, or go to a concert, movie or dinner, are met with the never-ending answer: "I have to go to a meeting," or, "I have to call." Hard, too, are the times when members tell me what a grand time they had when my husband visited them—what a marvelous personality he has, how much their children enjoyed him, how easy it was to discuss problems with him. . . . Then I know that he enjoys the company of his parishioners more than that of his own family. . . . And, a very personal note: In the night, after a particularly warm time together, I am lying on his shoulder. There is nothing in the world but him and I am feeling completely loved and happy. Then I'm sure to hear something like this: I think I'll propose to the Board that they elect Brother Jones as Charge Lay Leader!

As these comments indicate, the congregation can readily become a seductive mistress to the minister as well as a demanding and critical mother-in-law to his wife! In either case, it is not an easy situation for a young, inexperienced woman to cope with. For the ministry is a profession (and calling) which tends to change the relationship between husband and wife, as well as between wife and church. As one woman wrote in her diary after her husband's first sermon:

When he stood behind that huge pulpit in that hot little church, and saw the people, and began to speak to them, he was *all preacher*! He's been so happy since. . . . It's funny—I thought a man would have to *learn* to preach. Yet, he spoke with such assurance, such confidence, without hesitation. And I was astounded! As I listened, I was also aware of a strange chill in my heart. Oh—I was so proud of him! This handsome, assured man with the marvelous voice. But this man, standing in front of me was a stranger. I had never met him—in all the years I had known him. . . . And I know, as surely as I know anything, that the man who stands in the pulpits of churches for the rest of my life will be a stranger. . . . I want to cry to somebody—but he has been my whole life! What will happen to me if he moves so far away from me? There is no answer. Only a great sense of loneliness. In spite of this, I wouldn't have it any other way!

Therefore, a woman who yearns to be "close to her husband" (as do Kates in general) rather than to be "a teamworker with him" (Martha) or "background supportive" (Mary) can feel isolation in the midst of involvement. She can, moreover, in terms of congregational expectations that she assume "leftover jobs" or fill "unwanted slots," feel like a mere functionary. One woman expressed her sense of being exploited in this way:

> I feel that I'm just part of a *faceless procession* moving through this parsonage. When people telephone, they don't want *me*. They just want the present occupant of the position. The parsonage is a telephone switchboard, and I'm the operator. Operator 5, maybe. But not Kate Jones—a real, live person.

In the final chapter, on "Conclusions and Recommendations," we will discuss Kate again and the issue of how she can be helped to move out of rebellious withdrawal into a fulfilling involvement in her husband's ministry. Now, having examined the most common patterns of involvement and activity of MWs, and some of the variations on these general themes, we must see how these themes are orchestrated in a wider range of situations. This will involve considering both the basic story underlying the types presented and at the same time the individual styles in which that story expresses itself. The typology presented in this chapter represents a kind of bridge between general motivations and specific meanings.

CHAPTER 3

Motivations and Meanings

OTHERS MAY JUDGE in terms of involvement and activity. But primary for MWs themselves are the questions of motivation and meaning. No matter how appropriate the whats and hows, unless the whys and wherefores are relatively clear and consistent, outwardly model behavior may cloak inner contradiction and conflict. Acceptable response to the expectations of others concerning the proper role of the minister's wife will have brought denial of satisfaction, fulfillment—perhaps even integrity.

Getting the Information

Why, then do MWs involve themselves in their husbands' ministry and become active in the life of church and community? As the discussion of patterns of involvement and activity has indicated, motivations are varied. Moreover, they are usually complex, and analysis or even self-report of them most difficult and potentially misleading.

In this investigation, by necessity, major reliance was placed on written report, in response either to questionnaire items which forced choice from preselected alternatives, or to open-ended items, the responses to which the researcher categorized in terms of a constructed coding system. But the same wording may have variant meanings for different individuals, or even for the same individual over a period of time. A combination of motivations may exist, from which one must be chosen as most applicable.

Or, none may really fit, yet one is chosen, with reservations and qualifications.

Furthermore, motivations change with time, with the situation, and with increased maturity. Perhaps most basically—consciously or unconsciously—self-image (as well as social image) is at stake in this reporting of motivations and meanings. These are matters of importance for the individual and not just matters of fact.[1]

At least partly balancing these factors, however, which would tend to lead to superficiality or even deception in reporting, another major influence was operating. Participants in the study were, on the whole, grateful that it was being undertaken and honored that they had been chosen for inclusion. They viewed the investigation as an opportunity to present a more adequate and realistic picture of MWs than in previous literature. They wanted the story told as fully and honestly as possible this time.

For the respondent, this was also a valued and perhaps the first real opportunity to "think things through," with some structure and guidance provided. Thus a number testified that completion of the questionnaires had been for them "a kind of psychoanalysis," "the chance to express myself, and feel that someone was listening and understanding," "an opportunity to think things through, without false idealism or self-pity." As one would expect, therefore, the questionnaires were agents of change.[2]

How, then, was information secured?[3] Basic comparative data, used to construct the types described in Chapter 2, came from items 40-65 of the MW-5 precoded questionnaire (research instruments are found in the Technical Appendix). To probe more deeply into these matters and give greater freedom for adequate and full expression, an open-ended questionnaire (MW-6) was used and completed by approximately 600 of the original 5,000 respondents,[4] and approximately 60 depth interviews were conducted with respondents representing particular points of view, and with their husbands. The final stage of data collection came with the MW-7 questionnaire, completed by about 450 women who had previously completed the MW-5 and MW-6 questionnaires, and in most cases by their husbands as well.

Relationship of Motivation to Other Variables

As the discussion in Chapter 2 indicated, different motivations
tend to be associated with particular involvement and activity
patterns. As Marthas seek to express and fulfill a youthful call
from God to a Church-related vocation and/or to be a MW, so
Marys and Janes take part in their husband's ministry out of
belief in the purposes of the Church. As Dorcases, not certain of
either call or purposes, desire to contribute through useful work,
so Kates seek to be close to their husbands, and/or to fulfill
expectations of husband and/or congregation.

Taken as a whole, when forced to make a choice among the
alternatives provided, one-third of the approximately 5,000 respondents reported themselves to be motivated to take part in
their husband's ministry because of belief in the purposes of the
Church. Almost as many reported their motivation to be the desire to contribute through useful work (27 per cent) or the
experience of a call to be a MW and/or to a Church-related vocation (27 per cent). A total of 13 per cent reported being motivated either by a desire to be close to one's husband or by the
expectations of husband or congregation.

Reported motivation varied, however, according to denominational affiliation. While 47 per cent of Baptists reported call motivation versus 21 per cent purpose motivation, only 21 per cent of
Methodists reported call motivation versus 41 per cent purpose
motivation. There is almost complete reversal of relative emphasis between these two groups. Lutheran MWs are like Methodists in relative de-emphasis of call motivation, and Presbyterians and Episcopalians are like Methodists in relative emphasis
on purposes. Perhaps due to these denominational patterns, as
ministerial income goes up, emphasis on call motivation goes
down!

Moreover, the difference in reported motivation of MWs in
various religious traditions is reflected in the part they take in
their husband's ministry. While the ratio of teamworkers to detached is 30 per cent to 8 per cent for Evangelical and Baptist

MWs, it is 18 per cent to 14 per cent for Disciple, Methodist, and United Church of Christ MWs, and 10 per cent to 21 per cent for Episcopal, Lutheran, and Presbyterian MWs.[5] These differences in reported involvement are not simply a matter of self-report or self-perception according to norms of "woman's place." They are reflected in the amount and kind of activity the woman performs, and in her attitude toward church activities in general.[6]

Denominational contrasts may be illustrated in terms of the local church activity patterns of Baptist and Episcopal MWs.[7] Percentages of women who reported regularly doing and generally enjoying the following activities are:

1. Teach a Sunday-School class—74 per cent of Baptists versus 28 per cent of Episcopalians;
2. Lead a church youth group—40 per cent of Baptists versus 6 per cent of Episcopalians;
3. Leadership training—40 per cent of Baptists versus 6 per cent of Episcopalians;
4. Call on sick and shut-ins—63 per cent of Baptists versus 35 per cent of Episcopalians;
5. Counsel people with problems—42 per cent of Baptists versus 16 per cent of Episcopalians;
6. Hold office in a church women's group—42 percent of Baptists versus 18 per cent of Episcopalians; and
7. Lead devotional services—58 per cent of Baptists versus 16 per cent of Episcopalians.

Motivations are expressed, too, in what is considered a major joy or opportunity of being a MW. Forty-eight per cent of Baptist MWs emphasized showing people a better way of life versus 10 per cent of Episcopalians, while 43 per cent of Episcopalian MWs stressed knowing a wide range of people versus 16 per cent of Baptists. Likewise, 59 per cent of Evangelical MWs emphasized being of service to your fellow men versus 39 per cent of Episcopalians, while 53 per cent of Episcopal MWs stressed personal growth and fulfillment versus 25 per cent of Evangelicals.

Motivation to take part in one's husband's ministry and the actual *activity* pattern are, then, closely related, since *both* are influenced by the dominant understanding of Church and ministry, and of woman's place in them, held by the particular reli-

gious tradition. Yet the relationship is far from exact.[8] While
many more (36 per cent) of those with a call motivation report
themselves to be teamworkers than those with a purpose motivation (11 per cent), still almost two-thirds of those with a call
motivation *do not* report themselves to be teamworkers. In part,
this results from the heavy emphasis in the literature and in MW
groups on being a background supporter, rather than too dominant. But it also reflects the fact that in people, unlike theories,
neat, precise relationships seldom obtain.

Though it can be statistically demonstrated (at the .001 level
of significance for each pair of variables) that the reported motivation, involvement, satisfaction, and set-apartness of MW-5 respondents are not independent of one another, the actual
correlation of one variable with another is only of the order of
.30.[9] That is, it is difficult to predict reported involvement (or
satisfaction, or set-apartness) from reported motivation with
much confidence. Groups can be distinguished, but individual
predictions are risky.

With this caution, other relationships may be noted. First of
all, those motivated by a call *do* tend more often (40 per cent)
to regard themselves as set apart to witness for Christ than do
other MWs (10 per cent). In contrast, the purpose-motivated
more often see their main responsibility, after home and family,
as that of making their church what it should be. Call motivation
does tend to be associated with finding one's major joy in showing people a better way of life, while purpose motivation places
more emphasis on knowing more about the Christian faith. The
useful-work-motivated, in contrast, tend to emphasize respect,
knowing people, and personal growth.

Similarly, those motivated by a call most often feel that they
would have fewer opportunities if not a MW, while the closeness-
and/or expectation-motivated most often feel that they would
have more time, money, or freedom. Those motivated by either a
call or purposes feel *less* often that it is hard to be yourself as a
MW, while the closeness- and/or expectation-motivated *most*
often feel this way. Likewise, the call-motivated less often feel
that always being an example is a strain.

Mary Martha Mountain: Growth Toward Freedom

Statistics, though they may tell the most exact story, seldom tell the most meaningful one. More can be learned from listening to Mary Martha Mountain, the thirty-ish wife of a successful and effective Methodist minister in the South, than from hosts of tables. For Mary Martha, understanding motivations and meanings has been more than an interesting research problem. It has been a life-and-death struggle, through years of intensive psychotherapy.

When our Attitude and Experience Survey (MW-6) reached her in June, 1961, she was according to her own report, "too ill to know about it." With the encouragement of her therapist, however, she continued to participate in the study and completed all the forms, even after her second emotional collapse. And what struck her in August, 1961, was that

however changed my motives may be, and however differently I may approach life in the future, this *is* the life for me. With all its trials, and heartache, and loneliness, and however unorthodox my personal philosophy may be, I can do no less than be a Minister's Wife! If this study did no more good than affirm this in my own mind, it would have been worthwhile!

That, however, is near the end of the story, for as she reported a year afterward, "as this study concludes, a chapter in my own life—of years of psychotherapy—is also ending." Let us move back to an earlier point in the story, for as she herself states, "The roots of my illness reached far beyond the years of my life as a MW; however, my whole attitude toward this life was colored and often contorted by this warp of personality, and certainly the tremendous pressures of the ministry were what finally broke my set of defenses and made psychiatric help imperative." From all available data, this indeed could be made as a generalization: that when MWs are unhappy it tends to be as women, wives, and mothers, and not as MWs. While the church and community situation may involve *precipitating* factors to breakdown or general chronic unhappiness, the basic *roots* are in long-range personality and marital relationship patterns.

Where, then, do the roots of Mary Martha's later personality and behavior patterns lie? Certainly important is the divorce of her parents when she was 18 months old, resulting in her being reared by her grandparents. In her childhood home the dominant figure was her grandmother, "a domineering, mercurial, Calvinistic Methodist, who ruled the household with an iron hand. Punishments were frequent and often cruel psychologically, and every infraction was considered also a sin against God. Therefore, social law and moral law became confused in my mind. Children were to be seen and not heard." In contrast, she describes her carpenter grandfather as "a kind, patient, truly God-fearing man, whom I loved passionately. He may have disapproved of my grandmother's harshness, but he never defied her." Nor, we gather, did her mother—"a sweet, lovely, but completely ineffectual person," who "worked as a maid during most of my childhood."

Despite this description of her childhood home, she reports that

. . . as a very little girl, I think I was happy. I was a fairy-like child, everybody's darling. Probably the next really happy phase of my life, perhaps the happiest of all, came during my 14th and 15th years. My mother had remarried, and for the first time in my life I was out from under the pressure of filling a role. I acquired a nickname, and became a new person. I enjoyed the wider educational perspective of our new community, and was popular with teachers and students alike. For the first time, also, I "belonged," in the most satisfying sense. And I fell in love, purely and simply and completely.

Despite these happy periods,

my childhood, in general, was one long frustration, because I was reaching for stars and capturing so few. My later teens were discouraging because I came to realize that I was the bone of contention in my mother's otherwise ideal marriage. At 16, I left home, to solve the problem. Then began the years of struggle—for an education, for adequate finances, for love.

Therefore, "being a minister's wife has meant for me what I never had before—a sense of belonging," though "if I were not a minister's wife . . . I would have pursued my identity in a career

—most likely in medicine." "When I was younger, I did, or attempted to do, *everything* asked or expected of me," but now, "What is most important to me is to find myself as a woman—the real one, not an image." The congregation, collectively, is a warm, human entity, whom I love," but "In the future, I intend to seek fulfillment in activities unrelated to the church," for "the hardest thing to endure in this life is the loneliness," and "my closest friends are people outside the church, who do not expect me to BE anything." For her, "Always being an example became such a strain that I collapsed under it, confused as to who I really was."

In the struggle to achieve these goals, Mary Martha has had a number of things "going for her." As she states,

when I was 14 years of age, I looked at myself clearly and decided I had better capitalize on what good points I had, for I was short in the looks department! My assets include a good mind, a quick wit and a genuine liking for people (in spite of my fear of them). I have acquired a lively interest in the arts, attempted to cultivate social charm, and a knowledge of what makes people tick. Through my work with Dr. Bill in psychotherapy, I came to realize these drives were the products of a frightful fear, a lack of identification as a child, and guilt. I often take on more responsibility than I can handle; I am only just beginning to channel the anger and hurt of many years into more constructive areas.

Here, then, was a teamworker whose high involvement in her husband's ministry and the life of the congregation was

motivated by guilt, whose demands for expiation were impossible. Never certain of my own identity as a woman or as a person, my efforts to meet every demand made of me as a minister's wife ended, eventually, in breakdown. . . . Once I had faced and resolved the guilt, so deeply buried, I also felt that whatever "debt" I had "owed" the Church was paid! Re-evaluating my own motives to work, to service, will take much time and thought. This study has helped me greatly in this area.

As a result of examining her motivations and meanings, Mary Martha now is "sure of several things: whatever I do, as a minister's wife, will be done through real choice and not through the demands of compulsion. If I can become a whole, genuine, mature woman, the Church will be only *part* of my life, not *all* of it. I do not believe God asks that of me."

What Made Mary Martha Run?

Many factors influenced Mary Martha Mountain's patterns of involvement, motivation, and fulfillment. As a Methodist, she was less likely to stress call motivation than a Baptist would be, and more likely to be concerned with the purposes of the Church. That is, she was more apt to be intellectually idealistic (and therefore potentially critical when realities did not match ideals), and less apt to be unreflectively active. Nevertheless, as her fictitious name indicates, Mrs. Mountain combined Mary-type motivation with a guilt and resulting compulsion which led to Martha-type involvement. She was *driven* by her own inner dynamics, rather than responding to God's *call*.

Therefore, though Mary Martha matches almost exactly the group description of purpose-motivated background supporters found in Chapter 2, she did not find their general level of satisfaction and fulfillment. She was interpersonally oriented and had the religious commitment of a disciple. As the wife of a successful and effective minister, whom she admired both as a person and in his work, she was not subject to the disillusionment or despair of those less fortunate in these regards. Living in the South, she was expected to be more highly involved in church activities as a church hostess than if she had lived in the Northeast or Far West. But the pressure on her toward involvement was less for the fact that she was in a fairly large church in a medium-sized city. (*Church* size influences MWs' involvement and fulfillment much more than *community* size. The major issue is the size of the expectation-setting social unit.)

However, in Mary Martha's case, much more influential than situation was background. Her parents' divorce when she was 18 months old, and the resulting influence of her grandmother on her development, greatly affected the way she later functioned as a MW. As indicated in discussing Dorcases, *over*stability of home background—if protective care is provided at the price of independent selfhood—can produce problems for MWs, since they are so often forced to make decisions in ambiguous and otherwise risky situations. (For example, there are potential hazards involved in either accepting or rejecting an office in a church woman's group.) But in Mary Martha's case, *under*-stability produced the same results. Lacking basic trust from early childhood, she lacked the foundation for autonomy and identity.[10] She substituted industry, in the effort to justify and find herself.

Thus, as Mary Martha came to realize through psychotherapy, her high degree of involvement in church work and passive conformity to congregational demands and expectations represented "guilt, whose demands for expiation were impossible," even though she sought to meet "every demand made of me as a MW." Like other MWs who are driven by the desire to please others and/or by the cultural ideal of the MW, she found this an impossible combination of responsibilities to fulfill.

Moreover, she was often disillusioned by

the insidious political overtones of all aspects of the church, which I have seen at first hand, . . . as I slowly came to realize that the church —that pure Bride of Christ—the one perfect, infallible security of my childhood—was ruled by little, bickering politicians, . . . As I learned the value of figures, the obsession of the Powers That Be with positive statistics, my disenchantment became complete. The organizational church is a fascinating game, but the spirit of the True Church is not there! It is in the hearts of the worshipping Little People, who never suspect, or expect it to be anything more than a House of God!
In spite of everything, however, I believe in the Church. With my whole heart! . . . I remember standing alone in the empty church of my childhood, hearing the silence, feeling very, very small, and yet a giant. The afternoon sun streamed through the huge, beautiful windows, turning everything golden, lighting every object with joy— even me. I was, perhaps, only six or seven, but I've never forgotten the moment I first felt the presence of God—in a church. Unfortunately, the life of a minister's wife has practically destroyed that for me. One by one my idols fell, my refuges dissolved in the cold light of logic. . . . I gradually came to understand that I must find God again—or perhaps for the *first* time—for myself. Even in the depths

of my despair and aloneness, I have never doubted that He is there, and that I have built a wall of pain and fear and disillusionment between us. Now that I feel emotional health to be just around the corner for me, I have enough faith left to hope I can find God.

In part, of course, to "find God . . . for myself" will mean getting rid of the God of her grandmother. It will mean rebuilding her conception of God, and redefining the nature of sin and the bases for moral law. It will mean internalizing values to replace the consuming desire to belong, and therefore to please as the basis for belonging. And so, in a candlelight Good Friday evening service, Mary Martha heard the words of the anthem, "Gethsemane," and

. . . I looked at the people, struggling, human and sinful, even as I, yet reaching toward God, and I heard the first compelling phrase— "Come! Let us kneel, in sorrow and contrition. . . ."— . . . and I was praying to God, on my own behalf and the behalf of these people— "My sins, my sins, my Savior, they take such hold on me. . . ." (Dear God! Who knew this better than I!) "I know they are forgiven, but their pain to me is all the grief and anguish they laid, my Lord, on thee. . . ." I was only aware of sorrow, and forgiveness, and soul-shaking humility, as I saw the people come to Communion—the urban, sophisticated people, with tears streaming down their faces, and hope in their eyes.

And so we leave Mrs. Mountain—at an ending and a beginning. In her life story the variables previously discussed in terms of group statistics take on new meaning in the patterning of a particular personality. In some respects, Mary Martha represents most MWs; in other respects, she is quite distinctive.

Mrs. Mode: Summary of Questionnaire Responses

It is time now to turn to discussion of *general* trends in the motivations and meanings of American Protestant MWs. Fundamentally, each MW's motivations and meanings are unique. Yet, as we have seen, certain patterns do tend to occur more frequently for women with particular types of involvement and activity. And without sacrificing individuality to cultural stereotypes, factors can be identified which are shared by most MWs. What follows represents a summary of the modal (not model!)

pattern of responses to the MW-5 and MW-6 questionnaires, on the basis of the statistics listed in the Technical Appendix. To make these patterns more intelligible to the general reader, they will be presented in the form of a description of a representative composite woman, Mrs. Mode.

Quite properly, the word *mode* suggests a variety of connotations, as the following summary of definitions from Webster's unabridged dictionary will indicate. We will therefore be concerned with the patterning of tones of meaning, the structuring of the personal logic of motivation, the manner of expression, and the condition or state of being and living, that occur most frequently among American Protestant parish MWs.

No one MW will match this group portrait exactly. Each will wish retouching of outlines at some points. Almost every statement requires an "It depends," qualification. Nevertheless, in so far as *any* description of a group is valid, this one communicates the general thrust and flavor of responses to the questionnaires employed. With the plea of J. Robert Oppenheimer "not to treat too harshly those who tell you a story having observed carefully, without having established that they are sure that the story is the whole story and the general story"[11]—let the story begin!

Though at some points there is no real comparison between her present home and family life and that of her childhood, Mrs. Mode senses a general similarity. The major difference comes at the point of her sharing of family responsibilities with her husband, to a greater degree than was true with her father and mother. In general she likes this, though at times she wishes she had more relief and support. On the whole, she is happy in her present situation, and reports it as better than the home in which she grew up.

What she most admires about her husband is his devotion to his work, as well as the high regard in which others hold him as a person. At home the dedicated minister may, and often does, become rather rigid or inconsiderate in relation to the needs of his own family. But this is taken as the price of his calling.

In general, Mrs. Mode feels positively about herself as a person, though at times her shyness, lack of self-confidence, and impatience bother her. In her best moments, she views herself as basically a friendly, concerned person, whom others judge attractive. But she realizes that she holds a lower opinion of herself than others do, or than reality justifies, and wishes that she could increase in the sense of adequacy and security.

When things do get her down, however, it's hard to know to whom to turn. She accepts the general dictum that one should not have close friends in the parish, because of dangers of violated confidences and cliquishness. Her girl friends of school and/or college years live too far away to be real confidantes. Other friends, such as fellow MWs or fellow workers, are of some help, but she can't discuss certain aspects of church life even with them. Her husband wants to help, but is often too busy and concerned with church affairs to be readily available. Even when physically present he may not be really there. In a genuine crisis, she will blow off steam to him. But in less serious situations she tries to work it out by herself, through reading, writing, getting off by herself away from family pressures, or perhaps through having a good cry.

Though Mrs. Mode may feel put upon or neglected on a number of occasions, when her husband puts the church ahead of his family, she generally does not consider the church as a rival for his affections. She has learned to accept the situation rather than feeling sorry for herself or trying to get back at him. For she has slowly come to realize that her husband feels guilty about the situation, but sees no practical way out of it. Seldom, in any case, do the pressures of ministerial responsibilities keep them as a couple from fulfillment in the sexual love aspect of their marriage. More often is *she* too exhausted for love-making than he!

Thus for Mrs. Mode major satisfactions and fulfillments are found in the home rather than in the church, while for her husband the focus is the church. (Focus on the home would be less true for teamworker MWs, and more true for the detached—who, indeed, find major gratifications in neither home nor church, but rather in individualized pursuits.)

Yet, while major fulfillment is found in the home, church activities often do provide Mrs. Mode with genuine satisfaction as an individual. The part she takes in the life of a particular congregation will depend on its particular needs and available leadership. But in most situations she will focus on activities involving women and children, such as attending women's groups, entertaining in her home, leading a devotional service, or teaching a Sunday-School class when called on. In addition, she is likely to call on sick and shut-ins and *informally* counsel people with problems, and may hold an office in a church women's group, and greet parishioners with her husband after services.

She finds joys and opportunities in these activities, since they give her the chance to (1) share meaningfully in her husband's work, (2) learn more about the Christian faith, (3) be of genuine service, and (4) achieve personal growth and fulfillment. In other words, her motivation to involvement includes orientations toward husband, God, others, and self. She may, in her relations to others, stress knowing a wide range of people, or she may place the emphasis on showing people a better way of life. She may place herself in the role of disciple-learner, or in that of apostle-witness. But in any case, commitment, sharing, and growth are all emphasized.

Moreover, Mrs. Mode's involvement in her husband's ministry and the life and work of the Church expresses basic values, goals, and theological affirmations. In her ranking of the relative importance of various goals of life, devotion to God, as expressed in doing God's will, comes first, closely followed by her responsibility to provide love and security to her family as a good wife and mother. She seeks both to be genuinely concerned about other people and to achieve self-understanding and development, so that she may be a genuine person with a mature outlook. Less important to her, though not to be disregarded, are service to the community, self-sacrifice for the sake of a better world, achieving personal immortality in heaven, and preserving the best in human culture.

Devotion to God, for Mrs. Mode, is understood in terms of the creedal statements of the Christian Church. Seldom does she express conflict between her personal belief system and those traditional formulations. At the same time, she struggles to make tradition "her own," as expressed in the quality of her life as well as in intellectual understanding. She does not want simply to "repeat the words." She wants to know what the faith *means*, and what it *implies* for her daily, practical living. And, central to her understanding of the faith is *relationship* to God, as revealed through His Son—as made known through His Spirit—as expressed in His dealings with His children.

Such ideals tend, however, to bring frustration and conflict in terms of the constant sense of falling short. As a MW, she feels she should be a saint, yet the reality often appears closer to a devil. She aspires to *give* (to God, to family, to others), yet finds herself constantly yearning to *receive*. She has a mental picture of the MW as calm, cool and collected, poised, gracious and radiant. But she perceives herself as harried and distraught, overwhelmed and underpowered.

As she becomes older and gains more experience as a MW, frustrations and conflicts do tend to lessen, and joys and opportunities to increase. She has learned to adjust her ideals to the realities of situations, other people, and herself. She has learned how to lead from her strengths and compensate for her weaknesses. She has discovered how to say No graciously and creatively. She has, through a variety of experiences, found how to cope with a wider range of situations, so that she is less often confronted with the utterly new and threatening. More able to "be herself," rather than constantly trying to "prove herself" to her husband, the congregation, and ultimately to God, she is also less driven by guilts and insecurities, and more able to give of herself freely and spontaneously.

Yet, even with increased experience and maturity, certain problems do remain. Mrs. Mode still finds it hard, especially in small churches and communities, to have adequate expression and development of her artistic, intellectual, and generally creative abilities. She often discovers herself "doing more, and enjoying it less." At times, she looks back with a certain degree of nostalgia to her working days, when what she did was appreciated, and when she was treated with consideration—"not as a household drudge and unpaid assistant minister."

These, however, are minor complaints which in her better moments she regards as childish, and in any case shared by most young mothers. What bothers her most is that, though she has many acquaintances, she has few close friends in whom she can really confide. Time is a problem, too—in terms both of the limited amount for home and family, and of the difficulty in *planning*, because of her husband's irregular work schedule. And when there is the rare free evening, to "go out as other couples do, and not to another church supper" there just aren't the funds, especially when baby sitting is figured in. In the early years as a MW, more than now, there were the additional problems of moving so often that one never put down any real roots in a neighborhood or community. (How often is a parsonage part of a real neighborhood, anyhow?)

In general, though, parsonage living and finances are not the problems that books and articles about the ministry had led Mrs. Mode to expect. She does *not* usually feel herself to be in a goldfish bowl, under constant observation, but rather has the sense that her privacy and that of her family are respected. Her husband's salary certainly does not permit luxury living, and at times she wishes she had either the dishwasher and second car of the wives of other professional men, or a husband home more of the time like wives of men on a forty-hour week.

When she thinks deeply and honestly about it, however, she admits that what more than compensates for these frustrations and limitations is believing in the importance of what her husband is doing, and being able, unlike most wives, to have a meaningful part in it. Certainly there were some monstrosities of parsonages in the early years of her husband's ministry, but overall, parsonage committees have been very considerate. And there does seem to be a tendency toward provision of a housing allowance in lieu of a parsonage, when the minister and his family desire this.

Many months, it *is* hard to make ends meet. She *does* wonder where they will live after her husband's retirement, when there is no longer a parsonage provided. She does have concern about where the funds will come from for the college education of her children. Yet she recognizes that these are luxury-type problems which trouble most young middle-class couples. And when she gets out of these anxieties and takes the Sermon on the Mount seriously, she wouldn't swap her situation for another.

Value Orientations

In constructing and analyzing the questionnaires from which Mrs. Mode's story comes, the basic theoretical framework was that of a MW's system of interacting relationships. Of particular concern were the fulfillments and frustrations resulting from the expectations imposed and responsibilities assumed in relationships with God and His Church, self-ideal, husband, children, congregation, community, and people in general. In each of these relationships, there is a blend of self-assertion and yielding to others, of recognition by both parties of mutual rights and duties. These relationships have been implicitly discussed throughout this chapter, as well as in Chapter 2. Let us focus now on the goals and values of MWs, as these are grounded in theological viewpoints and devotional practices, and expressed in particular ways of life.

Needless to say, this is a difficult area of investigation, especially when one must depend upon written report. A person seldom fully understands his own values, and if he does, he may not desire or be able to communicate them. (For our purposes, a value may be defined as a belief upon which a person acts by preference, and which affects the direction his life takes.[12]) Moreover, there are inconsistencies and contradictions within each personality system, and levels of commitment to and expression of various values. There are verbal values and operational values, creeds as cultural artifacts and creeds as living testaments, forms of devotion and objects of devotion. Similar words may point to quite different realities, or carry different meanings.

With all these qualifications, what may be observed about the values and goals of the American Protestant MWs who participated in this study? Most obvious was their religious commitment and desire to be of assistance in their husbands' ministry. They wanted to serve God and husband, and believed in the purposes of the Church, whether or not they had experienced a specific sense of call to be a MW and/or to a Church-related vocation. Whether their motivation and involvement were those of a Martha, Mary, Dorcas, or Jane (Kates represent special issues), they wanted to be supportive and of genuine assistance.

Most MWs indicated, then, a high degree of religious commitment, expressed in a desire to share in their husbands' vocation, either as a fellow apostle showing others a better way of life or as a disciple learning more about the Christian faith. Conflicts sometimes came, however, between service to the congregation (as distinguished from God) and to one's family. For the majority of MWs, when a choice had to be made, devotion to God was expressed in family care (sometimes involving employment to supplement a husband's ministerial income) rather than in church work. For, with the exception of Marthas, the primary role orientation was that of wife and mother, not that of associate minister. Potential value conflicts were not limited, however, to family versus congregation, but involved other values as well.

If one omits from analysis the value of "achieving personal immortality in heaven"—which had widely varying meanings to respondents—three major value orientations are represented by the nine "goals of life" ranked by 427 respondents to the MW-6 questionnaire. (A total of 623 women completed MW-6, but mean rankings, in parentheses below, summarize the responses of MWs from only those denominations for which data were most solid: 100 Baptists, 33 "Evangelicals," 81 Methodists, 54 from the Disciples and United Church of Christ, 81 Presbyterians, 38 Lutherans, and 40 Episcopalians.)

For these MWs, relative emphases on three groupings of values (the names assigned to orientations are the author's, not the respondents') were:

1. *Propriate Service*—with a mean rank of *2.88* (1 = most important), when the following ranks are averaged: "devotion to God, doing God's will" (1.59); "providing love and security for one's family" (2.71); and "being genuinely concerned about other people" (4.34).

2. *Self-Development*—with a mean rank of 5.33, when the following ranks are averaged: "understanding yourself; having a mature outlook" (5.15); "self-development; becoming a real, genuine person" (5.30); and "peace of mind, contentment, and stillness of spirit" (5.54).

3. *Peripheral Service*—with a mean rank of *7.48* (10 = least important), when the following ranks are averaged: "serving the community of which one is a part" (6.70); "self-sacrifice for the sake of a better world" (7.21); and "preserving the best in human culture" (8.53).

These rankings indicate preference for *propriate* over *peripheral* service. (The term propriate connotes that which is central and "close to home," in personal importance as well as social distance.) One cannot, therefore, simply contrast emphasis on self with emphasis on service of others. It is a question also of *sphere* of service. For these women defined devotion to God and concern for others in such terms that serving the *community*, self-sacrifice for the sake of the *world*, or preserving the best in the *culture* were relatively de-emphasized. They tended to see their major sphere of service as home and family, while that of their husbands was the local congregation.

There were, of course, group as well as individual variations from this general pattern of value orientations. Thus, Baptist and Evangelical MWs placed more emphasis on devotion to God (mean rank of 1.24) and less on self-development (5.81) than did other MWs. Episcopal MWs made less value distinction between devotion to God (2.10) and love of family (2.20), or between preserving culture (7.52) and sacrifice for a better world (7.60), than other MWs. Lutheran MWs, though very different from the Baptists and Evangelicals in involvement and activity, were like them in relatively low emphasis on service to community (7.71) coupled with concern for achieving personal immortality (5.21 versus 8.18 for Presbyterians, 8.61 for Methodists, 8.64 for Disciples, and 8.73 for Episcopalians). Evangelical, Baptist, and

Lutheran MWs also placed relatively less emphasis on self-development and self-understanding than did other MWs.

These value emphases are consistent with the dominant theological positions—and preferred patterns of involvement and activity discussed in Chapter 2—of the religious traditions represented, as expressed by MWs from them. However, *across* denominations there was a dominant value orientation which seems related to patterns of need fulfillment, in so far as these can be inferred from the data. In a pilot program for wives of theological students, the rankings of values by 103 students' wives from four seminaries—Boston, Garrett, Southern Baptist (Louisville), and Yale—paralleled those reported above for 427 MWs.[13] And in personality profiles, these seminarians' wives were characterized by M.M.P.I. (Minnesota Multiphasic Personality Inventory) scores related to sensitivity and concern with the reaction of others, emphasis on femininity and marriage, social concern coupled with shyness, and a relatively low degree of rebelliousness and aggressiveness.[14] Likewise, on the *Edwards Personal Preference Schedule* (based on H. A. Murray's need-press theory) the needs receiving particular stress were nurturance (sympathetic care for others) and affiliation, followed by endurance, order, and deference to the wishes of others. There was less stress than by the general population on the needs for dominance and aggression, and particularly low emphasis on autonomy and exhibition.

Admittedly, these data relate to women averaging 22 years of age and two years of marriage, who are just starting out on the life of a MW, with limited experience and often considerable apprehension. Also, as a volunteer group, it contains a high representation of first-born children (48.5 per cent), and birth order relates to many of the characteristics listed above.[15] However, the personality type described by the test scores of seminarians' wives does seem to occur frequently among even experienced, mature MWs. Thus, in describing themselves on the MW-6 questionnaire, women—especially Disciple, Methodist, and United Church of Christ MWs from the South—often mentioned concern about their shy, retiring nature. In addition, the other aspects of personality with which dissatisfaction was most often expressed— impatience, perfectionism, moodiness, temper, and so on—indicated a tendency to turn feelings, especially negative feelings, inward rather than expressing them directly or spontaneously. Even the women who most often mentioned their friendliness and concern for others as a personal "strong point" (Episcopal, Lutheran, and Presbyterian MWs from the South) also often mentioned a felt need for further development in social abilities. For the life of a MW demands growth beyond initial shyness and insecurity; it demands transcending one's limitations.

It appears, then, that the religious commitment and resulting involvement in their husbands' work of MWs both (1) *produce* tendencies toward feelings of inferiority and insecurity, when they fall short of their ideals, which may lead to social withdrawal; and (2) may *alleviate* these feelings, through a sense of the worth of the goals to which they have committed themselves. Heightened ideals both frustrate and sustain. For the combination of situational *demands* (toward both Martha-type leadership and Mary-type social involvement) and personal *values* makes life worth while. But it also makes it difficult for many women to measure up to their own judgment of what they should be and do. Their ideal is that of a "calm Corinne," while the perceived reality is that of a "harried Hannah." There is an experience of "copelessness" as well as—or perhaps even because of—religious commitment and vocation.

In a way, the dominant value orientation (of propriate service ranked 2.88, versus self-development ranked 5.33, and peripheral service ranked 7.48) represents an attempt at resolution of competing, and potentially conflicting, goals. The demands of devotion to God and providing love and security for one's family seem so great, and one's capacities for fulfillment of these demands so limited, that other responsibilities to community, world, culture, and the rest must be narrowed. Ambiguities arise, too, with regard to the extent to which one can identify "doing God's will" with church activities. Most basic, however, is the problem of maintaining self-development (including self-understanding and basic contentment) in the midst of service which can so easily become frantic and compulsive. What apparently takes many women (and especially Dorcases and Kates) years to realize and work out experientially is that the two are not necessarily contradictory. Something of the dynamics of the process may be seen in the following summaries of the MW-6 questionnaires of two women written by a clinical psychologist:

Mrs. X seems a happy, well-adjusted, and secure woman. Though husband and family come first in her life, she gets many real satisfactions from church work and feels close to members of the congregation. She socializes easily, feels a part of the community, and is not lonely. Is busy and highly involved, but she is also secure enough not to feel guilty about her shortcomings or to be oversensitive to criticism. Can place her own needs and convenience above those of the congregation when necessary, easily, naturally, and realistically, without feeling guilty. Also, doesn't feel inadequate when she dislikes something or is unwilling to do certain things. Can discriminate among demands appropriately. Respects her husband and considers herself a helpmeet to him. Main limitation she feels as a MW is lack of a "home of my own." In values, places devotion to God first, followed by peace of mind, love to family, and self-development and understanding.

Mrs. Y seems to be a balance between feelings of frustration and fulfillment in the activities of this MW. Her major struggle seems to be with the development of a comfortable self-image. She feels inadequate and inferior and must keep reminding herself that she can do *something*. The relationships with her family seem good, and this is an area that is of paramount importance to her. When frustrations enter her life, she depends in large measure on her relationship to God to see her through. Her relationships with congregation and community are good, and she finds fulfillment in them. But she wishes her life were less chaotic, and she regards this confusion as related to her own incompetence, even though she is actively engaged in the work of the church and sees herself as a teamworker. Her theological statement reflects a useful-work emphasis. There is frustration and conflict between her perception of what is expected of her and her ability to accept these role expectations. In values, she puts God and family first. She is convinced that helping others is doing God's work, but at the same time feels that she is not doing enough in this work.[16]

In succeeding chapters we must, therefore, explore further those factors which contribute to a MW's *co-ordinating* fulfillment with involvement, rather than seeking to avoid frustration through either Dorcas-type withdrawal or Kate-type rebellion. At this point, only one factor will be considered: the devotional life and spiritual development of MWs.

Devotional Life and Spiritual Development

If values are difficult to investigate, devotional life poses even more problems for the researcher. Questionnaires and interviews do, however, yield certain clues and leads with regard to this area, which involves both concern and conflict. Thus, 51 per cent of MW-5 respondents agreed that "it's hard, as a MW, to have regular family devotions," and women of all denominational groupings shared this judgment. There was, however, real difference of opinion among MWs as to whether devotion to God could be identified with "devotions" or "devotional practices." Many would insist that devotion refers to the quality of a life, a dimension of all activities, rather than a specific set of practices such as Bible study and prayer. Also, because of guilt and conflict, this was one of the very few question areas in which the data from precoded (forced choice) questionnaires were not consistent at all points with those from open-ended questionnaires and interviews.[17] To admit "spiritual dryness" (or the other main area of ambiguous data, criticism of one's husband) required progressive development of trust in the researcher. Personal guilt was bad enough, without exposing oneself to the judgment of another.

On the MW-6 questionnaire, therefore, women preferred to state that their personal and family devotional life "can be improved" (24 per cent), rather than to state that they had no regular "devotional practices" (8 per cent), while 38 per cent indicated that unspecified "devotions" contributed to individual growth and stronger family ties. There was, in general, considerable vagueness in indicating what was meant by devotions or how often they occurred. Noticeable exceptions were Midwestern and Southern (but not Northeastern) Baptist and Evangelical MWs, who placed considerably more stress on the value of devotional practices than did other MWs (55 versus 31 per cent). It is interesting, too, that MWs who held full-time employment (usually as schoolteachers or office workers) more often than other MWs (49 versus 28 per cent) indicated that their devotional life had contributed to personal growth or family solidarity, at the same time as more of them (13 per cent) mentioned lack of any regular devotional practices. Apparently working MWs either developed meaningful practices or tended to drop them entirely.

Here again, however, denominational and regional differences operate. On the section of the MW-7 "Roles and Relationships—Wife's Form" questionnaire dealing with "Personal and Devotional Life," the percentages of those who marked the following statements "always," "usually," or "often" (in distinction to "seldom" or "never") were:

1. My husband and I hold family devotions together, on a daily basis: 74 per cent of Baptist and Evangelical MWs, 58 per cent of Episcopal, Lutheran, and Presbyterian MWs, and 38 per cent of Disciple, Methodist, and United Church of Christ [U.C.C.] MWs.

3. At a time of personal crisis or tragedy, I turn to Bible reading and prayer: 99 per cent of Baptist and Evangelical MWs, 92 per cent of Disciple, Methodist, and U.C.C. MWs, and 86 per cent of Episcopal, Lutheran, and Presbyterian MWs.

4. Rather than "set devotions," I "intersperse" reminders of God's presence through the day: 94 per cent of Disciple, Methodist, and U.C.C. MWs, 82 per cent of Episcopal, Lutheran, and Presbyterian MWs, and 57 per cent of Evangelical and Baptist MWs.

7. As a MW, "professionalized religion" makes personal religious life more difficult: 35 per cent of Disciple, Methodist, and U.C.C. MWs, 34 per cent of Baptist and Evangelical MWs, and 20 per cent of Episcopal, Lutheran, and Presbyterian MWs.

8. The fact that my husband is leader of worship detracts from my own worship, somehow: 22 per cent of Disciple, Methodist, and U.C.C. MWs, 18 per cent of Baptist and Evangelical MWs, and 11 per cent of Episcopal, Lutheran, and Presbyterian MWs.

Though it would be dangerous to generalize from these 450 MWs to MWs in general, since completion of three long, complex questionnaires represents a rigorous process of self-selection, the differences of emphasis among denominational groupings are suggestive. Rather clearly, from these as well as other data, Baptist and Evangelical MWs both assign more importance to devotional practices such as Bible study and prayer and maintain them more regularly than do other MWs. (The apparent contradiction of response patterns between items 1 and 4 seems due to interpreting item 1 in terms of family devotions and item 4 in terms of private devotions.) The trend in other denominations, especially for Disciple, Methodist, and United Church of Christ MWs is toward "interspersing" reminders of God's presence throughout the day, rather than set practices at a specific time. All groups (though the emphasis is less among Episcopal, Lutheran, and Presbyterian MWs) tend to turn to Bible study and prayer at time of crisis. Though the differences are not great, there seems also to be less conflict in acceptance of a minister-husband's priestly functions for Episcopal, Lutheran, and Presbyterian MWs than for other MWs.

Women from varying religious traditions, personal backgrounds, and family religious practices differ, then, on the necessity of having devotional life expressed in regular "devotional practices" of a specific type. Yet almost all agree that it is necessary for a MW to "practice the presence of God" if she is to gain the resources necessary for daily living. Almost all would emphasize that she must maintain regular spiritual as well as intellectual development, if she is to grow with her husband and be of service to others. Therefore, when MWs speak of the importance of "devotion to God, doing God's will" or "deepening your commitment to Christ and the Church" they are conscious of the necessity for growth in faith. As is indicated by the following excerpts from a recorded discussion of a group of MWs of various ages and denominations, there are many different interpretations of spiritual development.

You can talk very freely about God and about all sorts of aspects of God, but unless you have a realization and an awareness in your own mind, so that it's real to you, it's very difficult to make it real to anyone else. You can put up a pretense for a little while, and then you show through./Yes, but if you don't have something to start with, you may be sunk.

As far as a real sense of spiritual peace goes, you finish the day at

11:30 P.M. and by that time you're so completely exhausted that a real relationship with God may be blocked. Even in your family devotional life you're hurrying, because at any moment the phone may ring./ I haven't read a book in years! You just never get to the point where you can sit down and do something on your own.

But we need to remember that spiritual development is not exclusively something which requires aloneness. It happens in contacts with friends who worship the same God that I worship. Spiritual development to me means adjusting to people and finding that you're helping people—you don't have to be "in the clouds" . . .

I don't know about that. If necessary, anyone can draw aside for five minutes a day. You don't have to read the Bible or pray to God./ My striving is to get resources to give. What I can give is what I am. I must grow in grace each day.

For me, spiritual life is an awareness of God in all of life. Remind yourself sometime daily of this pervasiveness of God and reassure yourself or lift your mood by quoting verses. Then you feel a little bit committed to being glad./Going apart does not necessarily mean a division of spiritual and secular, but rather an inner evaluation./Yes, a need to try to understand better the nature of God and man and life, to understand why I tick the way I do in a given situation and why people do or don't.

Not always as easy as that, though, when you feel unequal to the burden of giving your children spiritual education./Right, and often without the help of your husband. But for me spiritual education is sharing what I have with them just as I share the food I prepare for them to eat. It becomes a way of life. There's no special program the wife has to carry on because the husband is too busy.

Maybe we're worried about being examples to the parish and community, and guilty about not filling the expected stereotype./And you worry about not giving devotions as your husband would—you're embarrassed if he comes in when you're leading a woman's group, for example./This may be due to lack of spiritual communication in the home./But it's also due to nervousness . . . you want to appear your best to him as he does to you—a sort of idol.

In all of this, you must have a core meaning in your own life, to resist getting pulled in all directions. The Christian life is something that you live in and try to develop.

Minister Husbands: Saints, Companions, and Lovers

To be a MW is first of all to be a wife, and the type of MW you are will depend, in most cases, more on your husband than on congregation, community, denomination, region, or any other variable except perhaps your own personality and commitment.

In this relationship, as in all others, it is the blend of demand with support that is critical. What does a MW perceive as expectations of her? What assistance is she given in meeting her own expectations? In this blend of demand with support, of expectations with rewards, of duties with rights, considerable role confusion can exist for a MW. For her husband is minister—the Rev. Mr. Brown—as well as husband Joe. He proclaims the Word of God and administers the sacraments to her, as well as making love to her and sometimes fighting with her. He has a special authority and a common humanity. She sees him in ministerial robe and bathrobe. She is aware of both his public image and his private reality.

Moreover, she lives out much of her own life through him. As one woman put it,

> . . . she suffers vicariously the frustrations and difficulties that her husband faces in his overburdened life. The mean tyrannical trustee, the petty critical officer in the woman's organization, all the "thorns in the flesh" that sooner or later turn up in the minister's life. Then, too, it is hard to accept the fact that one's husband is giving everything that he has to his calling, even at the cost of neglecting his family, is not adequately appreciated, or perhaps is not in a situation where he has the opportunity of using his training and skills to the full. This kind of thing is much harder for the minister's wife to take than the frustrations of her own life.

She is, then, immersed in her husband's work, his hopes and dreams, and yet often must remain a helpless bystander. She receives many confidences, but dares not communicate them to others.

She is also deeply involved emotionally in his professional advancement, and struggles with particular congregations and standards of evaluation.

> Is there a hierarchy in the . . . church? I see men getting degrees who are not dedicated men but who play "church politics," know the right people, and are men of fence straddling, not conviction. Men who have "press agents" to write nice things about them. Pastors who say black is white in order to be a "good fellow."
> Are pastors given recommendations when an opportunity comes for them by the amount of benevolence their particular church has been

paying? . . . The conflict in my life the past three months, as my husband has been passed by for "fly by night" pastors, has made me more aware of the need for Christ in my life. If it has bewildered me, I wonder what it has done to my husband.

This church had a long history of difficulties, but church headquarters never told us of them; indeed, we were encouraged to take the job. After several utterly discouraging years, we are leaving the church. . . . We have watched every hope and intention we had when we came out of seminary dashed to the ground. There has never been the slightest attempt to act as a Christian congregation. . . .

We love most of the people of the church, but due to my husband's challenging the established power structure, . . . we have now assumed the role of antagonists. My husband's every action is questioned and legislated.

We have had to face with every serious consideration the possibility that we are miscast. Through much counsel and a great deal of prayer, we have decided we will never be happy apart from this work. . . . We look forward to a church relationship where we see an honest effort made to carry out our Lord's demands, both on an individual and a church-wide basis.

The congregation thinks it wants a mighty man that they can point to with pride. But when it comes down to the living, the congregation will chip away at the character, dedication, habits, etc., of the educated suave minister.

But the tobacco-chewing, hair-flying, frayed-collar, shouting grammatical blunderer makes the congregation feel elevated. If he is morally degenerate, so much the better for they can feel righteous as well as elevated. For no matter how poor the representation, the minister represents God and is his ambassador to the congregation. This to me is the epitome of my frustration, and at one time, near breakdown.

As is apparent from the tone of these comments, there is little that so embitters a MW as the failure of congregations and of the Church in general to appreciate and live up to her husband's dedication and ability. She may feel, as many do, "I am the wife of a minister; I married him not because he was a minister, although it was the qualities he possessed as a minister that first attracted me to him." She loves the man; she admires and respects the minister. Thus, about half of MW-5 respondents mentioned their husband's "sincere faith and dedication" as what they most admired. If a MW's husband is five or more years older than she (true for 22 per cent of MW-5 respondents), then she will be even more likely to admire his faith, perhaps even saintliness.[18] Deference to an older, wiser man can further increase the emotional distance she may already feel with regard to a minister.

For most MWs, what is required and found, however, is not a saint but a companion and lover. Thus, in describing their husbands, while praising their dedication and ability, 23 per cent of MW-6 respondents also mention procrastination, general "sloppy" habits, and lack of discipline and organization, another 33 per cent mention rigidity and compulsiveness, and an additional 19 per cent refer to lack of consideration for family needs. (And what of the remaining 25 per cent of minister-husbands? They must be the saints!) It is not difficult, therefore, for most MWs to be aware of their husbands' humanity. They just wish that they had more time to be together, without interruptions and free from the constant preoccupation with church business.

> My husband is one of those wonderful, humble, lovable, understanding people that almost everyone likes, and I feel flattered daily that he loves me . . . if I stop to think about it . . . it gives me a terrific jolt in the ego to realize that I am so lucky . . . sometimes it's hard to share him with the rest of the world . . . and at times I literally hate the church for taking so much of his time. . . .

Therefore, on the incomplete-sentences section of open-ended questionnaires, respondents frequently indicated the belief that "if I were not a MW, my life would be different in that . . . I would have a minister and not a part-time husband," or ". . . we would have more time for each other, instead of the time of both of us going to the church." This frustration is the other side of the coin of the fulfillment of sharing in his vocation.

Despite conflicts regarding lack of time to be together, and difficulty in planning the available time, there is little evidence of problems in the sexual love aspects of marriage. When there are difficulties, they appear due to the personalities and histories of the individuals involved, not the ministry as such. Thus, in response to the MW-6 question concerning "problems in the sexual love aspects of marriage . . . [due to your husband's] physical and emotional exhaustion," one MW wrote:

There has never been a night, during the years of our married life, when Phil was too physically or emotionally tired to enjoy sexual love. Perhaps this sounds exaggerated, but it is true. I fill a very basic need for him, in that I am a sort of combination Earth Mother and Den Mother!

Yet, our search for compatibility has been . . . years long, and it is not ended yet. . . . We married young, and were subjected to a long, close relationship before marriage. The guilt I felt from heavy petting, and the emotional block I seem to have erected after our marriage was not surprising, but tragic. Phil was the kindest and gentlest of lovers, but I was unable to respond to him.

In contrast, a very different minister-husband posed this problem for his wife:

He gets great satisfaction from his work, and he tends to give, give, give, until he's at the point where he has nothing left to give. . . . The whole sex picture is one that we struggle with very definitely. But this just doesn't enter his head. He's preoccupied twenty-four hours a day, and so involved in large issues, personal problems with his people, etc., that sex is just relegated to a lower level, as less important. He looks at anything regarding his personal life, even sleep, as a waste of time, and he wishes he didn't have to do it. . . . Sometimes I'm objective about this, and sometimes I'm not.

These statements represent extremes in the husband-wife sexual relationship, of an unresponsive wife with a hyperactive husband, versus the preoccupied husband whose wife would like the opportunity to respond. Neither situation, nor any other, would be typical of MWs in general. As women, they vary as much sexually and emotionally as their husbands do as men, and the interactions between husband and wife are of an infinite variety. *From the data available,* there appear to be no significant differences between the sexual relationships of ministerial couples and those of couples in general—as revealed in studies by Kinsey *et al.* However, this may be a study which someone else will want to conduct!

In any case, as the research of Blood and Wolfe on *Husbands and Wives* in the metropolitan Detroit area revealed, *expressions* of affection and love are less important to most couples than the underlying feeling tone of *companionship*:

Companionship has emerged as the most valued aspect of American marriage today. . . . The primary emphasis is on companionship in leisure-time activities, not on merging every aspect of married life. . . . On the other hand, couples must take time to do things together if companionship is to exist. Such time is short if the husband works overtime, if he is obsessed with getting ahead in life, and if the wife is tied down with a large number of children. . . . During the child-rearing years, husbands and wives often cease doing things together, and grow apart from each other. . . . Such couples live the later years as relative strangers under the same roof, searching elsewhere for companionship or resigned to a life of increasing loneliness. . . . Companionship requires taking time and making a little effort. Most couples do—but not all.[19]

What was true for husbands and wives in the metropolitan Detroit area appears true for the MWs who participated in this study. And there are both particular potentialities and particular limitations on companionship implicit in the situaton of a MW.

Though this is difficult to evaluate, the over-all impression from questionnaire and interview data would be that MWs have *more time* with their husbands than do most wives. Indeed, for some wives, particularly when the study is in the parsonage rather than the church, this can be a problem in itself. But the distribution of this time is different from that of most families. And, more important, little of it is in a strict sense leisure time. To get away from the church, mentally as well as physically, is a great problem, and many MWs are bothered by a constant "two's company, three's a crowd" feeling at this point. How a woman responds to this degree of involvement of both of them in the life and work of the church depends, of course, on the person concerned.

For a Martha, to give all of herself in teamwork in the ministry is the richest fulfillment of what she is called by God to be and do. Others may not be quite so sure.

My husband was a student and a teacher early in our marriage. We had much in common then as we do now, but I was much freer. . . . He did the sitting while I did the running, or we would have cozy evenings at home with friends or just ourselves. Now life is just *too* hectic and purposeful, I sometimes think, to be really doing what you are intending to do. I think my attitude toward the church is much more that of a job that my husband loves, rather than a cause to which I am utterly devoted.

Thus, John Koehler discovered in a study among American Baptist Convention MWs of "The Minister as a Family Man" that, while respondents estimated the time husbands were at home with family (exclusive of sleeping) as averaging 26 hours a week, they nevertheless mentioned lack of time for each other and family as their main source of difficulty between husband and wife.[20] They referred to a monopoly of church business which made the family always come in second place and denied them any real social life or change of focus. When asked how many days off husband and wife had taken together in the past four weeks, about 50 per cent said that *no* day had been taken off, and less than 2 per cent reported a regular day off each week.

Those who had begun to solve the problem of planned time together, free from preoccupation with church work, as a basis for companionship, reported:

> His time should be so budgeted that it will reflect that his concern for family is equal to his concern for parishioners. Too many ministers have a queer "conscience" that makes them feel guilty if spending time relaxing at home. Time at home is so rare that they try to force recreation, family conferences, family devotion, instead of enjoying a more relaxed and natural sequence of family living.

> For the first seven years of our ministry my husband was "too busy" for regular days off. It was his physician who asked him if he were trying to save the world in the first ten years of his ministry and die or become disabled at an early age, or if he might consider pacing himself and being around to contribute his energies for four decades. My husband took stock of himself and his job and made the decision. He works like a beaver six days a week, arranges to be home for meals whenever possible, and plans the one day as a "date" with me or with the family unless emergencies keep him.

> I get hold of his engagement book, compare it with mine, and plan a month in advance on the "blank spaces." Planning together, working together, helps to bring about those enjoyable times when we can be together as a family.

These reports of Baptist MWs in Koehler's study reflect the wisdom of experience in dealing with potentially conflicting aspects of a MW's situation. For if a MW feels denied close friendship with members of the congregation, due to fears of implied partiality or cliquishness, it may be too much for her to bear if she also feels denied her husband's companionship. However, these and other issues cannot be considered adequately except in the context of a general pattern of fulfillments and frustrations. To this topic we now turn.

CHAPTER 4

Fulfillments and Frustrations

IF SO MUCH is demanded and expected of a MW, just what does she get in return? Are the rewards worth the necessary sacrifices? Or is any woman who considers marrying a minister thereby condemning herself to a drab, circumscribed existence of limited finances and time for herself and family, in which her life will no longer be her own? Is the reality as bad as the popular books and articles indicate, when they paint the portrait of a "poor thing" condemned to a hard, confined pattern of living? Or is this a good, fulfilling life, with opportunities for meaning and growth which ordinary women in our society miss—and the popular portraits mere caricatures?

Some Relevant Factors

In response to any question regarding the minister's wife, the answer must be that "it depends." Whether, in general, a woman finds being a MW primarily fulfilling and satisfying or primarily frustrating and confining depends on many factors. First of all, there is the issue of what she is seeking in, and from, life. Second, how many of those ideals and needs are, or can be, fulfilled in her family life and/or employment outside of the home? Third, what is her marital relationship—what demands does her husband make upon her, in relation to her ability to meet those demands, and what resources does he provide to assist her in her own self-expression and growth?

Fourth, what were her early "pattern-setting" experiences as a

MW—was there such an impossible combination of demands that she just gave up and/or rebelled, or were there supporting structures in the situation which encouraged her growth toward increased competence? Fifth, what is the nature of the present situation—what is her role, in terms of the defined expectations of others, the congregational history of previous ministers and their wives, and the system of rights and obligations to which she responds?

These questions indicate *a few* of the factors that help to shape the fulfillment and/or frustration of a particular MW. There are many more, and the number of possible combinations is practically infinite. Yet to leave the matter at the "it depends" level is seldom satisfying.

If any generalization can be made, it is that MWs much more often report themselves to have found being a MW satisfying and fulfilling than frustrating and confining. More than a third, in fact, state that the life has been *very* satisfying, while less than 5 per cent describe it as frustrating and confining, and only 10 per cent more describe it as "so-so." (For the approximately 5,000 respondents, the number of "satisfied" is over 85 per cent, versus 14 per cent "so-so" or "frustrated"—hereafter referred to as "so-so-frustrated"—and 1 per cent no response.)

What factors influence satisfaction as a MW? Certainly finances are important: a MW is much more likely to be satisfied if she judges her husband's ministerial income as "sufficient to meet her family's needs, with no scrimping involved." Satisfaction will be accented if she feels that "economically, your family is 'better off' . . . than your parents were, when you were a child."[1] She is more likely to be satisfied if she *does not* have preschool age children at home,[2] if she is over 50 rather than under 35 years of age, and if she married her husband *after* his seminary training, rather than before or during it.

She will probably be more satisfied if both she and her parents participated regularly in the life of the same denomination of which her husband is now a minister.[3] She will more likely be satisfied if she was born as the third, or later, child, in a family than if she was first- or second-born. There is a tendency, too, for daughters of farmers, and women whose husbands are five or more years older than they, to be more satisfied. But contrary to what one might expect, there is no clear relationship between the amount of a MW's education and her reported satisfaction.[4]

Moreover, one can estimate probable satisfaction in terms of a MW's *degree of involvement* in her husband's work. If she reports herself to be "very involved, as a teamworker, sharing in his ministry," then she is much more likely also to report herself as "very satisfied." If she describes herself as "involved, but no more than if he were in another vocation," she is more likely to state that she has in general found being a MW "so-so" or "frustrating and confining." (The ratio of very satisfied to so-so-frustrated is about 6:1 among teamworkers, 3:1 among background supporters, and 1:2 among the detached.)

She will more likely report satisfaction if she considers herself to have been "called to be a MW and/or to full-time Christian service" than if she reports her motivation to take part in her husband's ministry as based on "the desire to be close to your husband" or because "it's expected of you (by husband or congregation)." Similarly, those who describe themselves as "set apart, to witness for Christ" as a MW are much more likely to be satisfied; less than 1 per cent of this group report themselves to be "so-so" or "frustrated and confined," versus more than 50 per cent of those who consider themselves to be "an individual, for whom others cannot legislate" as a MW.

She will tend to be more satisfied if she sees her major responsibility, after being a good wife and mother, as "making the church what it should be," rather than "fulfilling your own potential as a person"; and if she sees her major joys and opportunities in religious witness, rather than in social contacts or personal growth. She will more likely report herself as personally fulfilled through her life as a MW if she spends relatively little time *worrying* about that fufillment, or whether she's "able to be her real self" or "achieve her true identity." The paralysis of analysis does operate, and one becomes easily mired in a bog of self-commiserating introspection.

Making such judgments, of course, moves beyond research report and descriptive analysis to evaluation and prognosis. Also, the fact that one type of MW will more likely *report* satisfaction and fulfillment (which may or may not be precisely the same thing as *being* satisfied and fulfilled) does not necessarily mean that this is the type of person you *should* be or will *want* to be. Rather, it indicates the kind of orientation and behavior which the husband-church-community social system rewards and supports.

With all these caveats, other factors can be reported which tend to be associated with *feeling frustrated and confined as a MW*. In general, those who are frustrated mention problems and conflicts which relate to lack of satisfaction of emotional needs (loneliness, set-apartness, etc.) rather than the "reality factors" (limitations of time and money) emphasized by the satisfied. Less often than other MWs do the frustrated recommend that young MWs "deepen their personal commitment to Christ and the Church." More often do they relate their frustration to the MW situation (rather than to themselves) and feel that they would have more freedom if they were not a MW. (Among the very satisfied, the ratio of those who emphasize "more freedom" to those who emphasize "fewer opportunities" if not a MW is 1:5; among the so-so-frustrated, the ratio is 11:1.)

Though considerably less active in church work as a group than the satisfied, the so-so-frustrated MWs still take considerable part: 12 per cent of them perform eleven or more activities (versus 27 per cent of the very satisfied) while 17 per cent perform five or less activities (versus 5 per cent of the very satisfied). These are real differences. But since the demands and pressures of the situation require a certain minimum participation, the difference between the satisfied and the frustrated is not so much in terms of *how much* they do as in terms of *what kinds* of activities they perform and *how they feel* about what they do. Though required to do a certain amount in the church, to "save face" or please their husbands, the so-so-frustrated will seldom perform "semi-pro" activities. And much more often (three times as often as the very satisfied, twice as often as the satisfied) will the so-so-frustrated feel negatively about church activities in general.[5]

On attitude items on which there is general consensus among MWs, the so-so-frustrated tend to share the consensus, but to feel more strongly about the issues than other groups. For example, they are more disturbed about "having many acquaintances but few close friends," and that their husbands do not "spend as much time with their families as do other professional men." While 71 per cent of the so-so-frustrated feel that "it is hard to be yourself as a MW," only 35 per cent of the satisfied and 21 per cent of the very satisfied share this opinion.

To summarize: In contrast to the so-so-frustrated, those who report themselves as very satisfied and fulfilled as MWs tend to be women of dedication and energy who are highly involved in their husband's work and the life of the congregation. They find expression for their religious commitment and the means to their own personal growth in church activities, and view themselves as witnesses for Christ rather than as "ordinary Christian lay-women."

The very satisfied Marthas are "higher-intensity" people (in activities as well as attitudes) than are the generally satisfied (but sometimes frustrated) Marys and Janes and the generally frustrated (but sometimes satisfied) Dorcases and Kates. They differ from the so-so-frustrated in that they perceive opportunities for service, rather than limitations of freedom, in the MW's situation. They accept lonely nights and set-apartness from others as part of the job for the wife of anyone in a position of public leadership. They have become reconciled to the fact that, for their husbands, church must often have first priority, before home and family. They seek to "love God and do my best," and are not often analytic or introspective about their situations. They have difficulty understanding why those who are frustrated "get so worked up."

Dorothy Taylor: Comfortable Within Limits

Though proportionately more teamworkers than background supporters report themselves to have found "being a MW very satisfying and fulfilling," more than a third of background supporters do make this judgment.[6] One such MW is Dorothy Taylor, the wife of a Congregational minister who moved from the Northeast to the Midwest in the course of this study. Dorothy is in her early forties, is a college graduate who married her husband when he was in the full-time parish ministry, and has two teenage children.

Dorothy takes part in her husband's ministry out of the desire to contribute through useful work. Her main joys as a MW come through sharing in her husband's work, personal growth and fulfillment, and learning more about the Christian faith. Problems and conflicts arise mainly because of her husband's irregular work schedule and the lack of close personal friends and time for self and family. But if she were not a MW, she does not feel that her life would be much different.

For her, "being a minister's wife has meant . . . a richer, fuller life—meeting some really fine people," though if she were not a MW, she "probably would not move about quite so much." When she was younger, she "thought mostly of having a teaching career," but what is most important now is "the fact that we are happy in our work." She enjoys contributing to the music of the church, as choir director and/or organist, and also likes Sunday-School teaching. But she is bothered at times by the lack of a "just pure social life . . . we are too busy with church meetings, events, and the like."

For, in addition to love for family and devotion to God, self-development and concern for others rate high in Dorothy's value system. She is somewhat disturbed that there is so little time to realize those values. Her theology is grounded in "the words of Jesus . . . what he said and did—that is enough to show me the way to what I can ever strive for, for myself and my family and my relationships with my fellow man."

When interviewed, Dorothy had recently accepted the position of choir director in her husband's church, and felt that she "would continue as long as they would like me to. It is something I love doing, working in music, and I feel confident working in that line."[7] She makes it a point, however,

never to get involved in any position of responsibility in the women's work . . . I feel I could get into difficulty there. I don't feel that I want to tell them how to run things; I think they know better. I will do Spiritual Life, or something like that, or if they want help on any project or ask me to serve on a committee, I'm always glad to do that. In the parish I try not to push myself in the musical field. If they wish me to do something there then I will assume responsibility and leadership. I have never gotten into any difficulty in so doing. It's not what you do, as much as your attitude.

Dorothy would never serve in a church other than her husband's, nor would she serve as both organist and choir director. Her general principle is:

I try to leave it, as much as possible, up to them, but let them know, too, how I feel. When we talked with the committee before my husband came here, they asked me very bluntly, "What do you do in the church?" and when they ask me things like that I tell them that I will teach, or work in the music line or work with the youth fellowships and will co-operate with the other groups, but not assume leadership because I don't feel capable.

Congregational expectations don't bother her particularly, since

99 per cent of churches feel that every minister's wife has certain abilities and talents which she can contribute if she is willing. I think they will accept that and not demand other things. . . . I don't think I have ever found that a parish is too demanding on a minister's wife. They expect you to go to meetings, to be there, to be seen, to be around, to be pleasant to everyone. I think they feel that every person, including the minister and his wife, has something to contribute, and if you are willing to contribute those abilities they are not too demanding.

Dorothy Taylor is like Dorcases in that she is shy and retiring, describing herself as "sincere, fairly easygoing, able to get along with my husband's parishioners—but still sometimes hesitant about introducing myself, a bit self-conscious, I would guess." Nevertheless, she has made an excellent adjustment to the life of a MW and is very happy in it. There are undoubtedly many factors contributing to this adjustment. She married a minister several years older than she, who had already had a number of years of parish experience, who was effective in his work, and whom she loved and respected. She felt she had something to contribute to the marriage as a person and woman and to his ministry as one trained in music and experienced in teaching.

As the only child of a farmer, she knew the demands of work.

I remember my father got up very early and didn't return from his work until sometimes eight in the evening. I guess, if anything, I probably saw my father less than my children see their father. My father worked hard, but he wasn't a prosperous farmer. I was brought up with my father and two aunts—my mother died at my birth. I remember it as a happy childhood but not seeing much of my father. He was gone for hours working on the farm.

Dorothy likes the security of having a parsonage provided, but feels "much more comfortable having my own furnishings." With regard to housing after retirement and saving toward children's education, she finds "most people in the same boat: 'How am I going to send my children to college and what am I going to do in my old age?' I think we are as comfortable as anyone and probably more comfortable than some. I think that our salary here is about on a par with many of the people and our financial problems are probably just about the same as theirs."

Initially, though,

. . . it was a great surprise to find myself ready to marry a minister. Perhaps I thought of ministers as I believe a lot of people do, as somebody a little bit different from anyone else. . . . I thought that it was going to be quite a responsibility—something that would make my life very different. But I don't think that it did, actually. I don't think my life would be terribly different now if I was married to a plumber. I think this mostly because my family has always been churchgoing people. They worked hard in the church. I can really say that I've enjoyed being a MW.

Perhaps the background experience which has helped Dorothy most as a MW was her training and experience as a music teacher. She developed tact and diplomacy, and you learn to meet people. . . . A teacher is more or less in the same situation as a MW. People sort of have the feeling, "There she goes, she's a teacher." Many times people say to you, "What is it like to be a minister's wife?" as though it were really out of this world. But it really isn't that different. And I think they have this idea about a teacher too. A teacher is watched very carefully. You hear comments that so-and-so smokes or was seen in a bar, and "Imagine, she teaches our children!"

When Dorothy was first married,

I think I was maybe overcautious. This idea that you can't have any intimate friends, that can be a problem in a way. When we first go into this business, of being a MW or teacher, it's new to you and you sort of have the feeling that everybody is looking at you and watching to see what you are going to do, and then you discover that they aren't. If you just go along in your own way and don't make too much of a point of it, I think you can be an individual and lead your own life pretty much the way you want. You can bring the feeling of set-apartness to the situation yourself, consciously or unconsciously. I think sometimes that we feel too much ourselves that people are watching us and are ready to jump on everything. I have learned that people are much more tolerant and understanding and kinder than we sometimes think they are.

Nevertheless, Dorothy confesses that she thinks of a MW as

rather plain, and I don't know why. I've wondered about that. Here again is that feeling—we probably never quite get rid of it—that people are watching us. I think sometimes we say to ourselves that if a MW gets very dressed up, not necessarily real expensive clothes but good ones, sometimes we have the feeling that people are saying "How can she afford those clothes on his salary?" On the other hand you don't want to underdress, and I think that most of us try to be a little conservative. I don't know that *plain* is the word, perhaps conservative is better, more like the norm or average. Anyhow, *I* like to wear earrings, and I do!

Dorothy, then, tends to be careful and somewhat conservative, but not at the price of complete denial of individuality. She has developed a pattern of living which brings her personal fulfillment and at the same time is not likely to bring criticism from others. *Within these limits*, therefore, she is free and doesn't need to worry about people "watching us and . . . ready to jump on everything." She can trust in people's tolerance and understanding, as long as she is "a little conservative." Nevertheless,

Dorothy differs from Dorcases in that over the years she has learned to be more outgoing. One expression of this is her practice of greeting parishioners after church with her husband:

> When we moved to a larger church, I discovered that there were people in the parish that I never saw except on Sunday morning. And I have always felt that I should know the parish—not as my husband does, because I don't call with him, but a little chance to know them and talk to them. They seem to like it very much. . . . This new parish we're in covers a large area, miles and miles, and these people I just don't see except on Sunday. As a matter of fact, my 16-year-old son has gotten in the habit of standing with us—we're forming sort of a line. It's a sort of family greeting. People seem to enjoy it.

Despite this kind of involvement, Dorothy in no way views herself as a teamworker with her husband:

> . . . all the problems and consultations are taken care of by my husband alone. I never enter into any of that. I don't feel qualified. Perhaps he may feel like a father to the parish, but I have never in any way felt like a mother to it. . . . I sometimes talk with the people about their concerns and their interests, but not really their problems. My husband and I do not discuss any of the problems which concern him and the parishioner. . . . It's like any other business: he has his job to perform and I try not to tell him how to do it. If you do get involved—I myself would tend to get involved emotionally.

Her contribution to her husband, then, is viewed not as fellow worker, but as woman and wife.

> When my husband walks in the door he doesn't want me to start asking him, "How's Mrs. so-and-so's problem today?" He's just finished discussing this with her and he'd like to think of something else— something we have planned together, or something about our children. Because, as you know, ministers have little enough time to be real family men. . . . You do want to keep your family and your church separated, in a sense. . . . It's important, in this connection, that the husband have a study in the church, so that the husband can go off to work, can get out of the house and to his business, even if it's next door.

Dorothy Taylor: Pattern and Person

Dorothy Taylor makes one realize once more that individuality cannot be categorized in any neat manner. She differs from most other "useful work background supporters" in the effectiveness of her adjustment, which depends on her own background, her growth over the years, and the nature of her husband as man and minister. Her church background and teaching experience made the transition to the life of a MW relatively easy. Her husband had already developed the basic pattern of his ministry before she married him, so there were not his "professional growing pains" to complicate marital adjustments. When they married, they were both mature professional people. Moreover, she limited her contribution to the church to areas where she felt confident—music and education—and saw her role as in the background as wife and mother.

In no sense was she ever competing with her husband, or with the "leading women" of the church. Also, marriage after her husband was already established in his ministry meant that she was spared some of the more acute problems of the smallest churches and communities, with often inadequate parsonages and salaries. In the relatively structured role of a MW, she was able to adventure in social relationships as she probably would not have dared otherwise, and to discover that people liked and accepted her.

But how would one describe Dorothy in terms of the typology presented in Chapter 2? Her pattern of motivation and meaning seems to be a mixture of the Dorcas and Jane types. Though very concerned about the judgments of others, she nevertheless has gained in security and self-confidence over the years, and this permits her to be increasingly inner-directed. As she put it with regard to the church deciding whether she should serve as organist or choir director: "I try to leave it, as much as possible, up to them, but let them know, too, how I feel." She tries not to "get into difficulty," as she might if she asserted leadership in women's work. She will never "push myself in the musical field," and never wants "to tell them how to run things; I think they know better." She has learned that "if you are willing to contribute [your particular] abilities [congregations] are not too demanding."

Dorothy, then, seeks to work out compromises which are appropriate both to the demands of the situation and her own desires, rather than simply yielding to the prevailing demands as a Dorcas would or rebelling against them as a Kate would. She is neither a "driver-type" Martha nor a "dreamer-type" Mary.

At the level of values, Dorothy puts "providing love and security for one's family" first and "self-development; becoming a real, genuine person" second. Following these in her value system are "devotion to God, doing God's will" (ranked first by most MWs, with "love for one's family" generally second) and "being genuinely concerned about other people" (ranked ahead of self-development by most MWs).

In comparison with Marthas and Marys, Dorothy's emphasis is more "secular" than "spiritual." (It is difficult to find value-neutral descriptive terms to represent this contrast.) She is personally concerned about "learning more about the Christian faith," but regards her husband's work more as "his business" than as "his calling." Her theology focuses on Jesus showing her "the way to what I can ever strive for, for myself and my family and my relationship with my fellow men." Her concern for others appears to focus more on their general welfare than on their "conversion" or "salvation" in a more strictly religious sense. There is little "witness" emphasis in Dorothy's approach to being a MW; she would regard apostleship as more her husband's business.

Dorothy spends little time in self-commiseration, since she regards her lot as generally a happy one.

I, like everyone else, have my problems and frustrations. At times like that, I feel—if my husband were only on a 9-to-5 job, then maybe *all* the family problems, as well as house and yard work, would not be my responsibility. But then, I think of my husband's capabilities in the ministry, of what his job is and what my job is, and how rewarding a situation is mine. Then, even though it gets frustrating and disillusioning at times, I can cope with it.

In summary: Dorothy *does not* match much of the "very satisfied pattern" described earlier in this chapter, and yet she *is* very satisfied. She is *not* highly involved in her husband's work and the life of the congregation. She does not seek expression in church work for religious commitment; rather, her church work is the fulfillment of her training in music and education. She regards herself as laywoman, wife, and mother, and not as teamworker or witness for Christ.

One can, then, depart from the general pattern and still be very satisfied as a MW. The key seems to be as much avoidance of the basic characteristics of the so-so-frustrated as matching the blueprint of the very satisfied. For Dorothy, though admitting problems of loneliness and set-apartness, does not brood over them, and she has learned how to improve her situation. She does not feel that she would have more freedom if she were not a MW. She doubts that the situation would be much different; if it were, it would probably be in terms of fewer social contacts and diminished opportunities for service and personal growth.

She does not feel negatively about church activities; rather, she has discovered those areas of church life in which she can exercise leadership and responsibility without competing with her husband or the "vested interests." She is not *situationally* frustrated, since she feels her way into a new situation and in general lets the congregation call the tune, nor is she *maritally* frustrated. She does not have the *chronic* frustration of those whose personality needs are so great that they cannot be gratified by any situation or any husband.

Dorothy shares the concern of the so-so-frustrated with regard to lack of close friends and husband's time, but she does not feel that "it is hard to be yourself as a MW." Basically a conservative person anyhow, she confines "letting herself go" to her earrings! Unlike the so-so-frustrated, she has come to accept lonely nights and some degree of set-apartness as part of the job. She does her best in the given situation and is seldom overly analytic or introspective about it. Basically, therefore, "how rewarding a situation is mine," compared with life on the farm—especially during high school, when she was "rather shy, self-conscious, and hard to know."

Donna Sykes: A Displaced Homebody

Like Dorothy Taylor, Donna Sykes reports her motivation to take part in her husband's ministry as based on her "desire to contribute through useful work." Unlike the background supporter Dorothy, however, Donna is "involved, but no more than if [my husband] were in another vocation," and in general she has found being a MW "so-so." It is hard for her to adjust to new situations, since she likes to "stay put and have a place to call home," and she feels that she would be freer to be herself if she were not a MW.

Like Dorothy Taylor, Donna is an only child, but unlike her, she is the daughter of a laborer rather than a farmer, and both her parents were living during her growing-up years. Donna Sykes is now in her early thirties, was married when she was 19 and therefore did not have schooling beyond high school, and has three school-age children. Her husband is a successful and effective minister in a quite large Disciples of Christ church in the Midwest.

For Donna, "being a MW has meant . . . a total new way of life," for "if I were not a MW, I would not be constantly on display and could live a more relaxed life." What is most important is "my family and the late evening hours when my husband and I can sit and relax; the hardest thing is trying to raise a family with a husband who is gone so much from home." Nevertheless, "My husband and I share a happy life in spite of the great demands on his time," and "The congregation has been considerate, helpful, and friendly." Also, "I had to accept that this was what my husband wanted to do, and I had to get accustomed to it." She has sought, therefore, to "realize that this is the way things are, become a part of my husband's work and help him where I can."

Unlike Dorothy's husband, who was settled in the ministry before their marriage, Donna's decided to go to college to prepare for the ministry after their marriage. It was a struggle to complete the B.A. and B.D. degrees, but he accomplished this through night school and part-time schooling, serving churches during both college and seminary. When he told Donna that he wanted to become a minister,

I wasn't too happy about it. I had gone to church before and had just never pictured myself as being a MW. But it was something he felt that he wanted to do and later, as I have been involved in his work more, it doesn't bother me at all now. I just feel like any other woman . . . even though your social life is not like other people's. When you do go out, it's always to church functions. I can't even recall a time when we have gone out with a couple that weren't part of the church.

Donna often wishes that she had "a little background in theology. I think it would be helpful. I myself never went to college. I just finished high school. . . . Sometimes when we go out and are with people that have had a higher degree of training, I feel somehow inadequate. In conversation, when different subjects are brought up, I feel entirely left out. When I have nothing to contribute, I just listen." Her adjustment to the life of a MW was harder than Dorothy's for another reason: ". . . my background just didn't prepare me. I was not much of a churchgoer and my family never went to church much. After I realized his duties and what it involved, it didn't bother me as much."

The church activities Donna participates in and enjoys are singing in the choir, attending church women's groups, and being a member of an adult Sunday-School class. Unlike Dorothy Taylor, she has not had training in any activity she can continue in her church life. She would not want to teach a Sunday-School class or lead a church youth group, hold any office or greet parishioners after services with her husband. "Useful work" for Donna is mainly in the area of helping her husband with telephone calls and typing some of his letters and sermons. On occasion, she will also entertain church groups in her home. She does not take part in any activities outside of the local church, though at some future date she might like to attend an interfaith group or the PTA, or engage in some sort of social service. Now, however, "with our own church activities and three young children, I have not found time for outside activities."

Clearly, the focus of Donna's life is her home and family. Unlike her activist, energetic, outgoing, adaptable husband, she describes herself as "rather slow and deliberate," "rather shy and timid," and "too rigid and perfectionist." "I am a compulsive housekeeper and make a neat appearance. I would like to be more tolerant and patient with my children and have a better understanding of my husband's work." In her value system, developing and understanding yourself rank highest, followed by providing love and security for your family, "peace of mind, contentment, stillness of spirit," and "devotion to God, doing God's will."

Like the Kates, Donna feels strongly that congregations in general, though not her own, err when they

feel a MW should be different from the wife of any professional man, doctor or lawyer. If a man becomes a doctor, I don't think any more is expected of his wife. He has had the training, his wife hasn't. Same with a lawyer's wife. . . . But churches sometimes seem to think a MW should have the same dedication as her husband, and I don't feel that. Everyone is an individual, and just because my husband became a minister doesn't say that I changed in any respect.

She describes her role in church life: "Personally, I don't care to be a leader. I don't mind helping out on things if I am asked, or I even might volunteer my services if I feel I can help any. I guess I'd just sooner be a follower." In her present church, she appreciates their attitude: ". . . they have never approached me with 'We think you should do this.' I think they feel that whatever I can do, I will do. I feel under no pressure, to force me into a pattern, at all. They have been very kind in that."

Life would be more comfortable for Donna, nevertheless, if she didn't feel she was always expected to be in the limelight and be some sort of example. "When you go out, you are always on your guard. People know you are a MW and you are looked upon a little bit differently." What bothers her most, however, are the demands on her husband's time. "At the beginning it was a little bit more frustrating. My husband was gone so much and I would just be so lonely at times. But now, I have become so accustomed

to his going out that it just doesn't bother me so much. I just wish
he had more time with the children, such as time to play catch
with our boy." At least, though, she has her own home.

When we were living next door to the church in the parsonage, I
never felt it was mine. We have been living for seven years in this
house that we are buying with a housing allowance from the church,
and I feel it *is* my home. Before, there were constant interruptions—
people stopping in on the way to a meeting, etc. Now, people come
only on invitation, with a few exceptions which I don't mind. Before,
the parsonage was an extension of the church. Now, it's my home.

Donna is no easier to characterize with regard to involvement
and motivation than was Dorothy. Though Donna is relatively
"detached," she has neither the purpose motivation of a Jane nor
the expected/closeness motivation of a Kate. Rather than being
satisfied, as are most Janes, or frustrated, as are most Kates, she
finds the life of a MW so-so. As her fictitious name indicates, she
is closest to a Dorcas, in that she withdraws rather than rebelling.
She resigns herself to the situation rather than actively protesting
or fighting against it. She would like to have more time with her
husband. She feels that she would be freer to be herself and
under less pressure to be an example if she were not a MW. In
these ways, she is like a Kate.

But at the same time she admires her husband's dedication to
his ministry and his success in his chosen profession. She enjoys
learning more about the Christian faith, sharing vicariously in her
husband's work, and having a place of respect in church and
community. She would urge other young MWs to seek first to be
a good wife and mother, to be in full sympathy with their husbands' work, and to be their own best selves—not worrying about
the expectations of others. Her motivation is, then, intrinsic to her
own value system, rather than extrinsic and deriving from the
expectations of others. This is illustrated in her perfectionism in
tasks important to her, such as household maintenance.

In her value orientation, self-development and self-understanding come even before concern for others or devotion to God. In
part, this is due to a theology which she describes as "liberal."

She is more of a doer (but with the focus on the home, rather than the church or community) than a be-er. With a different congregation and/or husband, she might be a Dorcas or a Kate. With further experience and maturity, she may become a Jane or even a Mary. At present, none of these labels fits her exactly.

Social Class and Personal Fulfillment

Implicit in the discussion of Dorothy Taylor and Donna Sykes, and other MWs as well, are issues of social class in relation to personal fulfillment. For factors such as occupation, income, and education do influence the dominant value orientations of both groups and individuals. However, the names given to social status groupings vary. Some prefer to speak of classes such as "lower-middle" and "upper-middle," while others distinguish between "blue-collar" and "white-collar" occupations. (In this connection, Blood and Wolfe's term of "high-white-collar" for business and professional men has interesting connotations in terms of clergy garb!)

In this study, the relative social status of respondents may be inferred in terms of: (1) father's occupation, with categories of business and professional men, farmers, and laborers; (2) husband's ministerial income in 1960, with categories of under $4,000, $4,000 to $6,999, and $7,000 or more; and (3) MW's education, with categories of high-school graduate or less, more than high-school but not college graduate, and college graduate or more. The respondents of highest social status, in these terms, would be daughters of business and professional men (38 per cent of all respondents, but only 28 per cent of Baptist and Evangelical MWs), whose husbands' ministerial income in 1960 was $7,000 or more (20 per cent of all respondents, but only 10 per cent of Baptist and Evangelical MWs), and who are college graduates (37 per cent of all respondents and 56 per cent of daughters of business and professional men, but only 30 per cent of Evangelical and Baptist MWs).

If one increases ministerial income by 15 per cent to take

account of housing provided, and considers only *husband's* (but
not father's) occupation, about 20 per cent of MW-5 respondents
would, in Lenski's terms, be members of the upper-middle class.
That is, they are in the family of a professional man with an income of $8,000 or more.[8] An additional 61 per cent of question-
naire respondents whose husbands' ministerial income is over
$4,000 would be classified by Lenski as of the lower-middle class.
If MW-5 respondents are classified according to these categories,
upper-middle-class MWs are found *most* often in the Northeast
and *least* often in the Far West. Upper-*lower*-class incomes (under $4,000) are found most often in the South and least often
in the Northeast. By denomination, upper-middle-class incomes
occur *most* frequently among Episcopal (32 per cent), Presbyterian (29 per cent), United Church of Christ (27 per cent), and
Methodist (26 per cent) MWs, and *least* frequently among
Evangelical (5 per cent), Missouri Synod Lutheran (7 per cent),
and Baptist (13 per cent) MWs. However, there is no evidence
that satisfaction and fulfillment are higher in regions and
denominations with higher ministerial incomes.

Yet matters are not quite so clear-cut. For social class depends
on other variables than just income. The relative prestige of the
occupation, which for the ministry would be considerably higher
than the income received, is important. This is particularly true
in groups such as Baptists, Evangelicals, and Lutherans, where
income is particularly low. Education, and the type of leadership
and general influence resulting from it, are also significant.
And 37 per cent of respondents were college graduates, while
82 per cent of their husbands were seminary graduates, with
seven years of "higher education." Even taking account of the
potential influence of nonrespondent bias in this study, ministerial couples do seem to be of a high educational level compared to the general population. (In the 1960 U.S. Census, only
8 per cent of females 25 years of age or older were college
graduates.)

Moreover, social status by its very nature is *relative*, involving
personal meaning as well as objective statistics. The general

social status of ministers differs in particular denominations, regions, community and church sizes, and even particular congregations. Thus, while social status of Baptist and Evangelical MWs may be relatively low in relation to other MWs, it may be relatively high in relation to members of their congregations. Personal background is important, too. (We do not know, incidentally, the *income* of fathers of respondents, but only their occupations, so we cannot classify them into upper-middle and lower-middle classes.)

Over-all, respondents are now in larger churches and communities than those in which they grew up. In general, they feel that their husbands' salaries should be more comparable with those of other professional men. (The Census figure for 1959 median earnings of those in business and the professions was $6,640, though the figure varied from a median of $5,984 in the South to $7,004 in the Far West.) While 64 per cent of MWs judge themselves as "better off" economically than their parents were, only 11 per cent judge themselves to be "worse off." Nevertheless, more than two-thirds of respondents judge their husbands' ministerial income as either barely sufficient for family needs (37 per cent) or insufficient—hard to make ends meet (32 per cent). Much depends, of course, on how one defines "needs" and "sufficient," but these judgments do appear to be largely reality-based.

Financial matters, discussed under "other situational variables" in Chapter 6, are not the major concern here, however. Rather it is a question of how a particular kind of value orientation may be related to social class (in terms of both background and situation) and thereby affect degree and type of personal fulfillment. In terms of the value orientations discussed in Chapter 3, MWs from lower-middle-class backgrounds tend to emphasize propriate service rather than self-development and understanding, while for those from upper-middle-class backgrounds the emphasis is reversed.

Indeed, self-fulfillment can be considered as a *luxury* value, which comes into prominence only when more basic needs are satisfied. Important, too, is the *kind* (as well as length) of education a MW has had. If education has consisted mainly of training for a vocation, then few issues of either self-fulfillment or culture-building may have been raised. However, if a woman has had an upper-middle-class liberal arts education, she probably has become aware of a great range of personal-fulfillment needs which she feels obligated (one might say "called") to satisfy. And, after introspection and analysis, she may have concluded that neither home nor congregation provide many opportunities for true self-fulfillment.

Moreover, social status itself tends to be ambiguous and uncertain for MWs. Farmers are certainly outside the main class structure in a way that laborers are not, in that many farmers combine aspects of the work of a professional, small businessman, and skilled laborer. But this is even more true of the minister and his family—even when he does not have to serve as church janitor and his wife as church secretary. For the position of a MW is a complex mixture of "ascribed" (i.e., defined by the expectations of others) and "achieved" (on the basis of one's own performance) roles. This becomes evident in Dorothy Taylor's discussion of proper clothing for MWs, which must be neither too luxurious nor too shabby, so that one neither "shows up" nor "lets down" the congregation. One's home may be in a rather good neighborhood and one's social position in terms of club memberships and general community leadership quite high. But the status is as much due to *position* as to person, and is shaky when it depends on the good will of the grantor, as in complimentary memberships. One is *given* a status, but does not often have the sense of having *attained* it on his own merits. At the worst, the minister and his family may be as subject to the favors and whims of their feudal lords (be it congregation or district superintendent) as were Anglican clergy of an earlier period. At its best, their status can have the security of respect and love, which is even greater than that of achievement.

In one sense, then, the minister and his family are *outside* considerations of social class. Despite status levels of denomination and the local congregation, clergy are allowed, and indeed required, to move across class lines much more than members of other occupations. The class structure is more flexible for ministers' families. But it is also more ambiguous, and can be more insecure. Conflicts exist even when both husband and wife are truly dedicated to fulfilling God's call in ministry. Even the most sacrificial and committed wife wants her husband to "get ahead" in his chosen profession. And the marks of professional success tend to be status symbols—including million-dollar "sanctuaries" —rather than the more intangible transformations of individuals and communities. For an "upwardly mobile" MW from a lower-middle-class background who aspires to upper-middle-class success, the struggle and tension will be particularly severe. For *all* MWs, issues of social class as these relate to *what* she is seeking from life and *how* she fulfills her goals, will be important.

CHAPTER 5

Ages and Stages

PATTERNS OF INVOLVEMENT and activity, motivation and meaning, and fulfillment and frustration all change, to at least some degree, through a woman's life cycle. Even though consistent life styles may characterize particular individuals across various age levels, significant changes do occur. And a woman does not become a MW simply through marrying a minister. Rather, a long-range series of adjustments and adaptations is necessary, in the effort to respond effectively to expectations of church and community without denying genuine selfhood.

Longitudinal and Lateral

In order to gain basic understanding of the ages and stages of MWs, longitudinal studies will have to be conducted, following groups of young women through the life cycle of a MW. This will be done, using two groups of subjects: (1) women under 35 years of age who completed all of the questionnaires used in this study, and (2) theological students' wives involved in an experimental program during 1962-63. Each group numbers slightly more than 100 women.

Since it will be many years before data from these longitudinal studies are available, other more limited sources of information have been utilized. One approach, of course, is to ask women to try to recall previous times of life and stages of growth, and to describe them in terms of the key variables of this study. This was done. But reported memory, especially when evaluation and not simply description is required, can involve considerable distortion. A cultural characteristic of Americans, moreover, as part of our "progressivism," is to describe the past (e.g., one's childhood) as worse than the present.

Self-report on the past, therefore, especially when protection of self-esteem is involved, can be a fallible source of information. Also subject to distortion is another approach used in this study: to compare women of one age with those of another. For this inevitably involves mixing two variables: historical difference (i.e., 35-year-olds in 1960 versus 35-year-olds in 1935) and developmental difference (i.e., 35-year-olds in 1960 versus 60-year-olds in 1960). Though theoretically the second relationship is being examined, there is contamination from the first, in that there is no way of knowing what the present 35-year-olds will be like when *they* are 60. Only a longitudinal study, not a "lateral" comparison of age groups, can avoid this problem.

For want of better information at this point, however, the data reported in this chapter come from comparisons of groups of MWs of various ages, supplemented by certain recollections of the past on their part. (All ages are calculated as of 1961, when data were collected.) Fortunately, there was good representation of the various age groups among questionnaire respondents. Of the 4,777 women who completed the MW-5 questionnaire, only 14 women failed to indicate their ages—a major research achievement in itself! Of those indicating their ages, 31.1 per cent were under 35, 44.8 per cent between 35 and 49, and 24.1 per cent 50 years or more of age. This compares with 1960 census figures for white females between 20 and 64 of 35.2 per cent 20-34, 37.4 per cent 35-49, and 27.4 per cent 50-64.[1]

Some General Patterns

Some of the differences between MWs of different ages depend on general trends in American society as they affect marriage and family. Early marriage is one such trend. While 64 per cent of MWs under 35 years of age were married while their husbands were in college or seminary, only 35 per cent of the age group 35-49, and 25 per cent of MWs 50 or over, were married this early. Like many other variables, this one is related to denomination. Considering all age groups together, 82 per cent of Missouri Synod Lutheran; over 50 per cent of other Lutheran, Episcopal, and Congregational; and 43 per cent of Presbyterian MWs married after their husbands had completed ministerial training. This is in marked contrast to Evangelical, Baptist, Disciple, and Methodist MWs, of whom only 20-30 per cent married after their husbands were in the full-time ministry. For *all* denominations, ministerial marriages appear to be occurring earlier: in college, when in previous periods it would have tended to be in seminary; in seminary, when earlier it would have tended to be after seminary graduation. Partly because of earlier marriage and partly because of the general religious and vocational uncertainties of present American young adults, a higher percentage of MWs than would have been true in earlier generations appear relatively unsympathetic to their husbands' vocational choice. They resent "anyone expecting anything of me just because I married a man who happened to become a minister." According to current evidence, the percentage of MWs with such an attitude will probably tend to increase, unless more effective premarital and postmarital guidance is provided.

Less often than in previous periods do women marry men who later *change* vocations to become ministers: only 8 per cent of women under 35 report such a change, versus more than 20 per cent of women over 35.[2] Like time of marriage, this variable is strongly linked with denomination, however. While only 2 per cent of Missouri Synod Lutheran and less than 10 per cent of other Lutheran, Presbyterian, and Congregational MWs report such a change, corresponding percentages for Evangelical and Baptist MWs are more than 30 per cent and for Episcopal MWs 20 per cent.

Partly because of earlier marriage and partly because of the general population explosion, MWs now tend to have more children than in previous decades:[3] 63 per cent of 35-to-39-year-old

MWs have three or more children, versus 48 per cent of the 45-to-49-year-olds and 47 per cent of the 55-to-59-year-olds. (The 35-to-44-year-old MWs average 2.4 children, which approximates the 1960 U.S. Census average of 2.57 "children ever born" for 35-to-44-year-old white females. For MWs, as many children have died as have been adopted.) The median "spacing" of children by MWs under 35 years of age is about two years, whereas for MWs now 35-49 it is about two and a half years, and for women 50 or over three and a half years. Thus, 83 per cent of MWs now under 35 years of age have at least one preschool-age child in the home, usually with the result of more limited involvement in church and community activities and greater possibilities of a sense of frustration and confinement as a MW. (This, of course, is but a variation of the "trapped housewife" lament of young middle-class American wives.)

MWs now marry younger and have more children spaced closer together. They tend less often than in previous periods to be farmers' daughters, and more often to be daughters of skilled or unskilled laborers; this undoubtedly is a function of the urbanization of America in recent years. (The percentage of MWs who are daughters of business and professional men has remained constant at about 37 per cent, including about 10 per cent daughters of ministers, over the last twenty years.)

While MWs under 35 years of age *more* often than older MWs come from homes where both parents were regular church participants, they *less* often judge religion to have been "very important in your home when you were growing up." There appears to have been relatively more involvement in the institutional *church* on the part of younger MWs, but less exposure to vital personal *faith*. For older MWs a *personal* decision regarding denominational affiliation (different from their parents) or even the Christian faith itself was more often involved.

Age group comparisons mentioned thus far undoubtedly reflect *general population* trends on age of marriage, number of children, occupational distribution, and religious life; they are not specific to MWs. This is true also of employment. Of MWs under

35 years of age, about 3 per cent hold full-time and 19 per cent part-time paid jobs. (Comparable figures for 35-to-49-year-old MWs are 13 per cent and 18 per cent, and for MWs 50 years of age or older, 16 per cent and 16 per cent.) "Working wives" will be discussed more fully in Chapter 6, but it may be noted here that 1960 census figures report 30.7 per cent of all "married women with husband present" and 19.2 per cent of women with children under 6 years of age holding regular paid employment. Apparently, about the same percentage of MWs as of American married women in general work outside the home for pay, but the percentage of *full-time* workers may be lower for MWs.

Since there are considerable research data to indicate that birth order tends to influence personality and behavior, it may be significant that 48 per cent of MWs under 35 years of age were first-born versus 20 per cent third-born or later, whereas comparable figures for MWs 35 years of age or more are 34 per cent first-born and 42 per cent third-born or later. In part at least, this is due to smaller family size during the depression years during which most of the younger MWs were born. Since first-born children tend more often than the later-born to be concerned about pleasing others, and to want to be with others when in anxiety-provoking situations, the current generation of MWs may possess more of these characteristics than previous generations.

In educational level, as we have seen, about 37 per cent of MWs are college graduates, though like many other variables (one related to education would be father's occupation) there is great denominational variation, reflecting the socioeconomic class composition of the various denominations. In terms of age groups, the greatest contrast is between those born between 1901 and 1905 (of whom 37 per cent are college graduates) and those born prior to 1901 (of whom 20 per cent are college graduates). The contrast is marked between the 25-to-34-year-old MWs (of whom twice as many are college graduates as are high-school graduates or less) and the MWs now over 60 years of age (of whom high-school graduates or less are twice as many as the college graduates). Since 1901, however, the percentage of MWs who are college graduates appears to have remained reasonably stable, even during the years of the "great depression." Since the percentage of female college graduates in the general population has greatly increased in this period, MWs are probably no longer the "educated women" of the community in the sense that they once were.

MWs under 35 years of age tend, therefore, more often than MWs over 50 years of age, to (1) have married younger, (2) feel uncommitted to their husbands' vocation, (3) have three or more children, spaced close together, (4) derive from a labor background rather than farming, (5) have participated regularly in the denomination in which their husband is now a minister, but experienced little "home religion," (6) be first-born children, and (7) be college graduates.

From these data, one might predict that present-generation MWs would tend to be more involved in their home life and less involved in "witnessing for Christ," more analytic and interpersonally anxious and less spontaneously activist, than previous generations. Only longitudinal studies will allow us to separate the historical from the developmental factors involved. Some clarification may come, however, through moving from comparison of *age* groups with one another to discussion of some of the *stages* in the life cycle of a MW.

Wives of Seminarians

As a basis for future longitudinal studies, as well as by way of an experiment in orientation of those later to occupy particular role positions, the Lilly Pilot Program for Theology Couples was conducted during the academic year of 1962-63.[3] This program assumed that the seminary situation for theological students and their wives involves certain basic transitions. What these transitions were became more clear through the five research instruments (personal data, role conception, and Minnesota Multiphasic, Edwards, and incomplete-sentences personality inventories) completed by 103 wives in four co-operating seminaries:

Boston, Garrett, Southern Baptist-Louisville, and Yale. (All five instruments were completed at the beginning of the academic year and the role conception and Edwards inventories about six months later.)

Clearly, for some wives the fundamental transition being experienced was from adolescent to adult. About 10 per cent of the women in the program were under 21 years of age. Some had only recently graduated from high school and had had neither employment nor college experience. For them, involvement in the seminary community brought real forced growth. Issues of personal identity had to be dealt with before matters of role and relationship were relevant. Their own growth might be complicated, moreover, by either an older, more educated, and experienced husband, in relation to whom there was great dependence and deference; or an insecure husband who was threatened by his wife's increasing competence and confidence.

Associated with the transition from adolescent to adult was the transition from single to married life. For the approximately 25 per cent married during the previous year (many during the summer just preceding), discovery of womanhood and wifehood had to take place prior to understanding of what it meant to be a minister's wife. Couples sought guidance on such matters as the establishment of common goals, values, interests, and communication patterns, as well as the development of a shared and mutually meaningful devotional life. For the recently married career woman, used to being on her own, there were particular adjustments involved in learning to live with another, and often to living on a lower economic level. And for the just married and now pregnant—especially when the pregnancy was unplanned—special pressures and potential problems arose.

All these transitions tend to lead wives of theological students, and probably most young wives, to feel that whereas all seemed so secure and placid before, now life is very insecure and pressured. Funds are in short supply and educational needs usually seem to take priority over family needs. (This is the wife's perspective; the seminary's may be just the opposite!) If the wife works outside of the home during the day, and many do, there is limited time in the evening to perform necessary household tasks, and even less for real communication and relationship with her husband. Moreover, both husband and wife tend to be exhausted and preoccupied.

Dynamics of husband-wife relationship can be further complicated by the "role reversal" involved in the wife being the family breadwinner over a long period of time. The time becomes longer with earlier marriage and longer professional training, and may stretch over six or more years. If the wife also feels homesick and sorry for herself, her husband's dependence on her may be even more trying. And if they are living in a student parsonage at a distance from the school, with the husband on a "split week," the transition for the wife may be still more difficult, especially if she is unprepared for small churches and communities.

As a result of all the pressures involved in seminary life, there may be a sense of growing apart from one another. The wife may feel cut off from the sources of her husband's intellectual and spiritual development. He is undergoing radical change; she tends to remain more static. There may be problems, therefore, in remaining a couple with shared commitments, beliefs, and practices, rather than two individuals with common housing and budget.

Many, if not all, of the transitions described above are common to the growth of all individuals and couples, and not peculiar to seminaries or the ministry. However, there is a crucial difference in that most wives of theological students understand and respond to the transitions in terms of their sense of involvement in their husbands' vocation. They realize that they and their children influence their husbands' vocational effectiveness. They tend to accept "semiprofessional" status and responsibility and consequently to express the need for some vocational preparation of their own.

In part at least, this is a function of the dominant personality pattern of the wives of theological students involved in this program.[4] In nontechnical terms, these wives of seminarians—according to personality inventory results—may be characterized as rather shy and retiring, but with a strong desire to relate to and help other people. They are conscientious, with a strong sense of responsibility to do a job well, but always seek to avoid being or appearing too dominant or aggressive. They would rather be in the background than in the limelight, dependent on their husbands rather than on their own. They are sensitive to and concerned with the reactions of others, and seek to appear to others as socially outgoing, helpful people.

This is a pattern which, moreover, remained quite stable when the wives were retested near the end of the academic year, about six months after the first testing. They continued high (in relation to female college students) in their emphasis on nurturance (care of others), affiliation, and endurance, and low on dominance and aggression. Deference and order, considered important at the beginning of the academic year, were stressed even more at the end. The major changes, which in general seem healthy ones, came in higher scores on exhibition and autonomy, bringing the average score close to that of college females; and on achievement, which now received more emphasis than was given by college females. These shifts appear to reflect an increased self-confidence developing through the experiences of the year, including participation in the program and general contacts with others in the seminary community.

In general, personality pattern is reflected in role conception, though this is also influenced by the religious tradition and geographic region in which a person grows up. (There are significant differences among wives from the four co-operating seminaries; these will not be discussed here.[5]) Like ministers' wives "on the field," these wives of seminarians tended to prefer being a background supporter to either a teamwork or detached relation to their husband's work. At the beginning of the academic year, about three-quarters stated that they expected to be background supporters; near the end of the academic year, about 80 per cent made such a judgment. In contrast, the percentage of those who anticipated being teamworkers with their husbands decreased from about 22 per cent to about 10 per cent over the six-month period, while the percentage of those who anticipated being "no more involved than if my husband were in another vocation" increased from less than 5 per cent to more than 10 per cent. Similarly, those reporting a "call" motivation decreased from about 40 per cent to about 29 per cent.

From these data, one might conclude that for *these* approximately 100 women at least (not knowing precisely how representative they are of wives of seminarians in general), the dominant role conception was that of background supporter, motivated either by belief in the purposes of the church or desire to contribute through useful work; and that life in the seminary community tended to strengthen this emphasis. More than 90 per cent reported that they expected to find the life of a minister's wife "in general satisfying and fulfilling," even though only about 50 per cent consciously desired to be a MW before marriage.

In part, this may be due to their religious background: 67 per cent of them reported their parents as inactive in church participation, while 17 per cent more reported their parents as active, but in a denomination other than that to which the wife now belongs. (This differs from—or perhaps carries one stage further—the general pattern for MWs under 35 years of age reported earlier in the chapter. Whether it reflects a decline of the "religious revival" only time and more adequate data will tell.)

The relatively recessive quality manifested in personality inventory results carries through, therefore, into role conception. The church activities which, as a group, they reported themselves as both feeling most *obligated* to perform and most likely to *enjoy* are: developing leaders, entertaining church groups, greeting parishioners, and calling on the sick. In lowest position in both obligation and expected enjoyment was holding an office in a women's group. "Semi-pro" activities such as teaching a Sunday-School class, leading devotions, counseling people with problems, and leading a youth group were all placed in the "may or may not" feel obligated or enjoy category. Like expected degree of involvement and motivation, reports on activities remained generally stable over the six-month period.

For these wives of seminarians, judging from their responses to incomplete sentences and other open-ended questions, the major goals as a MW will be to work with and help their husbands, but as women, wives, and mothers, not as church workers. Indeed, the emphasis was more on husband than on God, others, or self. They viewed the life of a MW as a challenge, in which they hoped to retain "true selfhood"; except for Baptists, seldom did they consider this to be *their* ministry, *their* opportunity to serve. Hardest, they expected, would be the pressure to do or be certain things which "don't come natural"; being an example was regarded as somewhat of a strain and certainly a demanding responsibility.

In the future, they hoped that they might grow as persons, in ability to get along with people, in religious dedication, in restraint of personal desires, feelings, and emotions. Yet they resisted the pressure of congregations toward making them more active, more interested, more responsible in church life, and felt that there was danger of loss of their independent thought and action, through conformity to the expectations of others. When retested six months later, they did, however, manifest increased ability to reject what they regarded as unfair demands. They were learning how to say No, but had not yet discovered how to do so creatively and graciously. Though the expected involvement was dominantly that of a Mary, the feeling tone was more that of a Kate.

Pilot Program respondents, therefore, focused their desire to relate to and help others, and to be a responsible, efficient person, on the *home* and not the *church*. With the exception of the Baptist wives, they were uncertain regarding both the value of most church activities and their abilities in relation to them. They were both institutionally critical and personally insecure. They were deferent, and sought to avoid dominance or aggression, and thus will probably not *fight* to protect their rights but rather choose to *withdraw* into the home.

Whether or not such opinions, attitudes, and behavior are maintained, following their husbands' graduation from seminary, cannot at this point be determined. To answer such questions is one purpose of the projected longitudinal study. It may be noted, however, that the data reported concerning these wives of seminarians in general support the trends hypothesized earlier in this chapter, on the basis of comparison of "younger" and "older" MWs. Early marriage, uncertain commitments to church and ministry, and lack of "home religion" in their backgrounds characterize these women, as they do the younger MWs now in the parish.

Like MWs under 35 years of age, these wives of seminarians tend more often than the general population to be first-born children (48 per cent), college graduates (70 per cent), schoolteachers (45 per cent), and daughters of business and professional men (55 per cent). It is surprising, however, that 41 per cent have come from families in which the income was less than $3,000; the ministry, for them at least, definitely represents upward social mobility. While 31 per cent are daughters of laborers, only 13 per cent are daughters of farmers. Note also that in other distinctive characteristics of MWs (birth order, education, and so forth) these seminarians' wives are *even more* distinctive.

Information secured through the Lilly Pilot Program for Theology Couples in general supports the predictions made earlier, after comparison of MWs now under 35 years of age with those now 50 years of age or older. There appears to be a trend toward higher involvement in home life and lower involvement in "witnessing for Christ" on the part of MWs. (This may parallel a trend toward the ministry becoming more of a profession and less of a calling.) These wives of seminarians do appear to be more analytic and interpersonally anxious and less spontaneously activist than earlier generations. But, again, what will happen to them when *they* are 50 years of age or older we cannot determine. Some clarification may be given, however, by drawing on recollections of the past—especially concerning the hardest ages or stages—on the part of mature MWs.

The Early Years

As noted earlier in the chapter, remembrance of things past may be distorted. Yet it is helpful to know which "ages and stages" are considered by MWs to have been most difficult, and this information is available through about 450 respondents to the open-ended MW-7 questionnaire.

For most women, the first five years or so in the parish situation are judged to have been the hardest. This is reported as due to the combination of *situational* factors—small church with limited lay leadership, low salary, poor parsonage, small children to care for; and *personal* factors—inexperience, lack of church background, immaturity, idealism, shyness, impatience, and perfectionism. Difficult transitions were often involved, too: from one part of the nation to another, from the city to the country, from one social class to another, and so on. And all other adjustments were compounded by the adjustments to one another in the beginning of married life.

In the early years as a MW, many women appear to have been driven by the desire to please others and to match the cultural ideal of what a MW should be and do. They found this an impossible combination of responsibilities to fulfill. In addition, they were often disillusioned when they found congregations to include self-satisfied, narrowly judgmental and moralistic, demanding, and unappreciative human beings. As one woman put it, "I cannot accept Christians as lying, jealous cutthroats." The stubbornness, the bickering, the intergroup conflict were in marked contrast to the ideals brought into marriage and the ministry. There was a tendency, too, "to take everything so seriously, and to try to please everyone . . . everything said about my husband hurt dreadfully."

Time, experience, and increased maturity solved many of these problems. Parish situations tend to get better the longer one is in the ministry, and one's ability to cope effectively with them also increases. The major discovery for many women has been that "we can't possibly please everyone; so, we've learned to do the

best we could, accepting my limitations and my husband's limitations, as well as the limitations of our congregation and our
denominational leaders." As another woman put it. "We've had
to learn that seminary ideals cannot always cope with reality. My
husband believed that he could change people and existing situations right away, and he lacked the patience to wait and to work
slowly. We both had an idealistic concept of what congregations
and ministers were like. We've had to learn to be realistic about
our faith, our congregation, and ourselves. We grew spiritually."

For some, however, the early years as a MW can involve a
growing apart from husband, family and friends, God, and even
one's inner self. The demands, expectations, and responsibilities
seem so great in relation to the limited personal resources to fulfill
them that the tendency has been either to plunge into hyper-
activism or to withdraw in hopeless resignation. In either case,
one's husband became a stranger, seldom home; and when home,
preoccupied with church business. Though there were many professional acquaintances, there were few real friends to whom one
could open oneself freely and honestly, and at the same time one
was cut off from previous friends and family.

Perhaps most serious, at the very time when God's assistance
was most required, there seemed to be most difficulty in "getting
through." Early patterns of personal and family devotional life
(often part of the idealism and perfectionism which were brought
into the ministry) proved hard to maintain. There was so little
time, so little peace and quiet, so little opportunity for genuine
prayer and communion with God. Indeed, there was little chance
even to "think things through" and discover what the basic priorities and values really were.

Sometimes, for improvement to come there had to be *situational* change. Thus, one woman reports her problems as focusing
on "the building of a new church building. My husband gave all
of his time and thought to his job and those who worked with
him. I felt left out. I didn't know how to be part of it. The
solution? The building was completed!" Or for another, the "small
salary and resulting inability to maintain a proper standard of

living" raised problems, especially when coupled with "my unwillingness to make all the sacrifices for the congregation." The solution came with "larger pastorates and my own work." One woman reports herself as bothered by a "nonprogressive church" since "I was too ambitious. I was unable to adjust to small-town conservatism. I needed more depth in my Christian life." Improvement came when "we moved to a growing city and a progressive church. And I deepened in my Christian experience." For still another, the hardest time was "when the children were babies. We could not afford baby sitters, and there was no family to help, so I stayed home too much. I resented being tied down, and the seeming unconcern of others." Things got better with "the growth of the children and the chance to work." For a number, their husbands' graduation from seminary and the end of the separation involved in a student pastorate was a real turning point.

Internal as well as *external* change was usually required, though. As one young MW described her years in a student pastorate: "We were too busy, too young, had too many babies too soon, and too little money." It was hard to cope with all this at once, since "I was immature, inexperienced in child-rearing and housekeeping." Improvement came with "gradual maturity and understanding." For another, "more dedication to do God's will" made it possible to adjust more adequately to "a complete change in our way of life." Others testify to the importance of "experience and much prayer and self-discipline," "knowledge and a little common sense," "training . . . and a desire to serve God," "husband's help, guidance, and understanding," "taking each day with its problems as it came," "understanding people more, and a deeper love of God," and perhaps most succinctly, "time, love, and effort."

For some, time, gradual maturing, and prayer were not sufficient, however. Professional help was required if the situation were to be improved. One woman, who testified to "just plain fright of the role I thought I had to play" and "fear of performing before an audience" found freedom and confidence through "depth psychiatry," as did another young woman when "my self-image as a MW crumbled." For others, marital counseling was required when there was "division of affection between my husband and our newly-born son," or when a "young and startled" wife discovered she could not stand her husband's "introversion and escape into excessive work," and he could not tolerate her "lack of commitment and understanding."

Time for increased experience and competence; professional counseling and/or personal maturation resulting in increased confidence, flexibility, patience, and realism; deepened commitment to and relationship with God; increased communication with her husband and with her "inner self"; better situations, with fewer frustrations and greater rewards and opportunities— all these contributed to making a difficult life easier for the young MW. For a very few, however, "all periods have been hard, and nothing has helped. I'm nearly out of my mind. It gets worse, and I'm ready to end it." While her husband hopes for resolution of the problems through "time, patience, and prayers," she considers "suicide or leaving my husband." While another has "just kept my misery hidden," others have encouraged their husbands to leave the ministry.

Entrance into the life of a MW is not, of course, so difficult for all women. Despite the complex adjustments required, approximately 20 per cent of MWs report having felt at home in this life from the beginning.[6] Over the years, they have found increasing opportunities for broadening and deepening their experience, for using their talents in dedication to God and service to others, for growing closer to their husbands through involvement in work in which both husband and wife deeply believe. They have become MWs without any conscious stress and strain, just as some pass through adolescence in blithe disregard of the textbook crises.

In personality, those who have found fulfillment through a natural growth process are usually extroverts rather than introverts. They have often had occupational experience, typically as teachers, in which they have already faced many of the problems of "fishbowl" living and community leadership, and have learned to cope with them. Usually, however, they are not career women, viewing their main responsibility as centered in the home and the congregation. While many are college graduates, many others have only a high-school education or less. Typically, whatever their level of education, they do not feel deprived of expression of unused talents or training in their present situation. Life is hectic and busy, but it is also exciting and fun.

Perhaps most basic, the "at home from the beginning" have generally grown up in close relation to the Church, in a family atmosphere which stressed religious values. They may have grown up in a minister's family (though ministers' daughters are less frequent than farmers' daughters!) and thoroughly enjoyed the rare privileges and opportunities afforded them in this position. Or, if this was not the case, then there have usually been admired ministers' wives as positive role figures in their childhood. Through these experiences, and their general life in the Church, they may have experienced an adolescent "call to be a minister's wife" which guided them in the choice of a life partner. For them, in any case, a minister represents "the best kind of husband."

If about 20 per cent of MWs might be described as "at home from the beginning," the remainder have found becoming a MW a complex, difficult, and painful process. Typically, they had little realistic understanding of "what they were getting into" when they married a minister. Consequently, for the first five years or so the range of situations and problems with which they had to cope was simply overwhelming. They had to grow up in a hurry. And five to ten years after marriage they are just beginning to "hit a comfortable stride." It has been a complex adjustment and assimilation process—a hard struggle, but worth it, in terms of resulting growth and fulfillment.

In personality, those who have had to "work out their salvation with fear and trembling" tend to be introverts rather than extroverts. They are analytic, reflective, and sensitive to the judgments of others. More often than is the case with the "at home . . . ," they are women of unusual intellect, talent, and education. They may have musical or artistic gifts, expression and development of which have been difficult in the churches and communities of the early years of their husbands' ministries. Often they have craved "stimulating" companionship and found the social contacts of the church very unsatisfying. In some cases they are more capable, even at church work, than their husbands, and perhaps have had as good theological training. In this case it is often hard to keep quiet and feel helpless in situations where they can see just what ought to be done.

Becoming an effective and fulfilled MW is for these women, therefore, a hard struggle rather than a natural process. In the early years, there were feelings of being "trapped in the church," deprived of close friends lest others regard them as cliquish, unable to exercise leadership capacities lest this be judged as "taking over." Now, however, they have found a comfortable place in church and ministry. They often wouldn't want to do it over again, and in a hypothetical next marriage might prefer not to marry a minister. But as of now they enjoy their life and find fulfillment through it. They have learned how to be their *best* selves in a way supportive of their husbands' ministry. They have learned, too, how to "speak the truth in love." They can be fulfilled, since they have become adaptable, flexible, and mature personalities.

The Middle and Later Years

For most of our respondents, the early years in the parish ministry were judged to have been the hardest. There were fewer reports concerning the middle or later years. Sometimes, though, the forties are mentioned as a difficult age and stage for both the minister and his wife. In addition to the physical change of life that may be involved, there can be a more general sense of declining powers. The first fires of enthusiasm have burned low, and the future is seen as a long haul. If a man has not yet achieved professional success, he realizes that he probably never will. By the forties, he has probably reached the largest church and highest salary of his ministry; in this profession, the top of the pyramid of achievement is indeed narrow.

MWs are particularly vulnerable to these pressures. They feel so deeply involved in their husbands' work, and yet can seldom directly influence their professional success. When their husbands are frustrated in their work, the wives are doubly frustrated: through suffering with them, and often through becoming scape-goats and targets for the frustration. As one MW put it: "The hardest time was from about 40 to 47. My husband's unrest over church problems led him to be hard on me. I took it personally and let it hurt too much." Sometimes, too, a change of church situation brings real pressures on a MW. She may have felt happy and secure in smaller churches and communities, but now finds herself projected into a larger, more complex situation for which her background has not prepared her. She may have to leave a familiar part of the country, where friends and family are located, for strange new surroundings, where she feels out of place and lonely.

For women whose main sense of significance has come in bear-ing and rearing children, there is a real psychic shock when the children grow up and leave the home. The vacuum can be filled in a number of ways. As will be seen in the next chapter, a number of MWs seek paid employment outside the home, once home responsibilities have lessened. In this way they can supple-ment family income and make use of their own education and training. Others invest surplus time and energy in church and/or community volunteer activities. For all, however, the middle years bring important changes in the pattern of living.

As retirement age draws near, a new set of forces becomes operative. Housing after retirement, if parsonages have always been provided, can be a real problem, since there are seldom sufficient savings to purchase a home. The denominational pension may be insufficient even for regular expenses. The decision must be made, too, as to where to live. After moving so much in the ministry, there may not be roots in or ties to any particular com-

munity or even part of the country. And to return to a community where one was previously pastor, now as an ordinary
resident and parishioner subject to another's ministerial leadership, poses its own problems. The very nature of the ministry is
such that it is hard to *stop* being a minister upon retirement.

Clearly, then, each age and stage of the life of a MW brings
its own particular problems—and its own special opportunities.
The key variable affecting adjustment to each stage is the individual's ability to be open to its possibilities and aware of the
internal and external resources available to fulfill them. Those
who seek to hang on to the past, or who live in constant anticipa-
tion or dread of the future, have little energy left for response
to the demands of the present. Likewise, those who seek to act
out a prewritten script of what a MW should be and do, fail to
discover and realize their own unique selfhood and the contributions which they alone can make. Openness to the fullness of the
present situation, flexibility and adaptability of response to the
unexpected and new in that situation, trust in God and in one
another: these influence greatly the meanings of the particular
ages and stages of a particular MW.

CHAPTER 6

Backgrounds and Situations

THUS FAR, the emphasis has been on diversity. We have met Marthas, Marys, Dorcases, Janes, and Kates, and still others, and have seen how they differ from one another. Not even these categories are sufficient, for few individuals fit them exactly. Rather, most MWs represent a very complex mixture of various tendencies, at various levels of personality, and in response to various situations. Moreover, the pattern of personality and role is not only complex; it is emergent with time, "forever the same, yet forever different."

Mary Martha Mountain demonstrated this emergence, as the motivations and meanings of her life became progressively clarified through years of intensive psychotherapy. Dorothy Taylor also gradually discovered how, as a shy and retiring person, she could best contribute to her husband's ministry through her training in music and education. For Donna Sykes, however, the road to fulfillment has been harder. Over the years, she has made gains in security and confidence. Nevertheless, she still feels ill-prepared for the roles she is called upon to play, and constantly seeks to withdraw from the limelight. For Mary Martha, Dorothy, and Donna, a complex series of adjustments and adaptations has been necessary, through various ages and stages. It is time now to examine how backgrounds and situations influence this process.

Background Resources

Women from the same sort of background do not necessarily think, feel, and behave alike, but they probably share similar "tool kits" of resources with which to cope with the situation of a MW. The majority of highly active, highly satisfied, "called" teamworkers (Marthas) discussed in Chapter 2 came from a home economically less well off than the one in which they now live, with fathers who were usually laborers or farmers. Their educational level and community status and respect are beyond that of their parents. They were not satisfied with just a high-school education, but on the other hand, few aspired to a career requiring graduate work beyond the B.A. They had had to work hard to get where they were, were grateful for what had been achieved, and were willing to continue to work hard in the future.

In contrast, purpose-motivated background supporters (Marys) tended to come from a higher social class background: 36 per cent of them were daughters of business and professional men (versus 26 per cent of the Marthas) but only 9 per cent daughters of laborers (versus 38 per cent of the Marthas). This may be one contributing factor to *purposes* being stressed by Marys, while *activities* are emphasized by Marthas. It may also relate to the Marys' predominantly interpersonal, rather than work-achievement, orientation. (In group dynamics terms, Marys tend to be group-maintenance and Marthas task-performance oriented.) Though Marys as a group had even more education than Marthas, the gap between their own and their husbands' education was greater.

For these and other reasons, Marthas are in general more highly satisfied as MWs than Marys. The difference is one of *adequacy*. *Objectively*, the life of a MW seems more adequate to a Martha, since she has not developed financial, social, and intellectual need patterns which are not fulfilled. *Subjectively*, she feels more adequate than a Mary would, since she is less analytic and introspective, and more confident of what she can bring to the situation. For a Martha, "witnessing for Christ" and "showing people a better way of life" represent great opportunities for use of what God has given her. For a Mary, witness, leadership, and being an example represent overwhelming and uncomfortable responsibilities, for which she considers her *husband* capable, but not herself. In part, the contrast may be due to the different educational and social backgrounds out of which they tend to come: for Marthas, job-oriented preparation which led one to feel adequate; for Marys, people- and idea-oriented preparation which led one to feel dissatisfied, if not inadequate. (This is not to assume that it is always best to feel adequate rather than dissatisfied; the latter may bring more humility and growth.)

Background supporters who report their motivation to be "the desire to contribute through useful work" (Dorcases) tend to come from more stable home and religious backgrounds than either the Marthas or the Marys. Indeed, the yearning for the stability of the safe and familiar, and the corresponding fear of the uncertain and new, determine as much as anything else the involvement and activity pattern of a Dorcas. While Marthas consider themselves partners with their husbands, and Marys seek to support and help them in terms of shared purposes and ideals, Dorcases are much less sure of what they have to give. They tend to be shy and timid in both Martha-type leadership and Mary-type social situations, and generally self-deprecating concerning their own abilities.

Why should a stable background have such a personality outcome? Apparently there has not been enough experience in decision-making with regard to complex, ambiguous situations, where each choice implies risk and potential opposition. Usually both of Dorcas' parents have been active in the church, and she went along with them and participated according to their desires. There was a strong religious influence in her home, which she accepted as part of life. Seldom did she have to make an *independent* decision: for or against the Christian faith, a particular denomination, a specific belief or activity. Her life was externally structured for her. While Marthas developed into apostles and Marys into disciples, Dorcases were obedient children.

Thus, though family religious participation tends to relate positively to satisfaction as a MW, a too stable (or more precisely, protected and insulated) background may not be desirable if security is given at the price of selfhood. While Mary Bernhardt reports little knowledge of the Christian faith as a child in a mixed marriage of Catholic and Baptist parents, Dorcas Patterson was the daughter of a minister, with most of her other relatives ministers as well. Apparently, this impeded rather than helped Dorcas' own development of a personal religious position, perhaps because she could never be sure if her judgment was the "approved" one. She increasingly withdrew from demanding or potentially conflictual situations.

For Janes and Kates the influence of background variables is much less clear than for Marthas, Marys, and Dorcases. In a sense this is inevitable, since Janes and Kates are by definition deviants from the modal patterns. They are individuals, either idealistically or rebelliously. And their patterns of involvement and activity may be as much influenced by situation as by background. For Janes in particular, being "involved, but no more than if [my husband] were in another vocation" usually expresses a theology of the ministry most often found in the religious traditions of Lutherans, Episcopalians, and to a lesser extent, Presbyterians. Also, relatively low involvement in their husbands' ministry usually is influenced by the other demands of the life situation, especially one or more preschool-age children in the home.

In summary, then, a MW's degree and kind of involvement in her husband's work are influenced by at least these factors: (1) her family's socioeconomic class, (2) stability—or more precisely, protection and insulation—of home and religious background, and (3) amount and kind of education. Thus, Mary Martha Mountain describes the period after leaving her grandparents at the age of 16 as "years of struggle—for an education, for adequate finances, for love." She yearned for social status and financial security beyond that of her childhood home—in which her grandfather was a carpenter and her mother worked as a maid. She wanted broader horizons than those possible in a home ruled by a domineering, moralistic grandmother, and saw the route to those horizons through education. But most important was to find a "sense of belonging" and "myself as a woman." For her parents' divorce when she was 18 months old, the nature of her grand-parents' home, and the realization in her later teens that she was the "bone of contention" in her mother's otherwise ideal remarriage: all these undercut basic trust in herself and her world as the foundation for later identity and intimacy.[1] They contributed to the guilt motivation which drove her life, and from which she sought to free herself through psychotherapy.

As illustrated in the case of Mary Martha Mountain, it is the *dynamic patterning* of variables such as socioeconomic class, family background, and education, not simply a given form or degree of any one of them, that is determinative. Also, in addition to these three factors others must be taken into account as well. As indicated in Chapter 4, the satisfaction of a MW will probably be greater if she is third-born or later, rather than first- or second-born like Dorothy Taylor, Donna Sykes, and Mary Martha Mountain. This probably relates to differential parental treatment of children of varying birth order, as this in turn influences prone-ness to anxiety and modes of coping with anxiety.[2]

Involved, too, is the size of the earliest social unit to which she has had to relate and in which she had to find her place. Training in social relationships with different kinds of people and in co-operative activities where others tend to take the lead may equip her better to be a MW. To be third-born or later (if she was "wanted") probably means, too, that she has entered a society whose leaders have gained some degree of security and confidence in interpersonal management. Unless she is spoiled through indulgence as the youngest child, there is also the experience of having to "pitch in" and help out with the family chores, perhaps more than would be the case in a one- or two-child family.

Similar factors may operate in the relationship between a MW's involvement and satisfaction and her father's occupation, as this influences socioeconomic class, which in turn influences family size and probable educational level of the children. As mentioned earlier, Marthas tend to be daughters of laborers or farmers, while Marys tend to be daughters of business and professional men.[3] Furthermore, a MW will tend to report herself as both more involved and more satisfied if she is the daughter of a farmer (like Dorothy) rather than the daughter of a laborer (like Donna). For a farm background can prepare one for being a MW in several important respects: the inclusiveness of a job which is always with you rather than on a 9-to-5 schedule away from the home, frequent absence of the head of the household from the home, probable limitation of the number of close friends, and necessary division of responsibilities among family members plus heavy burdens on the wife and mother. Moreover, the daughter of a farmer will, more often than other MWs, report motivation to involvement because of a "call"—perhaps due to the tendency of rural churches to have a more conservative theology and evangelical orientation than city churches.

Time of marriage and relative ages of husband and wife must be considered, too. For a MW will tend to be more highly involved, more "intrinsically" motivated, and more basically satisfied if she is married to a husband five or more years older than she and settled in his career before marriage (like Dorothy's husband), rather than someone her own age just beginning his studies (like Donna's husband). Marriage to a minister who has already graduated from seminary probably means that a wife is spared many of the initial struggles and trials, and the marriage may therefore be off to an easier financial (and perhaps psychological) start. Likewise, marriage to an older man tends to mean that he will already be established in his career, and that she is less likely to have to cope with the smallest churches and communities.

In addition, and perhaps most important of all, there is often increased deference and respect for an older husband, which fits the background supporter role model and makes it less likely that she will compete with her husband and/or leading church women. This *positive* association of age difference with satisfaction as a MW is of particular interest, since it is contrary to the general marital pattern reported by Blood and Wolfe: "Homogamous couples are the most satisfied. Satisfaction declines as the age gap increases in either direction."[4] Across age groups, the percentage of those who report themselves as "very satisfied and fulfilled as a MW" ranges from 46.0 per cent of those whose husbands are five years or more older, to 40.6 per cent of those whose husbands are younger, to 34.0 per cent of those whose husbands are the same age to four years older. Nor does this appear to be a matter of being more satisfied as a MW at the price of being less satisfied as a wife; rather, all available data would point to a positive association between role fulfillment and marital satisfaction.

Finally, a MW will tend to be more involved and satisfied if she (1) is over 50 rather than under 35 years of age; (2) grew up in a church of less than 400 members, (3) came from a home where religion was "very important" and both parents were active in the same denomination as her husband now serves in, and (4) *completed* either high school or college, but did not begin an educational program which was not finished. The influence of age on involvement and satisfaction is certainly due in large part to the difference of life situation when children are no longer at home, plus the factor of increased experience and competence. However, historical difference may be involved, as well as developmental difference. That is, changes may now be occurring with regard to both the *situations* into which MWs enter (including operative role models) and the *types* of women who tend to become MWs (including general population trends).

For if the portrait of involved and satisfied MWs presented above is compared with the characteristics of MWs under 35 years of age and wives of seminarians presented in Chapter 5, several significant trends become apparent. Compared to older MWs, younger MWs are *less* often (1) daughters of farmers, (2) third-born or later, (3) married after husband's seminary graduation to a man five years or more older, (4) from a home in which religion was "very important," and (5) graduates of the educational programs which they intended to complete.

One would expect, then, that future MWs would experience more frustration and confinement than MWs of the past unless (1) situations and role models change—and this research report may be one influence toward such change, and/or (2) more effective guidance and counsel are provided by the churches and seminaries. (The other alternative would be to "recruit" wives who match the characteristics of those now highly involved and satisfied. Even if this could be done, such a procedure would be highly questionable, since it would institutionalize current role models, as well as negating the freedom of individual choice of marriage partners.) Probably there will have to be *both* types of change: in the *situations* to which women must relate, and in their *preparation* for effective coping with the complex, the ambiguous, and the risky on the basis of personal commitments and values. In the recommendations presented in the next chapter there will be discussion, therefore, both of how situations and role models may be made easier to live with, and of the sort of supplementary growth opportunities that might be provided.

Denominational Groupings

If specific backgrounds provide "tool kits" of resources, specific situations make particular demands. (The converse may also be true of backgrounds producing demands, as in the case of Mary Martha Mountain, and of situations providing resources, as in the case of Dorothy Taylor.) Among the most important variables influencing the involvement, motivation, and satisfaction of MWs are religious denomination and geographic region. This is a matter both of background—as role models operative in various religious and geographic subcultures influence one's own conception of what a MW should be and do, and of situation—the present denomination and region of the husband's ministerial service, and the dominant expectations that exist there. What a woman does and feels will be strongly influenced, then, by the congruence between the *self*-expectations brought from her background and the *imposed* expectations of her situation.

In this study, groupings of denominations were formed empirically, rather than theoretically, in terms of clusterings of denominations whose MWs' questionnaire responses contained similar emphases. These combinations do not at all points follow customary distinctions of doctrine or polity. Nor do they necessarily reflect trends toward merger of groups—for example, between the Evangelical United Brethren (E.U.B.) and Methodist churches. Also, not all 37 denominations participating in the study were included in this stage of data analysis. Major findings have particular validity for the 18 denominations (reduced in number to 14 during the study, due to mergers) for which there were sufficient respondents and high enough response rates to give "solid" data. The resulting groups, with round-number 1961 totals of membership, "ordained ministers with charges," and "total contributions received"[5] are as follows:

1. BAP-EVAN (Baptist and Evangelical): American Baptist Convention, Southern Baptist Convention, Evangelical United Brethren, Church of the Nazarene, and Church of God (Anderson, Ind.). Thirteen million members, 44,000 pastors, and $665 million in contributions.

2. DIS-METH-UCC: International Convention of Christian Churches (Disciples of Christ), Methodist Church, and United Church of Christ (Congregational Christian and Evangelical and Reformed). Fourteen million members, 36,000 pastors, and $808 million in contributions.

3. EPIS-LUTH-PRES: Protestant Episcopal Church, Lutheran Church—Missouri Synod, Lutheran Church in America (Augustana and United), American Lutheran Church (A.L.C., E.L.C., and U.E.L.C.), Presbyterian Church in the U.S. (Southern), and United Presbyterian Church in the U.S.A. (Northern). Fifteen million members, 29,000 pastors, and $913 million in contributions.

Together, these denominations represent about two-thirds of the 64,000,000 members and half of the 219,000 "ordained ministers with charges" of the 227 Protestant bodies for which data are listed in the 1962 edition of the *Yearbook of American Churches*, and more than 90 per cent of the $2,500,000 in contributions received by the 49 Protestant and Orthodox bodies which report such data. As will be noted, the three groups contain roughly equivalent numbers of members, but vary in numbers of "ordained pastors with charges" and in church finances. The Bap-Evan group has 50 per cent more pastors but 25 per cent less finances than the Epis-Luth-Pres group, while the Dis-Meth-UCC group is intermediate in both respects. Contributing to these differences are several factors: percentage of "full-time" versus "part-time" clergy, standards of training and ordination, average size of congregation and number of "multiple charges," denominational social class composition, and so forth.

Collectively, the three groups contain more than 80 per cent of questionnaire respondents in this study, with about 1,000 Bap-Evan, 1,500 Dis-Meth-UCC, and 1,500 Epis-Luth-Pres MWs. More than 600 "other evangelical" respondents might have been added to the Bap-Evan group, but were not, for several reasons. Some denominations, such as Four-Square Gospel, Advent Christian, Cumberland Presbyterian, and Christian Reformed, had a very high response rate but a small number of cases. Other denominations, such as Assemblies of God and the Negro Methodist and Baptist churches, had low response rates. Still other groups, such as Mennonites and Brethren, had distinctive emphases which made it difficult to include them in the broad groupings. Even though major findings are presented in terms of the three major groups listed above, data were tabulated for all participating denominations and reported to their executives. And "other evangelicals" were used for "extend the continuum" contrasts with Bap-Evan MWs, as Unitarian-Universalists (very high response rate, but small number of cases) were contrasted with Epis-Luth-Pres MWs.

How, then, may the three major groups of MWs be characterized? (It is necessary to remember throughout that comparisons between groups of *MWs* may not be applicable to their *denominations* as complex, multidimensional wholes.) As the name given to the first group indicates, Bap-Evan MWs tend to have an *evangelical* (and evangelistic) emphasis more often than MWs from other groups. They view the Christian Gospel as truly *good news*, to which they are called to witness. Marriage represents teamwork with their husbands and the ministry their common calling instead of just his profession. Like other MWs, they most often describe their degree of involvement in "back-ground, supportive" terms, but the meaning attached to this is quite different.

For Bap-Evan MWs, to be a "background supporter" does not mean withdrawing from leadership in the local congregation. More often than other MWs, therefore, they hold offices in women's groups and other church organizations, call on the sick and counsel people with problems, take leadership in church music and religious education, and greet parishioners after church services. In an emergency, they may even conduct church services and preach sermons. More than other MWs, Bap-Evan MWs focus on church work, to the exclusion of other community activities. They may belong to the PTA but will seldom be involved in the YWCA, adult education, the League of Women Voters, an interdenominational or interfaith group, a community women's club, or even scouting or Campfire Girls. More than is true for MWs of other denominations, their world is the church.

In what they consider to be their particular joys and opportunities, Bap-Evan MWs differ from other groups, also. There is more emphasis on "showing people a better way of life" and less emphasis on "learning more about the Christian faith" or "knowing a wide range of people." (In these and the following contrasts, Epis-Luth-Pres MWs tend to make opposite emphases.) To a young woman marrying a minister, the primary advice given would be to "deepen your personal commitment to Christ and the Church," rather than to "be your own best self—don't worry about the expectations of others" or "become emotionally mature, with a sense of humor." More often than in other groups, they feel "called" to this life, "set apart to witness for Christ." In their value system, "devotion to God, doing God's will" receives even more stress than for other MWs, and "self-development" and "understanding yourself" relatively less emphasis.

Bap-Evan MWs, therefore, in comparison to other MWs, are more highly involved in the Church and its ministry at a semi-professional level, more often interpret this involvement in terms of a "call" from God, less often rebel against congregational expectations and demands, and more often combine a positive role image with a negative self-image. They more often report systematic personal and family devotional practices, and more often stress "personal immortality" and "peace of mind," but evidence less concern for "personal growth," "self-development," "self-understanding," or personal hobbies. Of all groups, they report the highest satisfaction as MWs.

These higher levels of involvement, "call" motivation, and satisfaction are influenced by the types of background out of which Bap-Evan MWs tend to come and the types of situations in which they now tend to be. They tend to come from a lower socioeconomic class background than other MWs, and are more often the daughters of laborers than of farmers. They tend to be third-born or later, rather than first- or second-born, children. Their average age is younger than that of other groups, perhaps due to expanding numbers of churches and ministers in these denominations; they may be quite well educated or of limited formal education, and have few children or large families. More often than other MWs, they are in a church less than 50 years old with fewer than 200 members, and have a family income of less than $5,000. This frequently means difficulties in "making ends meet" and the need for income from the wife's full-time, and perhaps also the husband's part-time, nonministerial employment.

As mentioned previously, Epis-Luth-Pres MWs tend to make emphases opposite to those of Bap-Evan MWs, while Dis-Meth-UCC MWs occupy more of an intermediate position. More often than in other groupings, an Epis-Luth-Pres MW may be relatively detached from her husband's work, since she tends to regard it as his profession rather than their common calling. An Episcopal or Presbyterian (but not Lutheran) MW tends to be more highly educated than a Bap-Evan MW, and to come from a higher socioeconomic class background. She is more likely to have developed financial, social, and intellectual need patterns which may be difficult to fulfill with a minister-husband. In addition, she is more likely to have, or want, a "career of my own," and to be dissatisfied with "just being a housewife and unpaid church worker."

In part at least, the emphases of MWs in the three denominational groupings are related to matters of church history. While Bap-Evan MWs are part of a religious tradition molded to a large extent by the particular nature of American society, in both its frontier and industrial stages, Epis-Luth-Pres MWs tend to find their identity within an ethos with clearer European origins and continuing connections. This tradition includes an educated professional ministry and clearly specified structures of church government and ecclesiastical procedure. In addition, there tends to be maintenance of older European judgments concerning "woman's place"; these, together with theologies of the nature of the Church and its ministry, influence conceptions of "the role of the MW" (which vary from the Episcopal "community leader" to the Presbyterian "manse hostess" to the Lutheran *hausfrau*, but all differ from the Bap-Evan "co-minister").

In these terms, as well as in relation to other contrasts presented, Dis-Meth-UCC MWs tend to be intermediate. Though deriving from European origins, these denominations responded to, and were shaped by, the emergent American culture more than denominations of the Epis-Luth-Pres tradition. Interpretation of data regarding Dis-Meth-UCC MWs in this study is made more difficult however by the fact, noted in Chapter 1, that wives of part-time and/or non-seminary-trained ministers are seriously underrepresented in the Disciple of Christ and Methodist samples, as is also the case for Southern Baptists. Since the focus of this study is on wives of *full*-time ministers, particularly those who are *the* minister of *one* church rather than in multiple-staff or multiple-charge situations, this sampling bias does not invalidate the study. But it is necessary to remember that the discussion of Dis-Meth-UCC MWs will not necessarily apply to wives of the part-time and/or student ministers who serve almost 40 per cent of Disciple of Christ churches, or to the wives of students and "approved supply" pastors who serve most of Methodism's smaller churches and have ministered to many New England Congregational churches throughout their history. As a result of these factors, the churches served by full-time, seminary-trained Dis-

Meth-UCC pastors tend to be larger than for comparable minis-ters of other denominations, and their salaries tend to be higher.

Before proceeding with other contrasts, however, two more factors must be considered: (1) *intra*group as well as *inter*group variations, and (2) *geographic* subcultures as these interact with *religious* subcultures. What has been presented regarding Bap-Evan MWs would characterize Southern Baptists more than American (Northern) Baptists, Church of God (Anderson) and Church of the Nazarene more than Evangelical United Brethren (E.U.B.) MWs. Thus, American Baptists evidence more concern for individual fulfillment, and E.U.B. MWs place relatively more emphasis on home and family life in contrast to congregational responsibilities. To apply to "other evangelical" MWs (and to the wives of non-seminary-trained Southern Baptist ministers, who are underrepresented in the sample), the description would have to be strengthened: e.g., Assemblies of God MWs almost twice as often report themselves to be "called" and "set apart, to witness for Christ" as do either Church of God (Anderson) or Church of the Nazarene MWs.

Likewise, even though Lutheran MWs "hang together" with Episcopal and Presbyterian MWs—and differ from Bap-Evan MWs—in level of involvement and satisfaction, they deviate from the Epis-Pres pattern in coming from a lower socioeconomic background and having less formal education. In addition, their theological and value system tends to be more like that of Bap-Evan than that of Epis-Pres MWs. That is, the general involve-ment level may be similar to that of an Epis-Pres MW, but the motivations and meanings are quite different; like Bap-Evan MWs, Lutheran MWs stress "devotion to God," "peace of mind," and "personal immortality" much more than other MWs, and "self-understanding" and "self-development" much less. There is more emphasis on dedication and less on fulfillment. Moreover, there are contrasts *within* Lutheranism, especially between Mis-souri Synod and United Lutheran MWs, related to different regions and type of community served, as well as countries of denominational origin.

Further distinctions could be drawn between "northern" and "southern" Presbyterians; among the component denominations of the Dis-Meth-UCC grouping—especially in terms of the particular characteristics of Disciples of Christ MWs; or even between the Congregational-Christian and Evangelical and Reformed MWs who compose the U.C.C. Such distinctions are, however, beyond the scope of the present report. And all the *intra*group differences do not obscure the basic and significant *inter*group differences: MWs within a given grouping do "hang together," and differ from those in other groupings, in their central emphases. Even though Bap-Evan MWs, like other MWs, most often describe their degree of involvement in background supportive terms, the meaning is quite different when Church and ministry are understood in terms of "winning the unbeliever to Christ" rather than "developing the institution." (This is never, of course, an either-or matter, but rather a question of relative emphasis.) Therefore Bap-Evan MWs are more often team-workers with their husbands than are Epis-Luth-Pres MWs (30 per cent versus 11 per cent) and are less often involved "no more than if [the husband] were in another vocation" (8 per cent versus 19 per cent).

Some Regional Emphases

Even more basic than denominational variation is regional variation within the three groupings. Thus, careful study of a subsample of 300 women who had completed all the questionnaires used in this study, and who represented equal numbers from each of the three denominational and three regional groupings, reveals differences of regional emphasis within a basically similar denominational grouping emphasis.[6] When *all* the responses of these women are taken into account, and not just their self-reports on the forced-choice MW-5 questionnaire, North Central Bap-Evan MWs are clearly more involved and satisfied than those from the Northeast and West regions.

In comparison both to Northeast and West Bap-Evan MWs

and MWs of other denominations, a North Central Bap-Evan MW places more emphasis on division of responsibility within the home, as well as on compensation for some of her husband's "letting-go" tendencies in his work. She more often maintains a balanced judgment regarding herself, considering herself to fall far short of the ideal but at the same time reporting consistent growth through her personal and family devotional life. Likewise, though she admits to occasional frustrations in relationships with particular congregations, and sometimes finds it necessary to defend her own rights and "peace of mind," she does not basically consider the church as a rival for her husband's affections. Therefore, though Bap-Evan MWs from all regions tend to be characterized by a high level of dedication to God and the Church, those from the North Central region appear more often able to temper this dedication with realism and to apply it with balanced flexibility.

In contrast, Northeast and West Bap-Evan MWs more often resent the demands placed upon them, and/or resign themselves to unpleasant situations. They report difficulty in expressing negative feelings and judgments, and more generally in being and feeling independent. Whether this is due to background and/or situational factors is difficult to determine. However, of all groups they are the youngest, most often "later born," in the smallest churches in the largest communities, from the lowest socioeconomic level, and least often daughters of farmers. Compared to other groups, they place relatively low emphasis on both "devotion to God" and "self-understanding." Instead, they stress "concern for others" and "peace of mind." Compared to other Bap-Evan MWs, they have less emphasis on "call" motivation and are considerably less involved in congregational activities. Yet, at the same time, they paint the rosiest over-all picture of what it is like to be a MW, presenting a multiple ideal and denying that others' expectations are unreasonable, the life lonely, or personal growth hard.

In general, southern Bap-Evan MWs are closer to North Central than to Northeast and West MWs in their major emphases.

However, they differ in their emphasis on interpersonal difficulties, to a point where they are tempted to "flee into the family" away from frustrating congregational relationships. Because of strong needs for their husbands as companions and confidants, they more often feel that his dedication to his work is at the price of consideration for them as persons. Like Northeast and West MWs, they have difficulty in making a balanced judgment on themselves, and generally avoid negative evaluations. Their emphasis on sharply defined doctrinal positions and on the necessity for attaining "personal immortality" is greater than that of other Bap-Evan MWs, in relation to whom they are more often first- or second-born children, have a lower level of education, and have larger families.

These regional differences in no way deny the *shared* emphases of Bap-Evan MWs of *all* regions, but rather represent the particular forms these emphases may take, or the qualifications added to them, in response to specific regional subcultures. This is true for other denominational groupings as well. However, in contrast to Bap-Evan MWs, the *least* satisfied Epis-Luth-Pres MWs are from the North Central region, in part because they are in smaller communities than others of their denominational grouping. In other respects also, North Central Epis-Luth-Pres MWs are quite distinctive. They see general similarity between their present family life and that of their childhood, and emphasize their husbands' sharing of home responsibilities. Nevertheless, they often feel that the congregation becomes a rival for their husbands' affection. Also, they tend to be critical of their husbands' "letting-go" or "holding-tight" (rigid, perfectionist, stubborn) tendencies. Of all groups they have the heaviest emphasis on congregational attitudes, rather than limitations of time and/or finances, as most frustrating. In their value system, both "devotion to God" and "concern for others" are ranked lower than by other MWs.

Southern Epis-Luth-Pres MWs present quite a different group portrait. They appear to be people of considerable interpersonal competence, who seldom judge themselves to be shy, retiring, or insecure. They emphasize family relationships and broader social concerns, but at the same time have the most hobbies and are most able to "blow off steam on their own" of all the groups. They are concerned with "being oneself" rather than passively yielding to role expectations or taking over unwanted jobs. Though from a generally high socioeconomic background, their educational level is not much above that of southern Bap-Evan MWs. Nevertheless, they tend to be analytic and to seek to determine the nature of a situation before taking action. Individualism and analysis do not prevent, however, a strong emphasis on traditional creedal statements. In general, perhaps due to large families, they limit their involvement in the local church. Least often of all groups do they work full-time outside of the home.

For this sample of women, at least, the background and situational characteristics of Northeast and West Epis-Luth-Pres MWs are quite distinctive. Of all nine groups this group of MWs is the oldest, the least active, in the largest churches (and therefore most often in multiple-staff situations and with the highest salaries), from the highest socioeconomic background and educational level, and most often third-born or later, but least often daughters of farmers. In marked contrast to North Central Epis-Luth-Pres MWs, those from the Northeast and West seldom mention relationships with the congregation as frustrating, in part because of their heavy emphasis on their own devotion to and care of their families. In general, they have a negative image of "a MW," and of all groups—in marked contrast to southern Epis-Luth-Pres MWs—express the most doubt regarding traditional theological doctrines. They are very much concerned with understanding themselves, and in general are dissatisfied with their present level of personal growth.

Epis-Luth-Pres MWs differ, therefore, from region to region as well as from denomination to denomination, and—most basically—from individual to individual, despite general characteristic emphases across all of these differences. Similar regional variation within a shared orientation occurs for Dis-Meth-UCC MWs. And for these women, like Epis-Luth-Pres MWs and in contrast to Bap-Evan MWs, the level of general satisfaction is lowest in the North Central region. In general, North Central Dis-Meth-UCC MWs consider their present family life to be similar to that of their childhood, and emphasize their husbands' lack of consideration of them as persons. Nevertheless, they express great dependence on them, and deny that their husbands basically put congregation ahead of family. They are proud of their own devotion to their families and satisfied as housewives, in contrast to congregational relationships, which they feel tend to frustrate their own personal growth and satisfaction. At the same time, they tend to have a generally negative self-image and "knuckle under" to demands on them, even though they seek to limit their involvement. In reality, most of them are very active in the church, despite the fact that twice as many report themselves to be "no more involved" than describe themselves as "team-workers."

North Central Dis-Meth-UCC MWs tend, therefore, to experience considerable frustration, even though their husbands receive high ministerial incomes and they seldom have to work outside of the home, in marked contrast to Bap-Evan MWs. They tend to be women of a middle-class background, more often than other groups daughters of farmers, and to be first-born children. They have a high educational level as a group and place strong emphasis on self-understanding, but are much less concerned about either peace of mind or personal immortality. They emphasize "devotion to God, doing God's will" as much as Bap-Evan MWs, but interpret this in quite different terms theologically, generally having a socal or ethical rather than pietistic emphasis. They frequently have a negative image of both "a MW" and "myself," and have difficulty sympathizing with and understanding the small communities in which their husbands' churches tend to be located.

While satisfaction for Bap-Evan MWs tends to be lowest in the Northeast and West, for Dis-Meth-UCC MWs it is generally highest in these regions. Characteristic of these women is emphasis on their husbands' professional ability, and on their own

skills and intelligence. They differ from other Dis-Meth-UCC
MWs in their relatively low emphasis on "devotion to God" and
on theology as a personal belief system, and have the lowest percentage reporting "call" motivation or regular personal and family
devotions of any of the nine groups. Like other Dis-Meth-UCC
MWs, they are more concerned with "self-understanding" than
with "personal immortality," and of all groups they place the
heaviest emphasis on "self-development" and have the most positive self-image. They are second only to North Central Dis-Meth-
UCC MWs in their level of education. Unlike North Central
MWs, however, they are seldom bothered by congregational attitudes. And unlike southern MWs, they seldom report limitations
of time and/or finances as frustrating. Rather, their greatest dissatisfaction is with their own level of personal growth and with
their husbands' "holding-tight" tendencies. On the whole they
are satisfied, though few report themselves as teamworkers with
their husbands. In part their satisfaction may be due to larger
churches and higher salaries. In part, it may be due to maturity
and experience, for like Northeast and West Epis-Luth-Pres MWs,
they are older than other groups.

If Northeast and West Dis-Meth-UCC MWs tend to be concerned with skills, those in the South focus on social relationships,
including those within their own families. They emphasize their
sense of limitation and inadequacy because of their shy, retiring
natures. Nevertheless, they have a positive self-image, which they
contrast with a negative image of "a MW." They report high general satisfaction, but their underlying frustration comes out in
criticism of the institutional church and of traditional doctrine,
and in emphasis on limitations of time and finances as a MW—
despite ministerial incomes which run above those of most other
groups. Their activity level in the local church is very high, but—
like North Central Dis-Meth-UCC MWs—they seldom consider
themselves to be teamworkers with their husbands. Nevertheless
they are proud of their own skills and abilities and may be
critical of either their husbands' "letting-go" or "holding-tight"
tendencies.

Such are some of the characteristics of the nine denomination-region subgroups. Like all brief characterizations, these are most inadequate, and can easily be misinterpreted if one emphasizes negative detail to the exclusion of positive context. It is difficult, too, to be descriptive without being evaluative, without loading the cards in one direction or another. At best, what can be presented is a series of hunches based on careful analysis of a great amount of material. Hopefully, these may serve as clues or leads which will stimulate others to investigation and reflection, rather than fixing premature caricatures which are used judgmentally.

Before turning to consideration of some other situational variables, it may be helpful, however, to draw together some of the threads of the discussion regarding regional subgroups. For issues appear to sharpen up when they are considered in terms of both region and denomination, rather than in terms of only one of these variables. For example, MWs in the South are more active, more often report themselves to be teamworkers with their husbands, and more often stress "witnessing for Christ" than MWs of other regions. Yet this is clearly denominationally linked, in terms of the predominance of Baptists in the South. It is only when one examines *combinations* of denomination and region that patterns become most meaningful. Furthermore, to understand regional subgroups (or individuals) involves consideration of other situational and background variables: church and community size, multiple charge or multiple staff, social class, education, birth order, and so on.

Pending further data analysis involving successive cross-tabulations with increasingly precise controls on variables such as those listed above, there do appear to be regional emphases which cut across the denominational groupings. Northeast and West MWs of all religious traditions, for example, manifest concern for individuality, are critical of the institutional church and its traditional doctrine, and reject cultural role images as limiting personal growth, more than MWs of other regions. For Epis-Luth-Pres MWs, these emphases tend to bring satisfaction and fulfillment, since they represent possibilities for breaking loose from role stereotypes. For Bap-Evan MWs, however, such an individualistic approach can bring real conflict and frustration. Even those who resent the demands on them as basically unfair usually are driven by a multiple ideal of what a MW should be and do. As a result, they tend to deny their own feelings and impulses and, in a kind of overcompensation, often paint a rosy picture of what it is like to be a MW.

If the emphasis in the Northeast and West is on individuality, that of North Central MWs is often on "useful work." For a Bap-Evan MW, such an orientation is generally welcome, as husband and wife work together in the home and church, and she feels that she can compensate at some points for his limitations. With the security of knowing that she counts for something, she is able to make a balanced judgment on both herself and her situation. She can admit to personal limitations and to frustrations with particular congregations, but sees growth taking place in relation to her basic purposes. In contrast, for a Dis-Meth-UCC MW the "useful work" emphasis can be frustrating and confining, and there is not—as with Epis-Luth-Pres MWs—the freedom openly to reject it. She may not see much point in church bazaars and bake sales, but still find herself under great pressure to work on them. Or she may be considerably more liberal theologically and socially than the members of her husband's congregation, but find honest expression of such positions dangerous.

For southern MWs, the key word is not individuality or work, but rather relationship. Though more active than MWs from other regions, and more often self-reported teamworkers with their husbands, the emphasis in the South tends to be more on interpersonal relationships than on simply getting the job done. In this context, to be a teamworker is far more satisfying than seeking to "be oneself" in an independent manner, since teamwork means closeness to one's husband and to God. This emphasis seems to be particularly congenial to Epis-Luth-Pres MWs, who are generally women of interpersonal competence who welcome limiting involvement in church work through playing more of a church hostess and/or exemplary homemaker role.

For Bap-Evan and Dis-Meth-UCC MWs—who more often report themselves to be shy and retiring people—the relationship orientation may produce more conflicts than it does for Epis-Luth-Pres MWs. Also, for them teamwork has a different meaning: activity rather than relationship.

Any such series of regional descriptions is, of course, an oversimplification, especially in terms of the limited evidence on which this one is based. Nevertheless, data from this study would indicate that Bap-Evan MWs will tend to be most satisfied and meaningfully involved in the North Central region, and least satisfied in the Northeast and Far West, while Dis-Meth-UCC MWs reverse this tendency. For Epis-Luth-Pres MWs, the dominant pattern is one of highest satisfaction and meaningful involvement in the South, and lowest satisfaction in the North Central region. It would appear, then, as if the "useful work" orientation best "fits" Bap-Evan MWs but is generally uncongenial to Dis-Meth-UCC MWs, who prefer an emphasis on individuality, and to Epis-Luth-Pres MWs, who stress interpersonal relationships. Such patterns may relate to the degree of congruence between the central emphases of a geographic region and a religious tradition, as both reflect the cultural history of the United (yet in a sense still separate) States.

Other Situational Variables

Multiple staffs and multiple charges. In this research report, the primary focus has been on the approximately 60 per cent of respondents who are wives of *full*-time ministers of *one* church as *the* minister of that church. Nevertheless, data were also collected for MWs whose husbands are involved in a "multiple staff" (more than one minister serving one church) or a "multiple charge" (one minister serving more than one church), in a specialized ministry such as a military or institutional chaplaincy, college or seminary teaching, or church adminstration; or who were part-time ministers. Consideration here will be limited to 383 MWs whose husbands are in multiple staffs and 408 MWs

whose husbands are in multiple charges, from the three denominational groupings previously discussed. Numbers in the other
subgroups are too small for judgment on the representativeness
of respondents.

In considering *multiple-staff* situations it is necessary, first of
all, to distinguish between Sr MWs (wives of "senior" ministers)
and Assoc. MWs (wives of "associate" or "assistant" ministers).
As one would expect, Sr MWs are generally older than Assoc.
MWs (median age of 42 versus 31), their husbands have a higher
ministerial income (median of $9,000 versus $6,000), their children are older (10 per cent with preschool-age children versus
40 per cent), and they are more highly involved in their husbands' ministry (17 per cent "no more involved" versus 36 per
cent). In a number of ways, the status and security of the
"established" Sr MWs are considerably higher than for the "not-
yet-established" Assoc. MWs.

But, here as elsewhere, denomination is important. Limited
numbers of Bap-Evan multiple-staff respondents (25 Sr MWs and
7 Assoc. MWs) make any comparisons tentative, but available
evidence would indicate that it is Sr Dis-Meth-UCC MWs who
experience the greatest satisfaction and Sr Bap-Evan MWs who
experience the greatest conflict in the multiple-staff situation.
This difference in satisfaction can be related to a variety of factors. The family income of a Sr Bap-Evan MW averages about
$500 less than for other denominational groupings, while it is
Sr Dis-Meth-UCC MWs who most often report themselves as
"much better off" financially than their parents were. (Epis-Luth-
Pres MWs report the least gain in comparative economic status.)
Sr Bap-Evan MWs also express the most concern about limited
personal friendships. In general, it would appear as if the "successful institution" approach usually connected with a multiple-
staff ministry is most congenial to Dis-Meth-UCC MWs and least
congenial to Bap-Evan MWs, who prefer a "small, dedicated,
friendly church family."

As a group, Assoc. MWs are much less involved in both local
church and community activities than are Sr MWs, and twice as

often work outside of the home. (Here, as at other points, Bap-Evan MWs differ since in this denominational grouping twice as many Sr as Assoc. MWs work; this is a matter of age, number of children, and economic status.) Differences between Sr and Assoc. MWs are, however, less marked in Dis-Meth-UCC churches, where Assoc. MWs appear to exercise more leadership. Assoc. Bap-Evan MWs are distinctive in their combination of high idealism and desire for further training with concern about the strains of personal example and "goldfish-bowl" living. Assoc. Epis-Luth-Pres MWs stress, rather, the limitations on personal friendships.

In some respects, multiple-staff situations present different sets of challenges and opportunities for MWs than do "one minister–one church" situations. In particular, there are the interpersonal dynamics of the individuals (wives as well as husbands) involved in the multiple ministry, especially with regard to its explicit hierarchy and implicit power structure. Nevertheless, the fundamental patterns of involvement and activity, motivations and meanings, fulfillments and frustrations, and so forth, do not appear to be different as between multiple-staff MWs and other MWs. There are very few differences in response patterns to research questionnaires for these two groups. Rather, the fundamental background and situational variables previously discussed appear to be most influential.

Multiple-charge MWs, however, live in a quite different world from multiple-staff MWs. Particularly striking are the great economic differences. While it is almost impossible to receive *less* than $7,000 in family income as a Sr MW, it is almost impossible to receive *more* than $7,000 as the wife of a minister in a multiple charge. In their median age of about 38, multiple-charge MWs are closer to Sr MWs than to Assoc. MWs, yet their median family income is about $1,000 less than for Assoc. MWs and $4,000 less than for Sr MWs. While less than 10 per cent of Sr MWs report their husbands' ministerial income to be "insufficient for . . . family needs" (and needs can be variously defined!), more than 40 per cent of multiple-charge MWs make such a judgment. For this and other reasons, multiple-charge MWs less often report themselves to be "very satisfied as a MW" than do Sr or Assoc. MWs. The differences between reported satisfaction of multiple-charge and multiple-staff MWs are particularly striking in the Dis-Meth-UCC denominational grouping.

Of particular concern to multiple-charge MWs are problems with regard to "being oneself." Apparently in a multiple-staff situation in a large city MWs experience relative anonymity, whereas in multiple-charge rural situations there is the sense of being observed and judged, not by just one church and community, but by several. In this connection, multiple-charge MWs also more often report having found it hard to have close friends from their husbands' congregations, and to have found being an example a strain. For Dis-Meth-UCC MWs the situation appears to be particularly difficult—despite higher ministerial income than in other denominations. For Epis-Luth-Pres MWs it seems somewhat easier, since as a group they are younger and more often consider this the beginning of their career, rather than a life-time situation.

Beyond questions of family economics and personal relationships, social status affects the relative situations of multiple-charge versus multiple-staff MWs. Considered in terms of the usual standards of professional achievement, someone in a multiple charge is "less of a success" than someone on a multiple staff. As a group, multiple-charge MWs do have less formal education than Sr or Assoc. MWs, and (except for Epis-Luth-Pres MWs) their husbands' ministerial training is more limited than for either multiple-staff or "one church–one minister" clergy. Both objective and subjective factors may lead, then, to the lower status of multiple-charge ministers and their wives. The "second-class citizenship" to which they are assigned, and the low rewards in relation to the heavy responsibilities, pose a problem, however, for the entire church.

Working wives. A MW who is employed full time outside of the home is in as much of a special situation as a multiple-staff or multiple-charge MW. However, the effects of employment on her involvement and satisfaction as a MW will depend on many other factors, one of which is the nature of the job itself and her reason for choosing it. The preferred jobs for MWs appear to be schoolteaching (about 70 per cent) and secretarial or other office work (about 20 per cent). For both teachers and office workers the major reason stated for working is financial—with "supplement my husband's inadequate salary" and "save toward children's college education" most often mentioned as specific purposes. For teachers, however, there is often also emphasis on personal fulfillment and service to others.

When asked concerning the effects on home and family life of their outside employment, both teachers and office workers emphasize positive benefits more than negative influences. However, the ratio of positive to negative is considerably higher for teachers than for women in other kinds of work. Positive benefits most often mentioned are "freedom from former economic tension and worry," "money for extras—a higher standard of living—a 'fun-type' vacation," "improved family co-operation and responsibility," and "a fulfilled mother is a better member of the family." Problems can arise, however, in terms of "can't keep up with housework—too much left undone," "life is hectic—we are pulled in too many directions at once," "the family is not complete without a full-time wife and mother, and time for exchange of ideas and feelings," and "I seem under strain and exhausted all the time." For office workers, there is more emphasis on "family life suffering" and less on "personal strain"; working hours are more difficult, but responsibilities perhaps less demanding.

While employed MWs show some concern about effects of their work on adequate fulfillment of their family responsibilities, they are almost unanimous in the judgment that their contribution to their husband's work and the life of the church suffers little, if at all. Most of them report that they still "take as active a part as before." The major change is in terms of "more focused participation, especially not being able to attend women's daytime groups. But I don't miss them!" Some do report missing "the chance to do more visiting among the people" or "the oppor-

tunity for deep, satisfying relationships," but the general effect
of employment on their church participation is generally seen as
positive: "when the church isn't my whole life, I can enjoy what
I do there more" and "our people now do things they always
thought the MW would do—it's been good for them, and for me."

As important as their own attitudes toward employment are
the attitudes of others, especially their husbands and their congregations, and here again the reported judgment is more positive
than negative. More than two-thirds of teachers report that their
husbands approve of their employment, and sometimes have even
suggested that they work, since they "recognize the value to me
as a person" as well as "the necessity of the work in terms of the
family's economic welfare." About one-third of the husbands of
teacher-MWs, however, are reported as "having divided feelings:
appreciates the necessity and my willingness, but doesn't like it"
or "would much prefer to have his wife home full time." For husbands of office workers, the judgment is considerably more negative, since about half of them "look forward to the time when I
can quit," "[my husband] objects when my job interferes with
church activities," or "objects to lack of our time together." Both
teachers and office workers report general acceptance by congregations of their outside employment, especially since "they
recognize how low my husband's salary is—and now feel less
guilty about it" and "after all, they only hired one person." There
are some criticisms about "missing meetings" or "not helping
more in the Sunday School," but these are definitely in the
minority.

For teachers in particular, there is a real sense of personal
fulfillment through their work: "the joy of service, usefulness,
achievement, and purpose—of shaping and influencing lives, helping children grow," as well as "winning respect and appreciation
for doing a job as a person in my own right, not because it's expected of a MW." They enjoy "the intellectual stimulation, study,
and growth" as well as the "companionship and stimulation of
other teachers and pupils." They feel, too, that in their wider
social contacts, their "influence as a Christian is extended beyond
the congregation." For some, too, it is a matter of "keeping busy

and expressing myself" with "less time to dwell on the short-comings of my husband and his church" and "something to do other than housework—to get out of the rut." In addition, there are economic benefits—including "going out without guilt for spending money" and the "sense of helping toward family goals." For office workers, the emphases are similar, though with less direct service motivation. Rather the emphasis is on "being myself, not a MW," "enjoying doing a job well—and being appreciated and respected for it," the "variety of experiences, people, and ideas—the general stimulation which keeps me growing, rather than busy-busy as a MW," and the economic benefits of greater financial stability and some "extras."

In general, employed MWs emphasize the benefits of their working much more than the losses. They regret being unable to do things at home such as cooking, sewing, entertaining, or hobbies, and the limited time to be with their family and to develop a "well-ordered home." But the emphasis on personal gain is much greater than on personal loss. Nevertheless, when asked whether or not they would work outside the home if their husband's ministerial income were sufficient for family needs, only 44 per cent of teachers and 32 per cent of office workers answer Yes. Here their guilt finds expression with regard to "helping my husband more, rather than expecting him to help with housework" and "mothers should be at home when their children need them," as well as the desire for "freedom to pursue other interests, and not be tied to a regular schedule."

Teachers who would continue to work even if it were not financially necessary feel that they are "making a contribution and accomplishing something worth while" as well as "filling a need in my life not filled by church activities—with stimulation and an outlet for my energy, and without competition with my husband," and that therefore to work is "better for him, for me, and for the congregation." For office workers the emphasis is on it being "better to have outside interests of my own" so that "petty grievances and worry about my husband's ministry and the congregation are put in perspective."

So much for self-report. What of the *actual participation* of

employed MWs? Does their outside employment limit their involvement in their husbands' ministry? For some, of course, it
does. But the striking fact is that, *as a group*, employed MWs are
more active in the local church than MWs in general. Twice as
often as other MWs, they report themselves to be "teamworkers"
with their husbands, and also report a "call" motivation more
frequently. They also express more willingness to "pinch hit" on
jobs such as Sunday-School superintendent, should the need
arise. Less often than other MWs do they mention the congregational situation as frustrating, and more often mention congregational relationships as a positive factor in their life situation.

Employed MWs, from all evidence, therefore, are as involved
in their husbands' ministry and as satisfied and fulfilled as other
MWs. However, their route to fulfillment appears to have distinctive characteristics. In part, this may be due to their being
older (7 per cent under 35 years of age, versus 31 per cent for
total sample), better educated (50 per cent college graduates,
versus 37 per cent of total sample), and more often married to
husbands three or more years older than they (43 per cent versus
32 per cent of total sample).

Whatever the reason(s), employed MWs appear to be women
who are more energetic and less analytic-reflective than other
MWs. Their self-judgment is generally positive, and at the same
time they appear more able than other MWs to combine a self-
ideal of church and ministry with rejection of cultural stereotypes. *Less* often than other MWs do they present a harassed,
harried self-image in their "mental picture of me," and less often,
too, do they offer a superwoman multiple ideal in their "mental
picture of a MW." They more often report personal and family
devotional life as contributing to growth, and less often state that
it "can be improved"; if it isn't helpful, they drop it. *Less* often do
they regard the church as a rival for their husbands' affections, or
report finding themselves (or their husbands) too exhausted for
love-making. *Less* often do they express concern about their
leadership abilities, or about being shy or retiring in interpersonal
situations.

As a group, then, employed MWs appear to be an unusually capable, confident, and energetic group of women—even in comparison to other MWs. Some of them may use outside employment as a means of withdrawing from, or defending against, the demands of congregation and/or husband. Some do report that the combination of outside work, home, and church responsibilities is more than they can physically manage. But in general, the women who do more outside of the home also seem to do more in the home, and in the local church. It is not so much a question of distribution of energy as of *amount* of energy available, and the manner in which the person *focuses* this energy. Employed MWs appear, in general, to belong to the "high, focused energy" group. Clearly, a number of women would not be employed if their husbands' salary were more adequate; but for many, employment represents self-fulfillment more than economic necessity.

Housing, finances, church size, etc. Among the situational variables which appear to influence a MW's involvement and satisfaction is the type of housing available to her. Some summary data on housing appear in the Technical Appendix to this report. Adequate interpretation of these data, like many others, must await further analysis. However, at this point it can be noted that the housing most often provided for ministers and their families is the unfurnished parsonage (about 78 per cent), with a furnished parsonage (15 per cent) or housing allowance (7 per cent) provided much less frequently. One notable exception is the Methodist Church, in which furnished parsonages are much more common, being indeed the usual pattern in some geographic regions. Methodist MWs are also distinctive in their high level of satisfaction with the type of housing they now have. Over-all, 80 per cent of MWs with a housing allowance report that they would desire this type of housing in their next parish versus 70 per cent of those with a furnished parsonage and 62 per cent of those with an unfurnished parsonage. (For non-Methodist MWs, the percentages of satisfaction with present type of housing are: 80 per cent housing allowance, 62 per cent unfurnished, and 44 per cent furnished.) Twice as many would prefer a housing allowance as now have it.

Although the common housing pattern, therefore, is that of a parsonage owned by the congregation but furnished by the pastor, the trend is toward a housing allowance with which the pastor may buy his own house. There are many pros and cons which affect the decision of parsonage versus housing allowance. In some communities, adequate housing is either virtually unobtainable or far beyond the resources of most ministers. The buying and selling of real estate certainly complicates ministerial moves, and may indeed deter one from a change of pastorate when that is otherwise indicated. Moreover, the housing allowance may not be (and often is not) adequate; it can be a way for the congregation to avoid responsibility for proper care of the pastor and his family. These are a few of the arguments for the parsonage system, especially within a denomination such as the Methodist Church with a tradition of itinerancy.

Yet many MWs feel that the advantages of a parsonage are far outweighed by the limitations. No one house can fit the family size and other requirements of a variety of ministerial families. Moreover, to live in tax-free property, especially if it is next to— and in a sense the continuation of—the church building, removes you from the category of average citizen. You may not be part of a real neighborhood. Having others responsible for repairs on your home may foster unhealthy dependence, and also make the most minor repairs a complex and frustrating "committee-type" process. And when retirement comes, there is no place to live and no equity to buy a home of your own.

There are, then, honest differences of opinion with regard to the desirability of a parsonage. Most MWs would agree, however, that when one is provided, it is best if it *not* be next to the church. Rather, "a healthy walk away—for both pastor and parishioner" is deemed preferable. This appears to be the trend in new parsonages. Indeed, the general report of MWs is that congregations are *on the whole* very considerate of their ministers' families' needs and desires. There is general respect for the privacy of ministerial homes and acceptance of the fact that they are *homes* and not just church property. Despite the descriptions of parsonages in popular magazines and novels, most MWs give a positive judgment regarding "your present residence, in terms of general adequacy for your family's needs [with regard to] location, space, facilities, upkeep, appearance. . . ." On these bases, about 50 per cent of MWs rate their housing "good," 25 per cent "fair," and 25 per cent "poor." For some individuals, and within some denominations and geographic regions, there are serious housing problems. But *in general*, congregations appear quite responsible in the housing provided for their ministers' families. Indeed, they may sometimes "overdo" in terms of luxurious accommodations—as a symbol of collective pride. And, there seems to be a steady and progressive upgrading of parsonages throughout Protestantism.

To evaluate ministerial salaries is even more difficult and controversial than to judge ministerial housing. Again one's judgment depends on the standard of evaluation: What do a minister and his family "have the right to expect"? For some MWs, the only true standard is one of sacrificial service; for others, one of professional status. For some congregations, the implicit assumption is that of vicarious suffering of the minister and his family on their behalf; for others, that of genuine empathy and concern. Also, there is considerable variation of ministerial income across denominations: in general, Bap-Evan MWs have the lowest family incomes, with the frequent need for supplementary income from the outside employment of wife and/or husband. (Until the end of the nineteenth century, Baptist preachers received no regular salaries, and until about a hundred years ago the "going wage" was only about $64 a year. If the wife had not taught school, many preachers' families would not have survived. Early American Methodism, likewise, with ministers on six- to eight-week circuits, expected men to remain bachelors.)

Despite all these difficulties of evaluation or indeed, comparison of denominations or individuals with one another, because of varying circumstances, some general trends are apparent. On the basis of MWs' reports of their husbands' 1960 "ministerial income (excluding housing allowance, but including utilities, car allow-ance, pension and insurance payments, fees, and so on)" the median ministerial income for Bap-Evan clergy was about $4,500 and for Dis-Meth-UCC and Epis-Luth-Pres clergy (excluding the Missouri Synod Lutherans) about $6,000.[7] Because of the heavy financial burden on Missouri Synod Lutheran churches of providing salaries of both parochial schoolteachers and pastors, ministerial incomes in this denomination are at the Bap-Evan rather than Epis-Luth-Pres level. The average 1960 ministerial income across denominational groupings is slightly below the median income for all families in 1959 of $5,660, according to U.S. Census data, and about $1,000 below the median earnings of persons in professional or managerial positions. It is difficult, of course, to assess the indirect economic benefits (especially with regard to provision of housing) and liabilities (especially with regard to unreimbursed professional expenses such as auto-mobile, education, books, telephone, and general office expense) with which to adjust cash salary to make it more comparable to that of other workers. In general, unreimbursed professional ex-penses probably more than offset indirect benefits such as hous-ing, especially for ministers on the lowest salaries, who least often receive fringe benefits.

Ministerial salaries, thanks to the efforts of the Clergy Com-pensation Project of the National Council of Churches, are im-proving. But they have a long way to go to catch up with incomes of other salaried workers.[8] Certainly the income re-ceived is in no sense proportionate to the training required. And this raises the issue of the average size of congregations served by full-time, seminary-trained ministers, which is especially small for Baptists and Evangelicals. (There are also the matters of the socioeconomic composition of denominations and their steward-ship practices.)

Church size is important for more than economic reasons, too, since it affects the part that a MW is expected to take in her husband's ministry and the sources of fulfillment and frustration connected with that involvement. Though it is difficult to establish an optimum church size, the available data would suggest that a congregation of about 400 to 700 members may represent close to the ideal membership with regard to a MW's involvement and satisfaction. A church of this size is large enough to have adequate program, staff, facilities, and volunteer leadership, but small enough to permit close interpersonal relationships and a genuine sense of belonging. Community size appears to influence a MW's involvement and satisfaction much less than church size.

The influences of these and other situational variables are being analyzed in the continuing stages of the research project. Yet beyond all statistical analysis are questions of religious motivation and subjective meaning. To the woman who feels called with her husband to sacrificial witness for Christ, housing and finances signify something quite different from their meaning to the equally sincere (and in her terms dedicated) woman whose major goal is to assist her husband in his professional advancement. As a group, MWs with preschool-age children suffer more frustration and conflicts than other MWs, but the way the individual copes with the multiple pressures of this period, and the balance of resignation and hope maintained in the midst of it, depend on her general value structure, marital relationship, and "sense of meaning" as a MW.

CHAPTER 7

Conclusions and Recommendations

FROM THE SAME data, different individuals can draw quite different conclusions. Moreover, the results themselves are conditioned by elements of research design—which questions are asked, of whom, and in what form? Therefore, any conclusions and recommendations must be regarded as tentative. Adequate validation can come only through future longitudinal research, investigations by other researchers, and—perhaps most important—the test of the experiences and insights of MWs themselves. In addition, since only a small percentage of the total amount of material (including file drawers full of letters) could be reported, the selection and organization, as well as interpretation, of data are subject to a researcher's biases and preferences. For these reasons each reader, in the final event, must draw his own conclusions. Many stories have been told; many more will be heard. Now we must consider which of our findings parallel those from other research on MWs.

Other Studies: Confirmations and Qualifications

While this is the first large-scale study of American Protestant MWs, there have been other, more limited studies in recent years, including Mary Suput's master's thesis at Northwestern University in 1953, Beverly Kaiser's master's thesis at Boston University in 1958, and Wallace Denton's doctoral dissertation at Columbia University in 1958, which after revision appeared in book form in 1962.[1] These studies involved small numbers of

MWs: Denton—30, Suput—52, and Kaiser—81. And each was limited in terms of denomination and region: Denton—Baptist, Methodist, Lutheran, and Presbyterian MWs from the metropolitan New York City area; Suput—Methodist student pastors' wives from Garrett Seminary, Illinois; and Kaiser—Methodist MWs from Illinois. Nevertheless, the results of these investigations, as well as those from less pretentious surveys by MWs such as Audrey Swett and Anne Jordheim, support at many points the results of this research.[2]

In particular, studies agree on the cultural image of "the ideal MW." Denton relied primarily on bibliographic research, supplemented by illustrative questionnaires and interviews. Kaiser used questionnaires, directed to 79 ministers, 69 laymen, and 85 laywomen, as well as 81 MWs. Audrey Swett mailed questionnaires to Congregational Christian MWs in New York State, receiving 33 responses. Anne Jordheim collected information on attitudes of Lutheran MWs in Wisconsin. Reports of these studies have particular emphases, in part dependent on the concerns of those who collected the information. Nevertheless, they concur on the basic lines with which a portrait of the "ideal MW" is drawn, in descriptions very similar to that presented in Chapter 1 of this book.

Kaiser's research is particularly helpful in contrasts of expectations held by MWs with those held by ministers, laymen, and laywomen, and in careful analysis of data—through a series of cross-tabulations. Her results indicate that the position of the respondent (MW versus minister, layman, and laywoman) most affected answers concerning the relationship of a MW to the church. But judgments with regard to personal and family life were more influenced by geographical location and age than by position. Altogether, MWs tended to expect more of themselves than did laymen and laywomen in some ways, such as teaching Sunday-School or working in the kitchen at church suppers, but less in such activities as accompanying the minister on pastoral calls and singing in the choir. Both ministers and MWs felt that a MW was of greatest service to the church when she found and developed local leadership, rather than taking office herself. But laymen and laywomen were more inclined to want her to assume direct leadership. With regard to personal and family life, respondents tended to permit a MW more freedom if they were: (1) from northern, rather than southern Illinois, (2) under rather than over 45 years of age, and (3) of a higher educational level —though on some issues those with a college education agreed with grade-school graduates more than with those who had postgraduate education. Kaiser found that the size of the respondent's church and community had less influence on answers than the other factors mentioned, though in general more direct leadership from a MW is expected in small churches and communities.

But what if the cultural role image proves to be more than a young, inexperienced MW can measure up to? Swett's respondents revealed two major emphases: (1) "be yourself," and (2) be careful, adaptable, patient, quiet, tolerant, "riding with the punch" and not "trying to do too much." Kaiser agrees, but gives more detailed advice to "any young woman" who, like herself, "is just learning to be a MW . . . as a help to her in forming her own conception of the role of a MW."

1. You must *want* to be a MW. You must feel that your husband is doing the most important work in the world, and you must be willing to help him do it. This is the only way in which you will be able to meet the demands that are made on your time and energy in a spirit of helpfulness rather than from a sense of duty.

2. You must decide what church work is most important to you and what church work you can do most effectively. Then you must learn to say No tactfully to the jobs which you think are less important . . . and you must learn to accept criticism.

3. Be grateful for the opportunity to become acquainted with so many people. . . .

4. Learn to love the young people. . . .

5. Show your interest in the women of the church. . . . Show that you are willing to help. . . . Seek out potential leaders and workers and help them to learn to do their jobs. . . .

6. Provide a Christian home for your husband and children. . . .

7. Be a real companion to your husband. He needs your suggestions and your criticisms (tactfully given), but most of all he needs your understanding and inspiration.

8. Be careful in your personal life . . . [so that you do not] hurt your or your husband's influence.

9. "You shall love the Lord your God . . . [and] your neighbor as yourself." If you obey these two commandments of Jesus, you can be a good Christian, and if you can be a good Christian, then you can be a good minister's wife.[3]

On such bases, a MW may determine the part she will take in her husband's ministry. Thus, Denton describes three types of MWs at the end of his dissertation: (1) the aloof-participant, comprising 10 per cent of his 30 respondents (cf. 15 per cent of MW-5 respondents who were "no more involved"); (2) the supportive-participant, comprising 77 per cent of his respondents (cf. 64 per cent of MW-5 respondents who were "background, supportive"); and (3) the incorporated-participant, comprising 13 per cent of his respondents (cf. 21 per cent of MW-5 respondents who were "teamworkers"). While data from other studies are not exactly comparable, since they often involve open-ended questions and responses which are difficult to categorize, the background-supporter pattern is always reported as the most common and highly valued. But, as in Denton's study, Marthas, Janes, and Kates are generally underrepresented, due to the combination of limits of region and denomination and the influence of self-selection.

In general, then, recent research on MWs, despite problems in statistical generalization, agrees on basic themes. However, other studies tend to neglect both individual differences and the relative influence of specified background and situational variables. Denton does attempt such specification in the twenty-three "propositions" in which he summarizes his findings. But even here there is too much emphasis on "the role" of "the MW" and not enough on specific patterns and the variables that influence them. Thus the proposition, "the role of the MW produces loneliness," while generally supported by MW-5 and MW-6 data in terms of concern for lack of close friends, fails to specify the conditions under which loneliness is most or least apt to occur. Similarly, one can say that "MWs without children tend to be more directly active in church activities than those with children" only if he is comparing MWs who have *no* children with MWs who have *preschool-age* children. Respondents in this study whose youngest child was *over* 6 years of age were, as a group, *more* active in their local churches than respondents with no children. (Percentages of those performing more than ten activities in the local church, by age of youngest child, were: no children—21 per cent; under 6 years—14 per cent; 6 to 16 years—26 per cent; and over 16 years—21 per cent.)

Of Denton's twenty-three propositions, those which the data of this research generally support, in addition to the one on loneliness, are:

1. MWs who express a sense of special call tend to be more directly active in church activities than those who do not express a call.

2. MWs who have worked to support themselves tend to maintain and express more individuality than those who have not.

3. The way a MW experiences and responds to the expectations of her church is a function of her own personality make-up.

4. The parsonage has been able to retain more of its traditional functions than many other homes in our society, thus contributing to the MW's sense of worth and value and averting a sense of uselessness characteristic of some housewives in our industrial society.

5. Role expectations of MWs in smaller communities are more clear-cut and insistent than in larger communities.

6. Role conflicts of the young MW are frequently attributable to the lack of experience necessary for acquiring and internalizing expectations of the role.

7. MWs endeavoring to choose between two roles, of relatively equal prestige, experience less church disapproval than those wives seeking to reject aspects of their role without assuming another role.

8. MWs perceive the supportive role as their main contribution to the husband and his work.

9. MWs frequently experience conflict between the satisfactions of their role and the concomitant sacrifices associated with the enactment of it.

10. The role of the MW differs from the role of another business or professional man's wife at the point of expectations of participation in the husband's work.

11. The church and community expect the MW to avoid extremes.[4]

Certain qualifications are necessary, however. Propositions 4 and 10 involve contrasts with other groups, for which exact comparable data are not directly available, and proposition 11 properly refers only to the *perception* of MWs. Propositions 3, 6, and 9 are in a sense axiomatic (as are other propositions not listed here), or at least apply to role performance in general. Proposition 5 would be stated more exactly in terms of *church* size, rather than community size.

Even more basic qualifications are necessary for the remaining four propositions (Nos. 1, 2, 7, and 8) in terms of considerations of motivation and meaning, age and stage, and background and situation. Particularly important are religious denomination and geographic region, since MW-5 and MW-6 questionnaire data contradict another of Denton's propositions: that "the denomination of the MW is not a significant factor in her attitudes about her role, other things being equal." For "other things" are seldom equal among varying religious traditions, as Denton himself indicates. The nature of Denton's group of 30 respondents (70, if one includes those on whom the questionnaire was pretested) was such that the variables of geographic region and religious denomination, as well as other variables influenced by these two, were simply not given the opportunity to operate. Proposition 1, in this connection, operates quite differently for Lutheran than for Evangelical MWs, in terms of doctrine of church and ministry. Proposition 2 depends on what *kind* of job she has had, and even more on what work *means* to the individual, her husband, and the power structure of her denomination and congregation. If a woman has worked, and/or now works outside of the home, primarily for financial reasons rather than motives of self-expression, there may be little maintenance or expression of individuality involved.

Likewise, what "relatively equal prestige" or "seeking to reject aspects of their role" means in No. 7, in relation to "church disapproval," will vary greatly by region, denomination, congregation, and the individual. Certain general tendencies may operate —e.g., that it is usually more acceptable to congregations for a MW to work as a schoolteacher than as an office worker—but concrete situations involve many qualifying factors. And while No. 8 applies to roughly two-thirds of the participants in this study, it does not apply to the other third, and it is highly doubt-

ful that Denton's conclusion that "the assistant-pastor type of
wife, whose life centers to a large degree outside the home, seems
to be passing" is justified for Baptist and Evangelical MWs.

Denton's great strength is at the point of defining issues, both
through an excellent summary of historical and contemporary
"looks at the MW" and in summarizing the dominant "role attitudes" of his 30 respondents toward "her husband's work," "her
family life," and "her church and community." His guidance is, in
general, sounder than that of other handbooks for MWs, in terms
of sociological and psychological analysis as well as reality-
grounding. But Denton's limitation, and that of most of the
literature produced by and for MWs, is at the point of failing to
realize sufficiently the variety inherent in the many factors that
operate—husbands, family life, parsonage, congregation, community, and so on—as well as the complex patterning of these variables for specific individuals. (Suput deals more adequately with
individual patterning, in her illustrative profiles of student pastors' wives with "healthy" and "unhealthy" attitudes toward life.[5])

This Study: Preliminary vs. Final Results

As the criticisms of other studies indicate, two conclusions of
this research are: (1) It is dangerous to make generalizations
about "the role" of "the MW," because of the great variation
among MWs on many dimensions and subject to the influence of
many variables; and (2) the patterning of variables for a given
individual is a very complex matter, with each variable taking on
a different meaning in interaction with other variables, and prediction of *individual* behavior much more difficult and ambiguous than description of group characteristics. In this report, therefore, the terms "MWs" or "a MW" have been used in preference
to "the MW." But since most readers will be interested in knowing what is true "in general," and will not be satisfied with "it
depends on . . . ," general trends of the data have also been
presented, as in the description of Mrs. Mode in Chapter 3.

Throughout, however, the goal has been that of understanding
involvement and activity, motivation and meaning, fulfillment

and frustration, at the *personal* level, through listening to the stories of Mary Martha Mountain, Dorothy Taylor, Donna Sykes, and others. Five broad types of involvement and activity (Martha, Mary, Dorcas, Jane, and Kate) indicate one dimension of variation. But, as we have seen, these basic themes are subject to infinite variation. And we must be aware, too, of how they are orchestrated in relation to specific personal data (socioeconomic class, family background, education, birth order, age difference between husband and wife, and so on), as well as situations (region, denomination, employment, multiple staff, church size, and the like). Moreover, the *time* dimension is important, as a MW moves through particular ages and stages, each of which will have particular meanings for particular individuals, even though general trends can be discerned.

Therefore, in order to understand variations on basic dimensions, characteristics of particular groups, and factors contributing to individual patterns of involvement and fulfillment, *many* women must be studied in *depth*. Large numbers are necessary if one is to "cut the cake" in various ways, in order to test interactions between variables with progressively more precise controls. To illustrate this point, let us examine the progressive gains in understanding of the two major "criterion" variables in this research—involvement and satisfaction—through various stages of the project, with increasingly large numbers of MWs involved. Fortunately, findings were summarized at each stage, so that comparisons can be made with some limit on the distortions of hindsight.

Of necessity, there must be some simplification here of both stages and learnings. But one important "gathering together" came in the summarizing of ideas expressed in 100 letters written by MWs. From these letters, the following picture of "what it is like to be a MW," in terms of major group emphases, was drawn:

1. Advantages of being a MW include the rich rewards of being able to devote oneself to what seems important, and share in husband's work, with respect in the community and exposure of the family to "the better things of life."

2. However, there are balancing disadvantages—the pressure toward exampleship, conflicts between family and church responsibilities, plus inadequate salaries and parsonages, and limitations of friendships.

3. Suggestions for a young MW include: the first duty of a MW is to her home and family, and therefore a wife should not become too involved in the church, and must learn how to schedule the time there is and make the best of interruptions.

4. Real division of opinion exists, however, on whether or not a MW should make calls with her husband, or entertain couples from the church, or have close friends from the church, despite agreement on her representative role and the need for her to be a gracious hostess.

5. There is emphasis, too, on a MW's spiritual life, with the desire to serve arising from love of God rather than a sense of duty, and the need emphasized for retreats and other means of spiritual refreshment.

6. With regard to church work, it is important that a MW be in the background, and not compete with her husband. She should give freely of her time, service, and understanding, but serve only in areas of interest and competence, recognize differences among congregations, and seek to develop lay leadership rather than accept positions of leadership herself.

7. This service, some maintain, should not be at the price of denying her individuality. But others recommend that she be adjustable, not overly sensitive, poised, uncomplaining, never bossy or nagging. And it will help if she is well educated and trained.

8. The situation of MWs would be improved if parishioners remembered that a MW is an individual, who must find her own way in the church, who needs some of her husband's time, and who appreciates kindnesses and a well-maintained parsonage.

Here we have the first tentative formulation of issues to be investigated, with more specification than in Kaiser's nine points. But there is little basis for judging the relative importance of variables or how they interact with one another. Nor is it possible to evaluate how representative these women are of MWs in general, or which factors influence their supplying information. Further clarification comes with summarization of responses of 332 MWs to the open-ended items on pretest questionnaires such as MW-3 and MW-4. With more respondents and clearer definition of both questions and categories for classifying responses, we now learn that:

1. Being a MW has meant great rewards (78 of the 332 respondents) in friendship (37), sharing one's husband's vocation (35), service (33), and fulfillment of a desire for full-time Christian service

(10) through the opportunity to serve one's Lord (17). There is spiritual growth (22), involving seeing *others* grow spiritually (6), as well as a greater general understanding of people and their problems (14), with wide social (8) and intellectual (10) contacts which bring challenge (8) as well as prestige (13). Nevertheless, for some the basic meaning is frustration (19), tension (7), and loneliness (10), compounded by a financial struggle (11), poor living conditions (9), the pressure of exampleship (10) and general sacrificial living—including uprooting moves (10).

2. If she were not a MW, she would have more time for her own interests (82) and could be more "herself" rather than seeking to please others (39), because she would not feel so personally involved or responsible for church activities (44). Her husband could spend more time at home (10) and she would have permanent roots somewhere (18) and less financial strain (18). But, others maintain, she would not have as much opportunity for service and growth (18), nor as many friends (17), and life in general would not be as exciting or fulfilling (28) since she could not share in her husband's work as much (13). Or, there might not be much difference (18). Or, one just doesn't know (7).

3. Major advice to a young MW would be that her first duty is to her home and family (50). At the same time, she must realize that dedication to Christian commitment is the most important prerequisite (40) and be ready to put church before family when necessary (45). Others would maintain that she must remain inconspicuous in church life (25) and be careful about close friendships in the church (11) and her appearance and behavior in general (7). In contrast, some feel that she should serve only in areas in which she is interested (16), and what is most important is that she become emotionally mature (32), love people (18), keep a sense of humor (9), and most important of all, love her husband (26).

4. Improvement of the situation of MWs will come through change in MWs—in commitment (9), education (11), adjustment and realism (8), and independence (9), as well as through parishioners' improving parsonages (19) or salaries (20) or kindness to ministers' families (13). Most basic, however, is that they attain a realization of a MW's individuality and get away from stereotyped expectations (67). Ministers, too, can help through setting more time aside for their families (17).

As the numbers in parentheses indicate, there are varying degrees of emphasis on particular issues, and one can begin to see both general "clusterings" of emphasis and possible patternings of variables for particular individuals. There are now clearer definitions of the *proportions* of those who, in general, feel satisfied and fulfilled versus those who feel frustrated and confined, and in addition the *meanings* of satisfaction (service, sharing, growth, etc.) and frustration (set-apartness and deprivations of freedom, time, money, etc.). Also, potential value conflicts between service to home, service to church, and self-development become apparent. And there is some indication of ways in which women deal with cultural stereotypes.

Clarification has come, then, at a number of points regarding sources and types of satisfaction and fulfillment. But the variable of involvement in one's husband's work (the second major criterion or dependent variable of this study) is much less clear. And there is still little reliable information on the variation of emphasis and practice by different subgroups: denomination, region, age, and so forth.

What can be learned, then, from the responses of 142 MWs from Indiana to the precoded (forced choice) items of the MW-4 pretest questionnaire? First of all, we note that 43 per cent reported themselves as, in general, very satisfied and fulfilled, 46 per cent as satisfied and fulfilled, and 9 per cent as "so-so," or frustrated and confined as MWs. (Cf. MW-5 percentages of 36, 50, and 14 per cent, respectively.) Likewise, 94 per cent of respondents felt themselves to be of help to their husband's ministry, at home in church activities, and liked and appreciated. The majority, however, would not consider a potential husband's being a minister as a major factor were they to marry again. They judged their contribution to the church to be "substantial" or "about average" rather than "very great."

With regard to involvement in their husband's ministry, 10 per cent of these Indiana MWs reported themselves to be teamworkers with their husbands and a total of 84 per cent reported themselves as either "very much" involved ("in a supportive role" —37 per cent), "much" involved ("through responsibilities I carry" —18 per cent), or "much" involved ("through general interest"— 29 per cent). The remaining 6 per cent reported "a little" involvement. (Though these are not directly comparable to MW-5 response categories, percentages there were 21 per cent teamworker; 64 per cent background, supportive; and 16 per cent "no more" or "not" involved.)

Many women contributed to church work through leadership in women's activities (28 per cent) or being a resource person (23 per cent), and teaching a Sunday-School class (18 per cent) and musical activities (11 per cent) were also mentioned. With regard to *motivation* for involvement, 37 per cent mentioned a call to full-time Christian service and another 19 per cent a call to be a MW, though others reported their motivation to be that of wanting to be busy in useful work (14 per cent) or close to their husbands (14 per cent). Participation was most often limited by having small children (36 per cent) or lacking leadership abilities (19 per cent). The majority admired either their husband's sincere faith and dedication (44 per cent) or his love for people (14 per cent), with other responses scattered. Many reported nothing to criticize in their husbands; faults most often reported were lack of disciplined work habits (24 per cent), poor preaching (13 per cent), failure to devote enough time to his family (12 per cent), and impatience and short temper (10 per cent). As to birth order, 47 per cent of these MWs were first-born. About 15 per cent had husbands five or more years older than they. In general, their father's occupation was either business and professional (38 per cent) or farmer (27 per cent).

With regard to expectations of a MW, these Indiana MWs agreed that she should attend women's groups regularly (63 per cent AM—absolutely must, and 31 per cent PS—probably should). But there was considerable consensus, too, that she should not be an officer in them (33 per cent MMN—may or may not, 35 per cent PSN—probably should not, and 21 per cent AMN—absolutely must not). There was general agreement, though less strongly, that she should sing in the choir if she has ability (10 per cent AM, 40 per cent PS, 39 per cent MMN), call on sick and shut-ins (17 per cent AM, 36 per cent PS, 42 per cent MMN), and entertain church groups in the parsonage (23 per cent AM, 23 per cent PS, 51 per cent MMN).

But there was much less agreement on whether a MW should

counsel women and youth with problems (22 per cent PS, 49 per cent MMN, 14 per cent PSN), do church secretarial or office work when there is no paid secretary (19 per cent PS, 36 per cent MMN, 23 per cent PSN), or play the piano or organ or direct the choir, if she has ability (18 per cent PS, 39 per cent MMN, 24 per cent PSN). In terms of qualities desirable in a MW, there was general consensus. The qualities most stressed were: to be a good wife and mother (93 per cent AM, 7 per cent PS), adaptability to different situations (88 per cent AM, 11 per cent PS), and awareness of the needs of others (85 per cent AM, 14 per cent PS). The two qualities which received least emphasis were: conservatism in dress and appearance (32 per cent AM, 4 per cent PS, 24 per cent MMN) and good education (28 per cent AM, 54 per cent PS, and 18 per cent MMN).

Though both questions and response categories required considerable revision prior to composition of the MW-5 questionnaire, the summary above indicates some of the gains in specification and meaningfulness arrived at in MW-4. Notice too, however, the points at which one might have been misled if he had generalized from the responses of these 142 Indiana MWs to MWs in general, or to a particular age group or region-denomination setting. In comparison to the 4,777 MW-5 respondents, these 142 MW-4 respondents are *over*representative of those who report themselves as "very satisfied," but—partly due to differences in response categories—*under*representative of those who report themselves to be teamworkers with their husbands. The figure of 18 per cent who reported teaching a Sunday-School class on MW-4 is quite different from the 62 per cent of MW-5 respondents who made such a report, since on MW-4 the item called for the *one* major activity.

Note, too, that 56 per cent reported *call* motivation on MW-4 versus only 27 per cent on MW-5, and the motivation of belief in the purposes of the Church doesn't appear, since it was not included in the response categories. (This indicates once more that if an issue is not "built into" a study at the point of questionnaire construction, it will not come out in the findings.) Also, the two "call" responses were listed first and second in MW-4, but fifth and sixth in MW-5.

Even before construction of the MW-5 questionnaire, issues of potential nonrespondent bias and the general unrepresentativeness of these Indiana respondents to MW-4 were apparent. Since names had been supplied through the Indiana Council of Churches, denominations such as Southern Baptist and Missouri Synod Lutheran, as well as a variety of evangelical groups, were not included. Since response rate was only about 50 per cent, there were factors of self-selection operating. This is evidenced in the high percentage of first-born, who generally volunteer more often than later-born. Also, there was overrepresentation of MWs from larger churches (36 per cent from churches of 700 or more members versus 19 per cent of MW-5 respondents). For some items (such as type of housing provided and location of housing) the percentage distributions are almost identical from MW-4 to MW-5. But on others, more strongly reflecting denominational, regional, and/or personality variables, there are great differences.

Because of these concerns, the MW-4 questionnaire was pretested further with two other groups of MWs—99 Methodist MWs from West Virginia and 189 Congregational MWs from Massachusetts. In a series of cross-tabulations, relating responses on one item to responses on another item, it soon became evident that interactions, and therefore meanings, differed according to geographic region. Thus, of those women who reported themselves motivated to participate in their husbands' ministry because of a "call to full-time Christian service," 58 per cent of the Indiana respondents reported themselves as participating "in a supportive role," versus 35 per cent of Massachusetts and 22 per cent of West Virginia respondents. Both "call" and "supportive," judging from other responses, appeared to have different meanings for the three groups of respondents. Some cross-tabulations produced even more surprising results, e.g., that of the *total* group of MW-4 respondents, 65 per cent stated that a MW absolutely must or probably should be *both* self-sacrificing to her husband's work *and* have a free and spontaneous naturalness!

Out of cross-tabulations of responses to MW-4 items, hypotheses were developed to be tested on the basis of MW-5 data. However, when this analysis was carried out, it was clear that most hypotheses had not been stated in a precise enough form, particularly in terms of the conditions under which a particular association of variables would occur. Therefore, of nine variables which were associated with reported satisfaction and fulfillment in MW-4 data, only two (home religion and church participation before marriage) "held up" on the basis of MW-5 data. Geographic region, kind of residence, and the size of church and community in which one grew up were not statistically significant "differentiators" of satisfaction. And for the remaining three variables, the association was of a different nature than that hypothesized: MWs tended to be more, not less satisfied when the parsonage was next door to the church or when they were over 50 years of age; but less, not more, satisfied when a first-born child. Similarly, of the six variables hypothesized as associated with reported involvement only two (highest degree of teamwork in the South and when a MW had grown up in a church of less than 400 members) were supported by MW-5 data. For three variables, the data were inconclusive. For the remaining variable, the association was different than hypothesized: MWs tended to be more, not less, involved if they lived next door to the church.

As the analysis of MW-5 data proceeded, with large numbers permitting more specification of "controls" (i.e., matching women by age, education, and so on), it became increasingly clear that seldom was any one variable responsible for satisfaction, involvement, or any other result. Rather, combinations of variables— such as denomination and region, church size and education, etc.) had to be considered. Some of the results of these "higher-order" cross-tabulations were reported in Chapter 6. More will be reported in future journal articles, as data analysis continues. At this point, however, one thing is clear: false conclusions would have been reached if research had ended with the MW-4 questionnaire. There simply were not enough respondents involved for the relevant variables to be given the chance to operate. Nor had the questionnaire itself developed to the point where the twin goals of precision and significant meaning could be realized. Therefore, another conclusion is that this study was worth doing, and that without all its stages the picture of American Protestant MWs would have been less complete. And the task of understanding is still far from finished.

Expectations and Selfhood

As we have seen, understanding of the involvement, motivation, and satisfaction of MWs requires study of *many* women in *depth.* For cultural stereotypes of "the role of the MW" fail to take sufficient account of the individuality of person, relationship, and situation. There is little connection between the ideal communicated in most of the literature and the reality. Indeed, the role image generally presented is not only historically anachronistic and personally impossible, but also theologically questionable. Cultural stereotypes, especially when expressed through congregational expectations, tend to produce unrealistic and unhealthy guilt, self-pity, rebellion, or passive conformity if an idealistic and inexperienced MW seeks to match them. Therefore, if a woman is to find meaningful involvement and fulfillment, it is often necessary for her to "puncture the role," so that she may become a person and not just a personage.

One reason that cultural stereotypes can create such pressures on young MWs is that stereotypes never change as fast as social realities. As the ministry has become less of a calling and more of a career in many denominations, professional rewards and status have become more important. This has meant less emphasis on "the salvation of the souls committed to her pastoral charge, and the alleviation of their temporal wants" by modern MWs, and more concern for "the advancement of her husband's ministry" in comparison to the 1832 MW who listed these three goals.[6] Even when "salvation of souls" remains a primary concern, as it does for many Baptist and Evangelical MWs, there is a more limited conception of a MW's pastoral charge than in an earlier

period. And while alleviation of temporal wants may be necessary, as in economically depressed inner-city or rural areas, this is
seldom seen in the evangelistic-paternalistic terms of earlier
"charity."

Most basic, however, is the changed conception of how a MW
can best advance her husband's ministry. In the nineteenth century, the general conception appeared to be that "in uniting herself to a Christian minister, she has bound herself to his work
and to his cross," and that "the proper qualifications of a pastor's
wife . . . should correspond in all important respects with those
demanded in the pastor himself." Some indeed went so far as to
state that "the minister's wife ought to be the kind of worker a
deaconess is; she has no business to marry a minister unless she
expects to be a pastor's assistant." While such positions are still
presented in some modern literature directed to MWs, and assumed by some congregations, they are questioned by most
young MWs. Many women insist, in fact, that they "married a
man, and not a minister," and that "no one has the right to expect
church work, or even personal faith, of a woman just because
her husband is a minister."

Such judgments may, of course, be questioned, on sociological
as well as theological grounds. For any woman, when she marries, chooses a way of life as well as a man. This is as true of the
wife of a salesman, factory worker, business executive, or doctor
as it is of a MW. For choosing a marriage partner inevitably
means choosing (usually unknowingly) a particular combination
of satisfactions and opportunities, frustrations and limitations. In
marriage, one has chosen a way of life, not as a cooky cutter to
be imposed on passive dough, but as a framework within which
a woman's individuality expresses itself. In this sense, every MW
married *both* a man *and* a minister. Nevertheless, the woman who
resists the pressures on a MW to be and do certain things which
lay people may not want to be and do, expresses a legitimate
concern.

Many young MWs express a desire, therefore, to be recognized
as a person, instead of as an extension of their husband or as part

of the "faceless procession" of MWs through a local church. They would like to escape the rush and pressure of parsonage living and "fly off to some desert isle." They feel so inadequate in leadership and faith, in relation to the expectations of others—and so guilty about housekeeping and family life, in relation to their own ideals—that the tension at times is very great. And early marriage and/or uncertain commitment to the Christian faith and ministry can make the situation even more difficult. If the *demands* for sacrifice and service are heavy, but the *motivation* for sacrifice and service limited, then frustration and conflict can be particularly severe, leading to either the rebelliousness of a Kate or the conformity of a Dorcas.

For the majority of women, frustration and conflict never reach this point, and problems are more than compensated for by the opportunities for sharing meaningfully with their husbands in a rich, satisfying life of service to others. Yet even those who are most meaningfully involved and fulfilled as MWs wish that congregations would accept their individuality, letting them find their own particular place in the life of church and community. They would like the freedom to *give* of themselves, rather than feeling that they must toe the line of someone else's expectations. They seek acceptance of the fact that they are primarily wives and mothers, not unofficial, unpaid pastors' assistants. They hope that congregations may come to realize that, just because a woman married a minister, she is not automatically an expert in theology, or an inspirational leader of devotions, youth, or music. They would like the chance to be woman-type people, not church-type operators.

These conflicts between social expectations and personal feelings are not, of course, peculiar to MWs. Any public figure and his family are aware that their lives are not their own. Anyone who represents a group to a larger community discovers that the price paid for respect, love, and privileges is being an example. But if a MW has sacrificed a certain measure of personal independence by her marriage, she has also gained the support, concern, and care of a wider family—the church. (As a Christian, she may have been in the family before, but now the inter-personal dynamics are different.) She has, in effect, married into this family and gained a whole set of new in-laws, beyond even those of her husband's parents and relatives. For the congregation her husband serves will play in many respects the role of mother-in-law to her, and she will have to learn how to be a good daughter-in-law. And, perhaps hardest of all, the mother-in-law to whom she must relate will probably change every few years.

For these reasons, the physical care of a minister and his family by a congregation—in housing and salary—takes on deep meaning. For it symbolizes a relationship which can be either mutually satisfying and rewarding or mutually frustrating and problematic. The parsonage and salary represent the caring rela-tionship in which the congregation must learn how to care for others without dominance, and the minister and his family must learn to be cared for without dependence. It is easy for providers to become tyrannical (even though oh-so benevolent), or for the dependents to become like children who incessantly demand more, while resenting and criticizing what has already been pro-vided. At its best, when a minister, his wife, and congregation share a common commitment and calling, the caring relationship expresses a covenant. At its worst, when a minister, his wife, and the congregation seek to protect individual rights and advan-tages against each other, there is only a contract.

In terms of this contrast between covenant and contract, there are no simple, universally applicable answers to such questions as whether a housing allowance is preferable to a parsonage, or what salary level is adequate, or how many hours a week a minister should be expected to work, or whether or not a MW should hold paid employment. If the congregation and minister's family decide together, in consideration of all issues influencing their mutual welfare, that a housing allowance be provided in lieu of a parsonage, this can be a very desirable arrangement. For some ministerial families, a home of their own in a neighbor-hood they have chosen, with "roots" in a community where they feel they belong, makes all the difference between satisfaction and frustration. For others, the responsibilities connected with the buying and selling of real estate, as well as home maintenance, divert them from the tasks to which they feel committed, and a housing allowance—especially if inadequate—can bring tension rather than release.

Basic to the decision regarding parsonage versus housing allowance, or any other issue regarding a minister's family, is the question of the advancement of his ministry. In order to serve effectively, he needs a certain level of security, comfort, and independence. What that level should be is, of course, a relative judgment, with false judgment possible on the part of both congregation and minister. Some clergy families clearly are called upon to make sacrifices and bear hardships which are unnecessary, and which the members of their congregations would not accept. In such cases, there is neither the covenant of love nor the contract of justice. As frequently, the minister and/or his wife make demands of the congregation which cannot reasonably be met without sacrificing important aspects of the church's total ministry.

In general, however, all available evidence would indicate that the majority of *both* congregations and clergy families move beyond a negotiated contract to a trusted covenant. Each party to the relationship seeks to consider the welfare of the other, and out of such mutual concern decisions are made. Indeed, for one who has read the popular literature concerning substandard salaries and antiquated arks of parsonages, the realities of ministerial income and housing are surprisingly good, and consistently improving, due to the united efforts of denominational leaders and local congregations. Admittedly, the situation of a substantial minority of ministerial families is extremely difficult, especially in small rural or inner-city Baptist, Evangelical, Disciple, or Methodist churches served by men without seminary training. But, the over-all situation is good, in terms of the nondominant, nondependent caring relationship which exists.

More fundamental than problems of finances and housing, for most MWs, are frustrations connected with limited time and friends of one's own. Here are the pressure points within the tight-fitting enclosure of expectations. Except for working wives, most MWs have little time or money for nonchurch activities, and few real personal friends in contrast to professional acquaintances. Particularly for Baptist and Evangelical MWs, but also in other denominations, the psychological environment is limited to the congregation. Such are the demands of church activities, in which MWs feel deeply involved emotionally even when theoretically not responsible, that little time or energy is left over for other community activities, or even for one's own home.

To carry most of the responsibilities of home and family is hard for any woman. It is a situation faced by many wives of business and professional men, especially those whose husbands are "on the road" a considerable part of the time. For MWs the situation is both easier and more difficult. It is easier because MWs, in general, believe in the fundamental importance of their husbands' vocation. It is harder because, unlike many other jobs, added work here does not produce added income. Also, if you believe in a vocation, it is harder to protect your rights against its demands. Despite basic dedication and good intentions, therefore, a MW may envy either the wife of a man with a 9-to-5 job whose evenings and weekends are free for the family, or the wife of a professional man with higher income, who thereby provides extras for the family. When a woman feels deprived of both time and money, the pinch is hardest.

To learn to live with your husband gone most of the time—especially when other "daddies" are at home; to avoid resentment when he seems more concerned about others than about his own family; to cope with family decisions and discipline on your own: all this is never easy. Much, of course, depends on the sort of person to whom you are married. If he makes disciplined, effective use of his time, if he is sensitive to the needs of his wife and children, if he is realistic about what can or can't be accomplished and avoids a Messiah complex, then the situation will be much easier; if not, the situation will be more difficult. Despite any good intentions of husband and wife, certain realities remain, however. The ministry can never be reduced to a forty-hour job. The dedicated, conscientious pastor can never feel that the work is done. Certain personal and family sacrifices are required.

Apart from outmoded stereotypes and the congregational and community expectations embodied in them, there are therefore certain realities about the nature of the ministry as a vocation to which any MW must adjust. Husbands' frustration, in terms of work left undone or imperfect, and wives' sense of neglect by their husbands may be inevitabilities of the human—or at least ministerial—lot. It is therefore necessary for a wife to learn how to create the sort of situation in which her particular husband can face (not must face) his family responsibilities, as well as those of his ministry. And it also requires that a wife accept the realities of marriage and ministry, avoiding unrealistic expectations which may lead to feelings of neglect and loneliness.

In order to preserve and enhance selfhood, a MW needs to learn how to deal creatively and responsibly with expectations—not only those held of her by others, but also those she holds of herself. Others must revise their expectations of her, so that account is taken of her individuality. But it is equally important that she adjust her own ideals to reality without falling into either cynicism or despair. Such an adjustment, which apparently takes many women the first ten years or so of their marriage, involves a delicate balance of commitment with detachment and humor. It requires separating seriousness about the Gospel from seriousness about yourself, accepting not only God's power and love but also your own finiteness and humanity. For, unless a MW learns how to "ride easy in the saddle of life," she is soon thrown by the multiple situations with which she must cope.

Commitment—Competence—Communication

What a woman does (involvement) and feels (satisfaction) will depend, then, on how well *self*-expectations match *imposed* expectations. If they differ greatly, or if either or both fail to take account of reality, problems will arise in involvement and/or satisfaction. Expectations must, moreover, permit self-development and expression as well as service, and define the sphere of service in accord with both realities and values, if involvement is not to be at the price of satisfaction. And in considering the meaning of involvement and satisfaction for a particular MW, account must be taken of motivation, age and stage, and background and situation. This inevitably involves considering the particular blend of *commitment, competence,* and *ability to communicate* possessed by a MW, as well as by her husband and his congregation.

Commitment is a matter of a MW's *values* and *goals,* of the personal future she is seeking to bring about through decisive moral choices that involve her in definite courses of action. Commitment involves, then, not just devotion to God, though this relationship is primary for most MWs, but also loyalty to family, concern for others, and a sense of accountability for your own self-expression and development. The degree of balance or conflict among these values influences the way in which a MW involves herself in her husband's work, and the satisfaction she finds in that involvement. As we saw in Chapter 3, in the discussion of value orientations, there are denominational as well as personal variations of emphasis. The most common pattern is that of placing greatest emphasis on the "propriate service" (God, family, others) cluster of values, with self (development, understanding, contentment) receiving relatively less emphasis, and the "peripheral service" (community, world, culture) cluster of values receiving least emphasis.

But it is not as simple as this. For example, there can be real conflicts between your understanding of the responsibilities connected with devotion to God—especially if this is interpreted in terms of church activities (which it *need not* be)—and those connected with loyalty and service to your own family. Because of the impossible combination of duties and ill-defined rights involved in seeking to fulfill *all* expectations held by yourself and others, there is usually a felt need to *delimit* your responsibilities.

That is, choices must be made, and some justification found for these choices.

There are at least three methods of delimiting responsibility common among Protestant parish MWs: (1) conviction that one's "first responsibility is to be a good wife and mother," (2) judgment that a MW has "the same responsibilities as any other church member" or "laywoman," and (3) concern for both personal integrity—"be your own best self; don't worry about the expectations of others"—and personal growth, "fulfilling your own potential as a person." (The quoted phrases come from items 40-43, 49, and 57 of the MW-5 questionnaire.)

If a woman emphasizes being a good wife and mother, she will tend to become a Mary who is involved in a background, supportive way—if she is motivated by "belief in the purposes of the Church." If she is not so clear about her own purposes, or her own worth and identity, then she will probably have a Dorcas pattern of involvement and activity, seeking to "contribute through useful work." However, if she judges her responsibilities to be the same as those of any other Christian (or church member, and these *may not* be understood as equivalent), then she will seek still less involvement in church activities. If her pattern is that of a Jane, she will be detached on principle, because of her conception of Church and ministry, and/or "woman's place." If, on the other hand, she is a detached-in-rebellion Kate, then the second method of delimitation will be combined with the third, and she will seek to protect her selfhood against being "swallowed up by the vacuum cleaner of the church," as one woman put it.

For a Martha, delimitation of responsibility may mean that the *congregation* becomes her community, world, and culture. Self-development, understanding, and contentment are likewise seen as based on devotion to God. And since introspection and analysis are not usually as important for a Martha as for a Mary or Jane (related to differences in theological viewpoint and socioeconomic class), Marthas make less distinction between *devotion* to God and *work* in the local congregation. Unlike Marys or Janes, Marthas seldom feel conflict between the purposes of the ideal New Testament Church and the work of the real local church.

For these reasons, a Martha who feels called of God to involve herself in teamwork with her husband in Christian ministry, and who may regard this involvement as the expression of her own adolescent call to "full-time Christian service," tends more often to feel very satisfied and fulfilled as a MW. The value structure of most denominations and congregations supports the Martha pattern and rewards her for it. She is rewarded for teamwork, that is, *provided* she does not become too assertive in her leadership, thereby competing with either her husband or the power structure of the congregation—especially the "leading ladies." (As we saw in Chapter 6, the Martha pattern is most typical of Baptist and Evangelical MWs and least typical of Episcopal, Lutheran, and Presbyterian MWs.) What many congregations seem to prefer, in fact, is the woman who can *act* like a Martha and *talk* like a Mary. For this means that she is willing both to play her part and to know her place.

Commitment, therefore, will mean different things to Marthas, Marys, Dorcases, Janes, and Kates, and to those women whose patterns of involvement and activity represent the infinite number of variations on these basic themes. For values differ, as do the choices made on the basis of them. Even in the narrower definition of commitment as devotion to God, great individual differences exist. In part, this is because committing yourself to another, in religious faith as in human love, is always a risky matter. One can never be "sure" of the other, in a rationally provable way. Commitment like faith is basically a trusting dependence on the faithfulness of the other, expressed in ethical obedience to the basic principles underlying the ultimate welfare of the other.

And we cannot grow in commitment until we first dare to commit ourselves. This is both an "all-at-once and forever" matter and a "piece-by-piece, day-by-day" matter. From the data of this study, it appears that young MWs find it much more difficult than older MWs both to make the initial commitment and to grow in commitment. Uncertainty of religious faith and vocation seems to be characteristic of our modern technological culture in its complexities, ambiguities, and rapid change. And the ability to trust in God and obey Him will certainly depend on, as well as influence, your trust in yourself, other human beings, and, ultimately, the world you live in. From the evidence of questionnaires and interviews, many young MWs find such trust and confidence difficult. And without trust there cannot be obedience. They may long for true commitment of all of themselves to all of God. Yet for many, growth has been arrested at an early stage.

Particular problems can arise, too, for those connected professionally with the Christian Church, or "semiprofessionally" as MWs. Many begin the married ministry with high goals and ideals, but when the "honeymoon" of the first few years wears off they experience increasing frustration and disillusionment. They find it difficult both "to let all men know your forbearance," and to "have no anxiety" (Phil. 4:5-6). The goals seem so important, and the people of the congregation so resistant and blind! A minister and his wife, entering their first parish, often want to accomplish *everything*, right *now*, and *directly*. It is hard to recognize that progress comes step by step, in small progressive developments. It is hard to accept the realities, and possibilities, of the Church as Sinners Anonymous—not Saints Acknowledged. And it is so easy, out of frustration and disillusionment, to fall into either the martyr ("I've suffered so much for the faith") or savior ("I alone am left") complex. Growth in commitment therefore involves learning to "speak the truth in love," without taking ourselves and our own limited understandings of the truth so seriously. It means combining the sense of ultimacy with the light touch, work with love, play, and worship.

MWs vary, then, in kind and development of commitment. So do minister husbands and congregations. As already indicated, frustrations and conflicts can arise for a woman if her self-expectations differ markedly from those imposed on her by her situation. And the two most important variables in her situation are her husband and his congregation. Denominational structure and officials, community and regional attitudes, other MWs—especially as organized in regional or national groups—and still other elements will also be important, but a woman can usually cope with these factors if the home base is secure and supportive. If the operative values and goals of either her husband or his congregation are opposed to those of a MW, and if any of the three parties to the covenant rigidly seeks to impose his values on another, then trouble lies ahead (the inadequate values may, of course, be the wife's, the husband's, or the congregation's). Or if husband and/or congregation have *no* clear sense of the goals of Church and ministry, while a MW does, she will be frustrated by uncertainty and inertia. In summary, general congruence of commitment (values and goals as well as the underlying faith relationship to God) is necessary if effective and fulfilling involvement of a MW is to take place.

But even shared commitment is not sufficient. For as commitment provides goals for life and ministry, competence provides means to realize these goals. The word competence as used here implies *physiological* factors, such as nervous system and endocrine glands—especially the thyroid gland—as these in turn affect potential energy level. Involved, too, are *psychological* factors such as anxiety, conflict, insecurity, self-confidence, and discipline, as these affect *available energy* and the focus or diffusion of it. For there may be plenty of womanpower, but the "emergency brake" may be locked on and the emotional equivalent of brake linings worn out, as both accelerator and brake are floored simultaneously. Or there may be slippage in the power transmission. Or the difficulty may lie in the steering mechanism. Finally, *social* factors are involved, as these affect *relevant energy*. For competence is relative as well as absolute; it depends on the needs of the situation as well as on innate talents and developed skills. It depends on *evaluations* by yourself and others of your actual or potential contribution, as well as on the contribution itself.

Problems arise for MWs in terms of competence as often as they do in terms of commitment, but they are much less often recognized in their true terms. Thus, when a MW's competence fails to measure up to a congregation's expectations, she may be criticized for inadequate commitment. (Similarly, when socially conservative congregations seek to unload a minister whom they consider too liberal or a trouble-maker, the reason given is seldom that of his supporting social justice and world brotherhood, but rather his theology, or "not calling enough" and "not preparing his sermons.") Also, when MWs themselves think of "the ideal MW" to whom they seek to measure up, they seldom consider the realities of varying personal competence. But, judging from the data of this study, MWs differ greatly in available energy, in terms of both *amount* and *focus*. Some, such as the Marthas, are clearly "higher-intensity" people than others, such as the Dorcases and Janes. Kates seem to direct their high intensity against what they consider to be unfair demands on them. Marys have a moderately high level of available energy, but their purposes do not focus it as much as the Marthas' "call." Competence as well as commitment, then, affect a woman's involvement in her husband's ministry. And more important than division of energy are its amount and focus, as we saw in the discussion of working wives in Chapter 6.

Competence, as this relates to personal intensity (or, in less elegant terms, "psychic oomph") affects attitude as well as activity, quality of life as well as performance. Thus, Marthas and Kates, on questionnaire attitude items, tended more often to give "strongly" agree or disagree responses; intensity as well as direction of attitude was a significant variable. In terms of problems of commitment, low-energy Dorcases tended to have difficulty in establishing secure trust and confidence, while high-energy Kates were more often concerned about issues of obedience. But both Dorcases and Kates were diffuse in terms of unclear values and goals. In contrast, the very satisfied Marthas described in Chapter 4 (with their high, focused energy) combine commitment with competence and have little "remainder." They are not aware of beliefs that are violated or gifts and training that are unused in their teamwork. (As observed before, this relates to the nature of beliefs and training dominant in specific denominations and socioeconomic classes.) Marthas, then, work full time as apostles intent on "showing others a better way of life," for they feel "set apart, to witness for Christ." Marys, on the other hand, consider themselves as disciples, not apostles, with the goal of "learning more about the Christian faith" and a social-emotional rather than a task orientation. Dorcases seek to win favor through being obedient children, and when forced to choose, prefer security to selfhood.

What a MW does and feels does not depend, however, simply on her own competence, but on that of her husband and his congregation. It is no wonder, then, that the early years in the parish are considered hardest by many MWs, as reported in Chapter 5. So many responsibilities must be assumed in a short period of time—those of adult, wife, mother, daughter-in-law, and MW. And just when *one's own* competence is most limited and one needs most support and encouragement, the competence of husband and congregation tend to be most limited and *they* need most support and encouragement. (Young MWs are only half-joking when they suggest that they be allowed to attend another minister's church, as doctors' wives go to other doctors for treatment.) For just when a woman is learning how to live with another person—and a man at that, and perhaps with little children—and discovering the realities in contrast to the romance, just then is when she is apt to be in small churches with inadequate lay leadership, low salaries, and poor housing. The competence of these churches to care for the minister and his family, or in fact even to exercise effective mission rather than focusing on institutional maintenance, may be very limited. As will be noted presently, this creates a real issue as to what size of congregation has the right, in terms of Christian stewardship as well as pragmatic efficiency, to claim the services of a full-time, seminary-trained minister.

Caught within such a network of competing pressures, just when she is in the midst of growing up and learning how to cope with situational demands, a woman can make one of a variety of responses. She can reduce the pressure somewhat through adjusting value priorities in such a way as to "loosen up" role expectations. This appears to be the response of both Dorothy Taylor and Donna Sykes, who placed "self-development" in a relatively higher position than "devotion to God" in their MW-6 ranking of values. Both also reported a liberal theology of a "to thine own self be true" variety. This adjustment appeared to work better for Dorothy than for Donna, for a variety of reasons, one of which is that for her the wife-and-mother focus is clearer. She is concerned with maintaining the separation between home and church, to preserve the little family time there is. She regards the structured situation of a MW as an opportunity for adventuring in social relationships, whereas a more outgoing person might regard it as confining and denying.

Dorothy has also discovered that congregations will accept the "certain abilities and talents" a MW has to contribute and "not demand other things," if she "is willing." She can express some individuality and find fulfillment without criticism, if she is careful and conservative. She has confidence in her abilities in music and education, and is able to lead from her strengths, whereas Donna does not yet seem to have discovered what her particular strengths and contributions are. Thus, Dorothy did not fall into the compulsion and guilt that plagued Mary Martha Mountain. She has difficulty in accepting her negative feelings and denies any criticisms she has made by asserting that "people are much more tolerant and understanding and kind than we think they are." But in general her adjustment is very good, due in large measure to her particular background.

This is true, too, for most Marthas, who tend to have moved up in socioeconomic status and community respect when they married a minister. They have attained a much higher educational level than their parents—their fathers most often were blue-collar workers—but Marthas usually have not aspired to a career of their own. They do not feel cheated of their own professional aspirations as a MW, but rather find fulfillment of their religious motivation. As indicated at the beginning of Chapter 6, "background resources" and corresponding need-fulfillment patterns are very different for Marthas than for Marys. Marthas feel more satisfied with life as MWs because they have not developed financial, social, and intellectual need patterns which are difficult to fulfill in the churches and communities to which they are called. In addition, they usually feel greater personal competence than do Marys. In general, Marthas have been trained to "do something," such as schoolteaching or music, rather than to "think about something," such as history or philosophy. They do not tend to be analytic or introspective: their "personal myth" is unbroken. And in addition, their education is more equivalent to that of their husbands than is true for Marys. One factor contributing to teamwork, therefore, is that they are "on the same level" as their husbands educationally as well as in commitment.

Marthas tend, then, to be both highly involved and highly satisfied as MWs. For many women, however, there are real problems of competence as well as of commitment. This is revealed in the mental pictures MWs have of "a MW" in contrast to "me," as expressed in the drawings and clippings attached to the MW-6 questionnaire: Calm Corinne versus Harried Hannah, angel versus devil, public leader versus household drudge, etc. (These contrasts involve accepting "a MW" but rejecting "me," the position expressed by about one-third of MW-6 respondents. Another third presented generally similar and positive mental pictures of both a MW and "me," and the other third were divided in equal proportions between "reject MW—accept me" and "reject both" responses. MWs from the Midwest, of all denominations, expressed the greatest self-rejection.) If a MW is to accept *both* her situation *and* herself, she must understand situational as well as personal dynamics. Unless she takes the relatively unreflective "love God and do your best" approach of many Marthas, she will need to develop increased skill in decision-making with regard to complex, ambiguous, and risky situations. This in turn will require knowledge of her own values and goals, as well as of the structures, processes, and realistic options of the decision situation. All this will be more difficult if she comes from the oversecure, overprotected background experienced by many Dorcases.

Competence involves, then, not only talents and training, but also their appropriate application to defined situations. A MW must calibrate the ideal to the realities, including her own particular form of finite humanity and that of her husband and his congregation. The question then becomes, not "what should an ideal woman be and do under ideal circumstances," but rather "what can I become and accomplish, under the *given* circumstances." To accept realities and calibrate ideals to them is not, however, to deny the possibility—indeed, necessity—of self-transcendence. For many women testify to another factor, beyond the "givenness" of yourself and the situation: the resources to which the Christian doctrine of the Holy Spirit testifies, namely a guidance, strength, and healing available to followers of Him who is perfect wisdom, power, and love. Growth in competence, as in commitment, means therefore learning how to renew and refresh, how to orient and ground your life, so that you do not burn yourself out in futile or undirected efforts. It means learning how to pace yourself, with alternating periods of different kinds of activity, and learning how to relax and enjoy recreation without feeling guilty about the work undone. Growth in competence is, then, fundamentally a matter of stewardship—of a MW's investment of time and, truly, herself.

She cannot do everything. She cannot emulate another person, from a different background and/or in a different situation. Despite, or perhaps because of, multiple crash programs of self-improvement, most of which last but a few days, she continues to fall short and to feel inadequate and guilty. To escape from this impossible burden of expectations, a MW must first work out priorities, on the basis of defined principles and values. In this way life can be structured from within, which includes learning to say No creatively and graciously. Otherwise, life will be structured from without, on the basis of expectations which may have little relation to her own commitment. In a stewardship of life based on clearly defined priorities and values, she can lead from her strengths ("this isn't down my alley") and compensate for her weaknesses ("seems like an opportunity for us to grow together"). In this way the "compete" is taken out of competence, so that a MW does not judge herself, or allow others to judge her, in relation to either a composite ideal or another person, such as the MW who preceded her.

Commitment provides a MW's ends, and competence her means. But both ends and means must be incarnated in relationships. Communication is giving and receiving, on the basis of the "wherefore" of commitment and the "what" of competence. It means learning what it is, in James Pike's phrase, to *do* the truth, as well as to do love, and hope, and faith. It means awareness of the *kairos*, the critical, appropriate time when action is not impulsive, premature, or strategically unwise. Involvement and satisfaction as a MW rest, therefore, not simply on commitment and competence, but on their expression in the communication of "the dialogical person":

. . . one who, by word or relationship, is in communication with his environment and open to the communication that environment offers . . . as a total authentic person . . . one who responds to others with his whole being and not with just a part of himself. . . . He is really present . . . he is able to learn as well as to teach, to accept love as well as to love, to be ministered unto as well as to minister . . . an open person—one who is known first by his willingness and ability to reveal himself to others, and . . . to hear and receive their revelation . . . one who responds to others and is, therefore, responsible.[7]

When communication of this sort breaks down between a MW and her God, her husband, her congregation, her community, her friends—when she feels isolated and alone—then the problems are most severe.

To grow in communication is, then, basic to everything else. But it is also difficult and, like the commitment on which it rests, risky. For what if you open up and the other does not understand? What if you give of yourself and the other scorns the gift? Monologue, which means controlling the situation, is always safer than dialogue. If you are open and revealed, you are vulnerable to hurt and misunderstanding. If you give, you are open to rejection. It is easier, therefore, to play intellectual and emotional chess games, moving the pieces according to accepted rules, then putting the pieces back in the box and going home. Much conversation and so-called relationship is on this level. For to be "really present" is both a strain and a hard discipline. One may be so wrapped up in his own preoccupations and concerns that he literally is "not all there" when with another person. There may be little to invest in him. And even more basically, few are strong enough to dare to be weak and dependent on another, to be ministered unto and cared for, as well as to minister and to care. These problems—of monologue, preoccupation, and accepting care and concern—seem particularly present among ministers and their wives, because of the nature of the vocation.

However, problems of communication involve not just MWs, but also their husbands and congregations. Communication can break down on either or both sides of all of these relationships. And problems of communication are made more difficult by changes now taking place both in the women becoming MWs and in the situations they enter. As discussed in Chapter 5, MWs now under 35 years of age—in contrast to those over 50 years of age—marry younger and have more children, closer together. They generally have a background of affiliation with the institutional church, and seldom have experienced a radical change of religious affiliation or viewpoint. But, though exposure to institutional religion has usually been high, there has often been little exposure to vital personal and family religion. As a result of these and other factors, the trend is for young MWs to be more involved in home life and less in witnessing for Christ, more analytic and interpersonally anxious and less spontaneously activist, than previous generations. These new-type MWs are not as acceptable to many congregations as the older models.

Communication between minister husbands and their wives may be affected, too, by the combination of longer ministerial training with earlier marriage, which results for many wives in a longer period of being family breadwinners. This may lead to a continuation of semiadolescent dependence on the part of their husbands. Denial of continued education through employment and motherhood may result, too, in "outgrown" wives. Minister husbands, through both longer education and wider experience, may grow apart from their wives, and may indeed find their major emotional gratifications in ministry rather than home life. Certainly these factors are not unique to the ministry; they appear to affect the family life of men in all types of business and profession. And for particular individuals the described factors may or may not operate, despite general trends in these directions.

Finally, there is the factor of communication with the community beyond the church. One of the disturbing aspects of data from questionnaires and interviews in this study, for anyone concerned about the Christian mission in the world, is the low degree of involvement of MWs in nonchurch community activities. As noted in Chapter 3, the competing pressures of family and congregational responsibilities are so great, especially when combined with a nagging sense of the resulting lack of self-development and expression, that "peripheral service" values are put in a relatively low position. Especially for Marthas, but to a lesser extent for most MWs, the local church (not even the Universal Church) becomes the practical equivalent of wider community, world, and culture. For many of these women, activities and social contacts are confined to a kind of religious ghetto composed of white, middle-class Protestant Christians who are active church workers. It is not that most women choose such a limited sphere of operation. Rather, circumstances appear to conspire toward this result unless vigorously resisted. And men now entering the ministry have had, on the whole, only limited contact with the world beyond the institutional church.[8] Theirs is not a "worldly holiness."

Recommendations

This research report has one central recommendation: that in any future consideration of MWs—by denominations, congregations, minister husbands, or MWs themselves—their individuality be recognized. There is no one pattern of involvement and activity which is appropriate for MWs of every denomination, region, congregation, age, education, socioeconomic background, relationship with husband, and so on. These factors and many more, especially a particular MW's unique motivations and meanings as these affect the patterning of other variables, must be considered. And patterns of involvement and satisfaction are both *emergent* (developing over time) and *relational* (to the needs, demands, and support of a particular region-church-community-husband situation). If this book and the study it reports do nothing more than break through stereotypes so that persons may be recognized, then its major purpose will be fulfilled. Listening to the stories of a number of MWs, a particular MW may gain deepened understanding, too, of her own unique way of functioning. No one type or case presented will fit another person exactly; but elements of the story may make sense and assist in personal clarification.

To be consistent with this primary recommendation would mean, in the extreme, that no further recommendations be made. For if infinite variation on multiple dimensions in complex interaction with one another is recognized, then general prescriptions certainly cannot be given. Furthermore, though parts of the report, especially Chapter 6, appear to be explanatory (if a background or situational variable exists, then a certain form or degree of involvement and/or satisfaction is more likely), in reality this is a descriptive, not explanatory, study. Rough mapping of the terrain has been completed. Relevant variables, and potential interactions between them, have been discovered. But the very nature of the research design, especially in the lack of a strict probability sample which would permit statistical estimates to be made with some assurance, precludes definitive generalizations.

For this reason, conclusions are, on the whole, *issues* warranting further exploration in research and concern in practice, not *hypotheses proven*. The major finding is that there are particular ways of being a MW, which can be described and made more meaningful in terms of tracing the interaction among defined variables. Beyond this description of basic themes and major variations on them—an achievement in itself—hypotheses have been developed concerning factors that influence themes and variations. Through future, more controlled statistical analyses and longitudinal study of specified subgroups of respondents, further substantiation, qualification, or repudiation will come for these hypotheses. Now that this first large-scale rough mapping has been completed, the investigations of future researchers in more narrowly defined samples of MWs and problem areas will be of great assistance. But, as indicated at the beginning of the chapter, the most fundamental testing of hypotheses will come in the experience and reflection of MWs themselves.

Yet beyond findings, or even hypotheses, are basic concerns about the implications of the data. It is always difficult to know which concerns have been brought into the study and have shaped it, and which have emerged from it. It is usually a matter of both the storyteller affecting the story and the explorer making discoveries that upset his most cherished assumptions and expectations. What one's concerns will be depends, of course, on background and situation, as well as one's particular religious tradition, theological viewpoint, and value orientation. For others the same data may give rise to very different concerns.

For this researcher, however, the major question is: What can be done to help MWs who are not effectively involved and fulfilled, specifically Dorcases and Kates? For in Karen Horney's typology, these are women whose backgrounds and situations lead to either withdrawal (moving *away* from people) or rebellion (moving *against* people). And as indicated in Chapter 6, present trends suggest the probability of a higher proportion of Dorcases and Kates in the future, unless two types of change take place: in the *situations* to which women must relate, and in their *preparation* for effective coping with the complex, the ambiguous, and the risky on the basis of personally meaningful commitments and values. Let us consider, then, first how situations and role models may be made less frustrating and confining.

Certainly a first step in making the situation of a MW easier to live with is that of clarification and reality-and-value-testing of expectations. As discussed in Chapter 1 and earlier in this chapter, the presently operative role images of "the MW" tend to be historically anachronistic and personally impossible. In addition, they are theologically questionable in a community of faith based on freedom within responsibility and love, rather than restriction by law. When a woman accepts the expectations and seeks to live up to them, the result tends to be compulsive activism, nagging guilt, and/or serious conflict and frustration. Either imposed expectations or self-expectations may fail to match reality and/or basic goals of the Church and its ministry. Or both sets of expectations may be realistic and relevant to the goals of the Church, but conflict with each other. Or, as is often true, the expectations held by individual members of a congregation concerning "our MW" may be quite appropriate, considered one by one, but impossible and sources of conflict when considered collectively.

Clarification and testing of expectations must take place, then, on *both* sides of the congregation-MW relationship. And minister husbands must be involved, too, in terms of their expectations of the congregation with regard to their wives and families, and of their wives concerning involvement in their ministry. Basic to all considerations is understanding of the nature of a covenant relationship of mutual care and concern. This is something quite different from a congregation making demands on a MW and seeking to exploit her as a worker, with little concern for her as person, woman, wife, and mother. It is quite different, too, from a MW seeking to maintain her rights but minimize her responsibilities—expecting that others will provide the best for her in housing, finances, and so forth, but have no right to expect anything of her in return. When commitment, competence, and communication operate on both sides of the relationship, then a congregation may grow in its capacity to care for others without dominance, and the minister and his family in their capacity to be cared for without dependence. On these bases, the relationship between a congregation and a minister and his family is covenantal, not contractual.

Denominations which seek to communicate such a covenant theology in Christian education curricula and program need, then, to develop ways of making this theology manifest in church structure and function. At the point of the call or appointment of a minister to a new pastorate, in particular, it would be useful if some means were provided to assist a congregation in clarifying its expectations of a minister and his family. And indeed, denominational guidelines, with regard to not only housing and salary, but also reasonable expectations, might be provided.

For example, for young ministers with small children there should be realistic facing of the cost of baby sitting for meetings attended by a MW. Either the expectations should be lowered, or some provision of volunteer help and/or financial assistance made. The question should be raised as to whether it is considered necessary, or even desirable, for her to attend all of the women's groups of the church, and what sort of involvement in community life beyond the church may be acceptable, or even desirable. Other issues that might be considered—little things in themselves but important cumulatively—include: a discretionary fund for small parsonage repairs; the location and equipment of any new parsonage and related consideration of an office or study in the church; the general issue of hidden professional costs such as church conferences and meetings, car expense, general office expense, books, and telephone; and—perhaps most basic—the time of minister and his wife invested in secretarial and/or janitorial work, etc. This is but a small sampling of issues to be considered in terms of both covenant and stewardship. Ultimately each denomination—and preferably, each congregation in relation to each new minister and his family—must consider which issues are relevant and of importance to them. But it is critical that communication take place.

For unless there is real two-way communication, implicit expectations will be imposed which are never brought together into any pattern and evaluated. It is this situation that leads some MWs to flash with defiance, especially when Mrs. Brown says, "You must sing in the choir, and teach this Sunday-School class, for after all, you're our MW." Ultimately a MW, like any other Christian, must decide what she is to do and be. But, in any group setting, it is well to be aware of what the other members of the group are thinking and feeling, so that relationships may be as harmonious and effective as possible.

Even beyond problems of communication, however, are some knotty reality issues, especially that of church size in relation to ministerial income. And ministerial income below $4,000 simply is not adequate, under most circumstances, for support of a minister's family; this is the subsistence barrier. An income over $4,000 but under $7,000 probably provides for basic needs in most cases (living standards vary, of course, by region, community size, number in the family, and supplementary gifts—especially in farm areas). But the comfort barrier, in which there is some provision for cultural amenities for oneself and one's children, is probably only passed for most families with two or more children with a ministerial income of $7,000 or more.

Thus while finances and housing, as discussed in Chapter 6, are fairly good, there still are real "pockets of poverty" in the ministry. And financial hardship of ministerial families bears a direct relationship to the size of the employing unit, that is, the local congregation. While it would be desirable, and indeed is the practice in some denominations in some countries, to have ministerial income based on family need, length of service, and so forth, rather than church size, there does not seem to be immediate prospect of such a development in American Protestantism. For one thing, some form of "connectionalism," in distinction to congregationalism, is required. Nevertheless, the question should be raised—yet seldom is, in discussions of ministerial recruitment or seminary enrollment with regard to filling pulpits—as to *which* congregations require full-time, seminary-trained ministerial leadership.

As long as churches continue as voluntary organizations, most of which call their own pastors rather than having them appointed by an ecclesiastical office such as a "bishop's cabinet," mergers of congregations pose difficult issues. There are family and personal histories involved, as well as many vested interests in existing power structures and processes. Changes usually take

a generation or more. But, even apart from issues of church renewal and the viability of the neighborhood church as a structure
for mission in present-day and future America, other issues must
be faced. Current trends indicate a variety of future ministries
in other spheres of society to supplement (but I would maintain,
not replace) the traditional parish ministry. Compensation for
such service as a missionary-in-society will have to have a basis
different from the present one of the combined membership and
"giving power" of a congregation, whether or not a multiple
charge or staff is involved.

Full exploration of these issues cannot take place in the context of this report. (Fortunately, the Clergy Compensation Project of the National Council of Churches, in a long-range research
and action program, has considered many of them—for a narrower range of denominations than that involved in this study,
and in terms of the ministry as a career requiring appropriate
economic compensation in an "open market.") But even if the
present bases for ministerial compensation continue, denominations still have the responsibility for evaluating (1) the *competence* of a given congregation to provide support for a minister
and his family, and (2) the *need* of a given congregation for full-
time seminary-trained leadership. For the allocation of leadership
resources—which involves an awareness of the total ministry and
mission of the total people of God, including both "ordained" and
"lay" ministries—is not simply a matter of filling pulpits.

We have explored, then, a few of the issues in the situation
of a MW which can be improved, to the benefit of women who
feel forced into either Dorcas-type withdrawal ("it's too much
for me") or Kate-type rebellion ("they have no right . . ."). More
basic to positive change than denominations and congregations,
however, are minister husbands. For, as noted at several points
in this report, it is easy for the ministry to become a seductive
mistress which demands all a man's interest, time, and emotional
investment. A minister husband has to *work* at home and family
life, or it will be lost by default. He has to schedule time to be
with his family, as for his own renewal and growth, on the same

level of priority as his other responsibilities. For if he is married, then his covenant includes marriage vows as well as congregational call. As husband and father, he has a basic parish of his own family, where God's love must be as manifest as in his beyond-the-home ministry. It is important, then, that he listen and respond to his wife and children, as well as their listening and responding to him. Their concerns must become his concerns, as well as his concerns theirs, if true communication and community are to develop. And if his wife has the insecurity and lack of self-confidence of a Dorcas, he must assist her in growth and security. If his wife is a rebellious Kate, he must examine the relation of the demands he makes on her and the support he gives her to the way she operates.

Most basic, of course, in the improvement of the situation of a MW is the woman herself. Many recommendations regarding ways in which growth can take place have appeared in the discussion of "Expectations and Selfhood" and "Commitment–Competence–Communication." These need not be repeated, except to note that different women have different needs and require different types of assistance. No one program or set of materials, even within a given denomination and region, will be of assistance to all. Some are doing well as they are and should be left alone, not coerced into a program for the sake of the program. Others find it difficult to accept assistance even when it is offered, and here the first task is that of developing trust and confidence as the basis for possible help at a later date. Some find great benefit from the sort of inspiration and guidance which retreats and conferences for MWs often provide.

After survey of growth opportunities provided, and experimentation in the pilot program for theology couples, the most fruitful line of future development would seem to be in the area of workshops in decision-making. Preferably these should include: (1) casebook material, presenting the sort of situations a young MW faces, (2) guidelines for clarifying the principles on the basis of which evaluations and decisions are made, (3) experienced and winsome MWs of various patterns of involvement and fulfillment

as role models and discussion leaders, and (4) small-group interaction over a period long enough so that real confidence and
honesty may develop. Such materials, so far as can be provided in
writing, will be covered in the sequel volume to this report, under the tentative title of *Memo to a Young Minister's Wife*. In
the meantime, groups of seminarians' and ministers' wives can
experiment in developing their own materials and processes, as
long as these include reality-confrontation, principle-clarification,
and feeling-expression. For the "love God and do your best"
Marthas, such materials and processes are not only unnecessary
but probably also undesirable, since they arouse a type of introspection and analysis which may diminish rather than increase
their effectiveness and fulfillment. However, for a woman who is
seeking to think through her situation, and particularly for
Dorcases and Kates, training in decision-making—which involves
both analysis of situations and clarification of priorities on the
basis of accepted values and goals—seems highly desirable.

This report now ends, but the search for understanding must
continue. The final recommendation, therefore, is that further investigations should proceed, in defined subgroups, on the basis of
hypotheses formulated in this study, and from the perspectives
of ministers, congregations, denominational leaders, and general
culture as well as MWs themselves. Yet the basic search for
understanding will inevitably be an individual one, which for
most will take place through the very process of living. For some
this search will require group structure. For others, as in the case
of Mary Martha Mountain, professional counseling and guidance
may be required. (Names of counselors, or sources of information
regarding counselors in a particular area, may be obtained by
writing to the author.) For many, the search will be one aspect of
devotional life, which may be expressed in regular Bible study
and prayer. There is one Way, but many ways. Each needs the
other, yet walks alone. But let each walk—and relate—as a person,
not as a stereotype.

Notes

PREFACE

1. Charles Merrill Smith, *How To Become a Bishop Without Being Religious* (Garden City, N.Y.: Doubleday & Co., 1965), pp. 19-28.
2. In "Psychology in Theological Education," a chapter in Hans Hofmann (ed.), *The Ministry and Mental Health* (New York: Association Press, 1960) and "Religion," a chapter in Norman L. Farberow (ed.), *Taboo Topics* (New York: Atherton Press, 1963).

CHAPTER 1

1. London: Holdworth and Ball, 1832. The copy consulted is in the Harvard Divinity School Library.
2. From the Foreword, p. v. Succeeding quotations are from pp. 194-95, 204, 8, 16, 47-48, 75, and 101.
3. Cf. Neal Gross *et al.*, *Explorations in Role Analysis* . . . (New York: John Wiley and Sons, 1958).
4. Cf. Max Weber's analysis of *The Protestant Ethic and the Spirit of Capitalism*, trans. by Talcott Parsons (New York: Charles Scribner's Sons, 1958). In a sense, the compulsive activism recommended is a kind of spiritual capitalism, which is Puritan in stressing a rigorous moral code opposed to indulgence or pleasure-seeking.
5. Boston: Crocker and Brewster, 1835. The copy consulted is in the Library of Congress. Quotations are from pp. 1 and 39.
6. Philadelphia: American Baptist Publishing Society, 1898, p. 54. Topics discussed in this book include: "Chosen as a Wife," "Living Within One's Income," "The Gift of Silence," "Making Changes," "Declining a Mold," "Our Homes and Our Intimate Friends," and "The Pastor's Wife a Widow."
7. New York: Lane and Scott, 1851. He considers the basic qualifications of a MW to be common sense, literary ability, knowledge of the Bible, and experimental piety.
8. Paper read by the daughter of Harriet Angell Anthony (Mrs. R. C. Dexter) at the Radcliffe Women's Archives Workshop, on March 17, 1954. Used with permission.

9. [Eunice W. (Mrs. Henry Ward) Beecher], *From Dawn to Daylight* (New York: Derby and Jackson, 1859).

10. London: Faber & Faber, 1943, pp. 196-98.

11. Copies of these letters are preserved in the Women's Archives, Radcliffe College, Cambridge, Mass., from a paper written by Mrs. Blanche H. Sprague. Used with permission.

12. For list of books consulted, see the "self-help" literature section of the Bibliography.

13. In evangelical and small-town Protestantism, ministers have probably retained a higher status. Negro ministers have, in recent years, been displaced in community status by lawyers, doctors, and other professionals, which has apparently been a major factor in reducing the number of Negro candidates for the ministry.

14. Simeon Stylites [Halford Luccock], "New Look in Preacher's Wives," *Christian Century*, 72:1489 (December 21, 1955). See also the comments of "Simeon Stylites" in the June 25, 1952 and January 20, 1954 issues of the *Christian Century*.

15. Wallace Denton, *The Role of the Minister's Wife* (Philadelphia: Westminster Press, 1962), pp. 29-30. Chaps. I and II, on "A Historical Look at the Minister's Wife" and "A Contemporary Look at the Minister's Wife," are good summaries of much of the literature on this subject.

16. See books published since 1960 in the Bibliography.

17. Two examples are: Laura Berquist and James Hansen, "The Many Lives of a Minister's Wife," *Look*, 20:99-103 (May 1, 1956) and Elizabeth Dodds, "What Are You Doing to Your Minister's Wife?" *Good Housekeeping*, 148:88-89 (June, 1959). Berquist and Hansen emphasize that "the wife of a parson marries her husband's profession" and must share him with it; and Dodds states that "many fine men are leaving their pulpits . . . because they are unwilling to subject their families to the distorting pressures of life in a parsonage."

18. Data on self-conception vs. role-conception were secured through two sections of the MW-6 open-ended questionnaire: A. Sentence Completions (especially 1 and 2) and F. Art—Just for Fun. See description of the questionnaire in the Appendix.

19. These articles were included in William H. Whyte, Jr., *Is Anybody Listening?* (New York: Simon and Schuster, 1952). See also *Fortune*, 44:86-88+ (October, 1951) and 44:109-111+ (November, 1951).

20. *Life*, 32:32-34 (January 7, 1952); *Nation*, 174:204-205 (March 1, 1952); *Saturday Evening Post*, 224:10 f. (April 5, 1952); *Coronet*, 34:67-74 (January, 1954); and *Reader's Digest*, 71:137-40 (October, 1957). Similar articles appeared, during the period of 1952-60 in *Colliers* (May 31, 1952); *Good Housekeeping* (January, 1956); *Cosmopolitan* (May, 1957); *Mademoiselle* (February, 1958); *McCall's* (July, 1958); and *Newsweek* (February 1, 1960).

21. *Family Weekly* (September 11, 1960), pp. 10-12. Debate con-

cerning women's route to self-fulfillment has continued in recent years, as in the writings of Betty Friedan and Phyllis McGinley concerning the "feminine mystique" and the profession of homemaker.

22. Proposal submitted to the Lilly Endowment in October, 1958. Subsequent quotations are from project progress bulletins distributed to advisory committees and co-operating denominational and seminary administrators. Three progress bulletins were prepared, in the springs of 1959, 1960, and 1962. (Questionnaire mailing occurred in the spring of 1961.)

23. The consistency, and more generally validity, of questionnaire responses was tested qualitatively in a number of ways, but not quantitatively. Husbands' reports in both questionnaires and interviews, with very few exceptions, substantiated the factual aspects of wives' reports, but also indicated the different meanings attached to facts by husbands and wives. There was little, if any, evidence of intentional distortion in reporting, but varying perspectives were clearly important. Data from interviews matched, and clarified, data from both open-ended and precoded questionnaires. And research assistants who did "progressive analysis" of questionnaires reported that responses to various sections of the questionnaire "hung together"—themes and emphases carried through the entire questionnaire of a given individual. Responses to the eight criterion items used in establishing the typology reported in Chap. 2 were consistent in terms of theoretical constructs represented.

24. All IBM cards were verified after key-punching. Coding of open-ended responses always involved the effort to achieve valid, reliable coding categories, through use of at least two independent coders, and pretesting of categories on a subsample of the data in order to achieve at least a .80 level of agreement among coders. Whenever possible, tabulation and analysis were checked by an independent, alternate method as well as individual. Tests of group differences involved chi-square statistics, despite recent debate concerning such techniques when (as in this study) one cannot assume a probability sample. (Cf. H. C. Selvin, "A Critique of Tests of Significance in Survey Research," *American Sociological Review* [October, 1957], pp. 519-27, and responses to Selvin in later issues of the journal.)

25. As Benson Y. Landis notes in each annual issue of the *Yearbook of American Churches*, the most accurate source of statistics regarding American Protestantism: "There are no complete, annual compilations of church statistics." But best available information would indicate that in 1960 there were about 250,000 ordained Protestant ministers, of whom about 160,000 were serving local churches. This estimate, made from denominational statistics prior to selecting names for the sample used in this study, was substantiated by the list of about 8,000 names which resulted from selecting a one-in-twenty sample of clergy, and eliminating those who were in administrative, teaching, institutional, or other nonparochial ministries. A danger involved in use of a

systematic sample is "periodicity" in the listing of names; no evidence of this could be found in this case, but it remains a possibility. Also, the condition of random start in listings of names was not fulfilled for all denominations—an error discovered too late to rectify.

26. Half of the MW-4 questionnaires were stamped with an identifying number and half left anonymous. The response rate was slightly higher for the questionnaires with an identifying number, for as women indicated in their written evaluations of the questionnaire—"if no one knows or cares, why bother?" There was no significant difference in response rates when prestamped (vs. postage paid) envelopes were used. All open-ended questions were coded by two or more research assistants, with checks on coding reliability. Pretesting permitted refinement of each stage of research design, from questionnaire construction through to communication of results in the form of a report of findings distributed to co-operating denominations and individuals.

27. Twenty-four additional MW-5 questionnaires, 90 per cent or more complete, were returned too late for key-punching onto IBM cards. Response rate is 70.8 per cent if it is calculated on the basis of the number of questionnaires returned 90 per cent or more complete (5,001) versus the maximum number who could have received it and to whom it was applicable (7,062). A follow-up letter was sent to nonrespondents from low-response denominations. (June 14, 1961: ". . . I am particularly anxious that we hear from those of you in the South and/or of evangelical orientation, since you are presently underrepresented. . . . Whatever your attitude concerning the study and your part in it, please FILL OUT AND RETURN THE ENCLOSED POST CARD. Only in this way will we know how representative and adequate our study has been. . . .") The post card asked for information on age and education, and indication of whether the questionnaire would be returned, was misplaced and another should be sent, or was not completed because not applicable, objectionable, too difficult, and/or time-consuming. Forty-two reported that they had never received the questionnaire, with 23 of the 42 from one denomination—the Church of the Brethren. These were women who received a second mailing, but not the first—when both were sent to the same address. This may indicate problems of mail going to a church (rather than a home) address, with minister-husband as communication medium. Fifty-nine indicated that they preferred not to complete the questionnaire, but only 4 indicated that they found the questionnaire objectionable, and 8 others that it was too difficult and/or time-consuming. For the other 47, the questionnaire was not applicable, because of retirement, not being in the *pastoral* ministry, sickness, death of husband or wife, or there "being no Mrs. Jones." Twenty-two per cent of MW-5 questionnaires were returned during the first two weeks after mailing, 55 per cent during the following two weeks, and 23 per cent thereafter. When questionnaires were distributed according to week of return, there were no significant differences in response

patterns. Therefore, it was not possible to estimate characteristics of nonrespondents in terms of differences between early respondents and late respondents.

28. Personal correspondence with denominational officials, particularly Thomas E. Wood, then Executive Director of Ministerial Services. In Dr. Wood's letter of December 20, 1961, he also stated that only 56 per cent of their full-time ministry were serving as parish pastors, and that about 1,900 of their 5,000 churches were served by students or part-time ministers. Many of these churches were very small.

29. "Evangelical" as used in this context refers to concern for witness to the unbeliever. Rationale for groupings is given in Chap. 6. During the course of the study, several mergers took place, particularly among Lutheran bodies.

30. By denominational groupings, there were the following frequencies represented in the twenty-seven cells of a three-by-three-by-three (denomination versus region versus basis of selection) table: (1) Baptist and Evangelical: from the Northeast and Far West, 6 random, 4 employed, and 11 dissatisfied; from the Midwest, 12 random, 14 employed, and 8 dissatisfied; from the South, 14 random, 21 employed, and 10 dissatisfied. (2) Methodist, Disciple of Christ, and United Church of Christ: from the Northeast or Far West, 13 random, 13 employed, and 13 dissatisfied; from the Midwest, 11 random, 5 employed, and 14 dissatisfied; from the South, 9 random, 11 employed, and 11 dissatisfied. (3) Episcopal, Lutheran, and Presbyterian: from the Northeast and Far West, 13 random, 15 employed, and 12 dissatisfied; from the Midwest, 10 random, 12 employed, and 14 dissatisfied; from the South, 12 random, 5 employed, and 7 dissatisfied. Total N is 300, with 100 from each denominational and regional grouping, as well as 100 randomly selected MWs, 100 employed, and 100 who reported themselves on the MW-5 questionnaire as in general frustrated and confined as a MW. Note the sizes of cell frequencies, which are as comparable as available questionnaires permitted.

31. The fullest report of this program is found in Robert I. Ayling, "The Role Anticipations of Student Ministers' Wives" (unpublished Th.D. dissertation, Boston University School of Theology, 1964). Mr. Ayling was associate director of the pilot program, with the author as director and major researcher. Some of the data collected in this program are contained in the section on "Wives of Seminarians" in Chap. 5.

32. Of the 4,777 women whose MW-5 questionnaires were included in data tabulation and analysis, 31.1 per cent were under 35 years of age in the spring of 1961, 44.8 per cent were 35 to 49 years of age, and 24.1 per cent 50 years of age or older. However, of 385 nonrespondents to the MW-5 questionnaire for whom data are available, 17.7 per cent were under 35 years of age, 42.1 per cent were 35 to 49 years of age, and 40.2 per cent were 50 years of age or older. For MW-6 respondents, the distribution is: 31.4 per cent under 35, 40.2 per cent 35-49, and 28.4 per cent 50 years of age or older.

CHAPTER 2

1. All names used are fictitious, though information given is factual, taken from questionnaires filled out by respondents, who have given their permission that this material be used. See the Technical Appendix for the MW-5, MW-6, and MW-7 questionnaires from which this material was drawn. Ideal types were established on the basis of the following MW-5 items: 40, 41, 42, 46, 47, 49, 52 (total no. of church activities), and 54 (semiprofessional church activities). Thus, the pure-type teamworker (40-1) reported herself to be motivated by a call (41-5 or 6), set apart to witness for Christ (42-3), very satisfied and fulfilled as a MW (46-1), finding joy in showing people a better way of life (47-2), and stressing the deepening of commitment to Christ and the Church (49-4). She performed eleven or more activities in the local church, at least four of which were semiprofessional (such as calling on sick and shut-ins or leading devotions). Selection of these eight criterion items, and specification of the specific response pattern associated with a particular type of involvement, were based on both theoretical and empirical grounds.

2. Based on the projective (sentence completion, and mental pictures of "a MW" and "Me") sections of the MW-6 questionnaire, as well as on item 46 of MW-5 and the general tone of all questionnaire responses.

3. The section of the MW-6 questionnaire from which these data are derived is adapted from a "Goals of Life" questionnaire used by the Educational Testing Service in its study of the ministry. The underlying theory is that of Charles Morris' "ways of life" (Charles Morris, *Varieties of Human Value* [Chicago: University of Chicago Press, 1956]). See Chap. 3 for the section on "Value Orientations."

4. From the cartoons used to illustrate her mental picture of "a MW" and "Me" on the MW-6 questionnaire. The calm Corinne vs. harried Hannah contrast was one of the most common, as was the dumpy, dowdy vs. young and attractive contrast.

5. Two hundred in 1,000 women reported themselves as teamworkers with their husbands in his ministry, but only 4 in 1,000 reported the very intense involvement, motivation, and satisfaction, represented in the pure type specified by the eight MW-5 items described in n. 1 above. Thirty of 1,000 women approximated the type, in that they had a 40-1, 41-5 or 6, 46-1, and 52-11 or more response pattern to the MW-5 questionnaire.

6. Seven of the eight pure-type teamworkers come from the South (three from Florida, and one each from North Carolina, Georgia, Oklahoma, and Texas) and the eighth from the southern section of Missouri. None of the eight, however, is from the rural Deep South of Mississippi, Alabama, or South Carolina, perhaps due in part to low response rates from these regions. Of the eight, five are Southern Baptists, two others are "Evangelicals" (see discussion of "Denomina-

tional Groupings" in Chap. 6) from the Church of the Nazarene and the Church of God, Anderson, and one Methodist. Five of the eight are in churches of less than 200 members, though they represent a wide range of community sizes. As a group, they tend to have had two years of posthigh-school education. In age and number of children, they are distributed about the same as MWs in general, except for underrepresentation (only one of the eight) of women over 50 years of age.

7. These eleven women were selected by computer on the basis of a specific response pattern to the same eight MW-5 items used to discriminate the eight pure-type teamworkers. The purpose-motivated background supporter pattern, as specified theoretically and then identified in terms of specific individuals, was: 40-2, 41-4, 42-2, 46-2, 47-5, 49-3, 52 (activity), five to ten, and 53 (semi-pro), two or three.

8. While 53 per cent of teamworkers report the life of a MW to be *very* satisfying, only 37 per cent of background supporters make such a judgment. As may be evident from the quotations from questionnaires and interviews, Marys tend to be lower-intensity people than Marthas, more often dreamers and less often drivers.

9. Five of the eleven come from the South (Virginia, Georgia, Alabama, Kentucky, and Texas), four from the Midwest (Ohio, Illinois, Michigan, and Iowa), one from the Northeast (Massachusetts) and one from the Far West (Oregon). Pure-type MWs may be less often found in areas of greater population fluidity and changing way of life, such as the Northeast and Far West. Denominationally, five of the eleven are Methodist, two Baptist, two Lutheran, one Congregational, and one Presbyterian. Six of the eleven are in churches of over 700 members, three in churches of 2-700 members, and only two in churches of less than 200 members—a very different pattern than for pure-type teamworkers. Four are in cities of more than 50,000 population, three in cities of 10-50,000 population, and four in towns of less than 2,500 population, or open country.

10. Of the eleven, only one is under 35, and three are over 50 years of age; only 18 per cent have preschool-age children, versus 40 per cent of all respondents. Their education averages about three years of college, and all of their husbands are seminary graduates, often with graduate work beyond seminary. Their social-class background may be judged by fathers' occupations: 36 per cent business and professional (vs. 26 per cent of teamworkers) and only 9 per cent labor (vs. 38 per cent of teamworkers).

11. Cf. the two types of group leadership discussed by Robert F. Bales and others in *Family, Socialization and Interaction Process* by Talcott Parsons and Robert Bales (Glencoe, Ill.: Free Press, 1955), especially pp. 259-306.

12. Only two of the ten Dorcases are in churches of less than 200 members and one in a church of over 700 members, but seven are in churches of 2-700 members.

13. Only two of the ten Dorcases are under 35 years of age, and only one has been a MW for less than nine years.

14. Response pattern for a Jane to the eight criterion items on the MW-5 questionnaire is the same as for a Mary, except that Janes describe themselves as "no more involved . . ." (40-3) instead of as background supporters (40-2). This does not seem to be merely a verbal difference, in the way one *describes* her involvement, but rather expresses a different orientation (more "detached") toward church and ministry. It seems as if, for some, the "Jane" orientation represents a stage, in the early pressured years of life as a MW, in the development of a "Mary" orientation. For others, the "Jane" orientation is the one favored by the religious tradition of which one is a part, in terms of the doctrine of the ministry and the dominant conception of woman's "proper place."

15. Response pattern for a Kate to the eight criterion items on the MW-5 questionnaire is as follows: 40-3, 41-1 or 3, 42-1, 46-3, 4, or 5; 47-3, 4, or 7; 49-2, 3 or 8; 52 (activity)—four or less; 54 (semi-pro)—none or one.

CHAPTER 3

1. Gordon W. Allport, in *Becoming* . . . (New Haven: Yale University Press, 1955) makes this contrast in discussing propriate processes, those central to the organization of personality.

2. About 70 per cent of respondents gave exactly the same response to items concerning *involvement* and *satisfaction* on the MW-7 questionnaire as they had on the MW-5 questionnaire about a year earlier. Less than 5 per cent moved more than one point on a five-point scale, in reported involvement and satisfaction. However, only 50 per cent reported the same *motivation* on the two questionnaires, a year apart. Other data and follow-up interviews indicate that this is not primarily a matter of questionnaire validity or reliability, but rather of new understandings, attitudes, and even ways of life produced through both experience and reflection on that experience. Filling out questionnaires, with the type of analysis they involved, was for a number of women a major influence toward change, at a behavioral as well as cognitive and attitudinal level.

3. The section on "research methods" in Chap. 1, and the corresponding notes, should be consulted by those seeking fuller and more specific information than that presented in this context.

4. To be exact, MW-6 questionnaires were mailed to a randomly selected 10 per cent sample (478 MWs) of the 4,777 MW-5 respondents, plus 184 who reported themselves as "frustrated and confined" as MWs on the questionnaire, and 217 MWs who held full-time employment. Of 879 MW-6 questionnaires mailed, 623 were returned 90 per cent or more complete in time for data processing. This is a response rate of 71 per cent. However, the response rate is at least

80 per cent if calculated in terms of those who actually *received* the questionnaire and to whom it was *applicable.* In analysis of data from the MW-6 questionnaire, three subgroups of 100 women each were kept separate: the randomly selected, the dissatisfied, and the employed. These 300 MWs, out of the total of 623 respondents, were selected on a quota basis, to ensure equal representation of the major denominational and regional groupings. See Chap. 1, n. 30 for further information.

5. Cf. discussion of "denominational groupings" in Chap. 6. No group differences are reported unless, by the chi-square test, they reach at least the .01 level of statistical significance; most are at or beyond the .001 level and would occur less than one out of a thousand times on the basis of chance. *Statistical* significance does not necessarily mean *theoretical* significance, however, nor do *group* differences necessarily provide the basis for prediction of relationships for *individuals.*

6. Thirty-nine per cent of self-reported teamworkers performed 11 or more activities in their local churches, versus 18 per cent of self-reported background supporters and 8 per cent of the detached ("no more involved . . .") with this high level of activity. And, there is a qualitative as well as quantitative difference: 46 per cent of teamworkers performed four or more "semi-pro" activities, versus 8 per cent of the detached. The 8 per cent of the detached who performed 11 or more activities, with 4 or more of them semiprofessional in nature, were apparently hyperactive women who would be as active, no matter what their husbands' work. They were truly "no more involved . . ." but they were not detached in the sense that other women who made this response were.

7. The summary of MW-5 responses contained in the Technical Appendix does not contain data concerning the specific activities contained in item 51-52. Sixteen local church activities are listed, with the respondent requested to make one of the following responses: (5) Do this and enjoy it; (4) Do this, but do not enjoy it; (3) Do this occasionally to get it done; (2) Don't do this, but would like to; or (1) Don't do this, and would rather not. Data were tabulated for 2,863 MWs whose husbands served *one* church *full*-time as *the* minister of that church, including the 472 Baptist (both American and Southern Conventions) and 146 Episcopal MWs contrasted here. For the total group, the following activities were most often performed: 95.5 per cent attended church women's groups; 71.5 per cent entertained church groups in their homes; 67.6 per cent led devotional services; 63.5 per cent taught a Sunday-School class; 58.4 per cent called on sick and shut-ins; 49.7 per cent held office in church women's groups; 48.7 per cent greeted parishoners after services with their husband; 41.4 per cent sang in the choir; and 40.8 per cent counseled people with problems. (Included in the per cent figures are those who reported "do this, but do not enjoy it," which varied from less than

1 per cent to almost 7 per cent.) In factor analysis these activities proved to be quite "independent" of one another.

8. Major cross-tabulations were calculated for 1,000 wives of *full-time* ministers of *one* church as *the* minister of that church. Each of two matched samples (groups A and B) included: 150 Evangelical, 150 Disciple and United Church of Christ, 150 Lutheran, 200 Methodist, 200 Baptist, and 150 Presbyterian MWs. (There were not enough Episcopal MWs for a separate group, and they did not "fit" with any other group.) Group A was used for cross-tabulations of involvement, motivation, set-apartness, satisfaction, "hard to be yourself," and joys and opportunities—versus all major MW-5 items. Group B was used for cross-tabulations involving community size, church size, ministerial income, age, father's occupation, and education. Some group A cross-tabulations were replicated for group B, and vice versa; in no case was there a significant difference between results from the two sets of calculations. These were all first-order (no controls except type of husband's service) cross-tabulations. Some hypotheses developed in this manner were explored further with a subsample of 106 MWs under 35 years of age, who had been a MW 5-9 years, and who had preschool-age children. With $N = 1,000$, for a 2 x 2 table of call (yes-no) versus 11 or more activities (yes-no), chi-square equals 28.07. With one degree of freedom, this means that P is less than .001. However, C is only .16. (See following note.)

9. For a 3 x 3 table of motivation (call, work-purposes, closeness-expected) versus involvement (teamwork, background, detached) chi-square equals 85.76 and P is therefore less than .001, but C (the coefficient of contingency) is only .28. The upper limit of C for a 3 x 3 table is .82, but nevertheless a value of .28 is not high enough to predict reported motivation from reported involvement, or vice versa, with much confidence. Likewise, for the 3 x 3 table of motivation versus satisfaction (very satisfied, satisfied, so-so-frustrated) chi-square equals 107.64 and P is therefore less than .001, but C is only .31. For motivation versus set-apartness, chi-square equals 133.32, P is less than .001, and C is .34.

10. Erik Erikson, in *Childhood and Society* (2d ed.; New York: W. W. Norton & Co., 1963) and *Identity and the Life Cycle* (New York: International Univ. Press, 1959), provides the best discussion of the development of secure identity on the basis of autonomy and trust. He relates basic trust to faith, and identity to ideology and illustrates how these variables interact in his incisive case study of *Young Man Luther* (New York: W. W. Norton & Co., 1962).

11. From Oppenheimer's address to the Sixty-third Annual Convention of the American Psychological Association, in San Francisco, September, 1955, as quoted in Bruno Klopfer *et al.*, *Developments in the Rorschach Technique*, Vol. II (New York: World Book Company, 1956), p. x.

12. Derived from Gordon W. Allport's discussion of values in *Pattern*

and Growth in Personality (New York: Holt, Rinehart, and Winston, 1963). See also Charles Morris, *op. cit.*, and John Tisdale, *Psychological Value Theory and Research: 1930-1960* (unpublished Ph.D. dissertation, Boston University, 1961). The section of the MW-6 questionnaire from which data concerning values and goals are derived is adapted from a "Goals of Life" questionnaire used by the Educational Testing Service in its study of the ministry. The format of that questionnaire was different from MW-6, and ten additional value statements were included. The studies begun by the Educational Testing Service, in the development of the Theological School Inventory, have been carried on by the Ministry Studies Board, 1810 Harvard Blvd., Dayton 6, Ohio.

13. Data from this program, of which the author was director, are reported by Robert Ayling, the associate director, in *The Role Anticipations of Student Ministers' Wives* (unpublished Th.D. dissertation, Boston University School of Theology, 1964). See Table 52 (p. 189) of this dissertation for report of value rankings by 103 seminarians' wives. Mean ranking of propriate service values was about 2.9, self-development values 5.0, and peripheral service values 8.9. The mean ranking of propriate service is identical to that of the 427 MWs, and the mean ranking of the self-development values is only a third of a rank higher. However, the mean ranking of peripheral service values by the seminarians' wives is almost one and a half ranks lower than for the experienced MWs. And in two of the four seminaries (Boston and Garrett) the ranking of peripheral service values was significantly (at the .05 level) lower at the end of the year than at the beginning. Boston and Garrett seminarians' wives were also distinctive in ranking "self-development; becoming a real, genuine person" significantly higher the second time than the first.

14. In general, standard scale means on the M.M.P.I. for the 103 seminarians' wives were close to general population norms for females, and differences between means may be due simply to random variation, in terms of small numbers involved. However, there is a tendency for these seminarians' wives to have higher scores on scale 3 (Hy): mean of 21.49 and standard deviation of 4.71 versus general female norms of 18.80 and 5.66; scale 5 (Mf): mean of 40.62 and standard deviation of 3.27 versus general female norms of 36.51 and 4.83; scale 6 (Pa): mean of 9.87 and standard deviation of 2.45 versus general female norms of 7.98 and 3.32; scale 7 (Pt): mean of 27.72 and standard deviation of 4.75 versus general female norms of 25.21 and 6.06; and scale 9 (Ma): mean of 17.67 and standard deviation of 4.19 versus general population norms of 16.12 and 4.11.

15. Ezra Stotland of the University of Washington, in "Birth Order as a Determinant of Social Behavior in Adults" (dittoed paper, no date) points out, after summary of relevant research and theory, that first-born children tend more often to be obedient and submissive to authority, and to develop patterns of giving and receiving nurturance

(care of another). Cf. the conclusions of Stanley Schachter in *The Psychology of Affiliation* (Palo Alto, Calif.: Stanford Univ. Press, 1959), p. 132, that "ordinal position of birth is one effective discriminator of the magnitude of the affiliative tendency" and that for the first-born ambiguous situations and feelings lead to the desire to be with others as a "means of socially evaluating and determining the 'appropriate' and proper reaction."

16. These summaries were written by a female doctoral candidate in clinical psychology who was a research associate. In developing coding categories for MW-6, one stage was the composition of such summaries, based on progressive coding of various sections of the questionnaire, to see how they "hung together."

17. In general women reported more consistent devotional practices, and less conflict, on the MW-6 open-ended questionnaire than on the forced-choice questions on the MW-7 questionnaire. In interviews, this turned out to be a particular problem area for many ministerial couples, in terms of relatively few being able to maintain consistent and satisfying practices, at the same time as they felt they should, and often urged others to do so.

18. When asked, on item 37 of MW-5, "What do you most admire about your husband, as a minister?" 49 per cent of respondents chose "sincere faith and dedication." The group which most often (67 per cent) made this response were MWs 35 to 49 years of age whose husbands were 5 or more years older. In general, MWs under 35 years of age gave this response less frequently (42 per cent) than other MWs.

19. Robert O. Blood, Jr. and Donald M. Wolfe, *Husbands and Wives* . . . (Glencoe: Free Press, 1960), pp. 172-73. In the Detroit area, 48 per cent of 731 urban wives and 53 per cent of 178 farm wives chose "companionship in doing things together with the husband" as the most valuable aspect of marriage, ahead of love, understanding, standard of living, and the chance to have children.

20. John G. Koehler, "The Minister as a Family Man," *Pastoral Psychology*, Vol. 11, No. 106 (September, 1960), pp. 12-15. Data came from 119 American Baptist MWs, 79 per cent of those to whom the questionnaire was sent.

<h3 style="text-align:center">CHAPTER 4</h3>

1. About two-thirds of MW-5 respondents reported themselves to be "better off" economically than their parents were. This is partly a matter of upward social mobility, through both education and marriage, but even more a result of the "times" now being better for the population in general. Of those who reported themselves as very satisfied as a MW, 69 per cent said they were better off economically than their parents were; of those who reported themselves as feeling "so-so" or frustrated as a MW, 51 per cent said they were better off. (To put it otherwise, of the "better off," 41 per cent reported themselves as

very satisfied and 11 per cent as so-so-frustrated; of the "worse off" 27 per cent reported themselves as very satisfied and 28 per cent as so-so-frustrated.) Of the very satisfied, 32 per cent reported their husband's ministerial income as sufficient for family needs, versus 15 per cent of the so-so-frustrated.

2. Actually, in terms of age of youngest child, those with *no* children most often (22 per cent) reported themselves as so-so-frustrated, followed by those with preschool-age children (17 per cent), children aged 6-16 (11 per cent), and over 16 (7 per cent so-so-frustrated). In part, this is a function of the MW's age and experience, but the relationship holds up even when age is held constant. Of women under 35 years of age, 19 per cent reported themselves as so-so-frustrated, versus 13 per cent of those 35-49 years of age, and 7 per cent of those 50 years of age or older. Of those who married their husbands after he had completed seminary, 10 per cent reported themselves to be so-so-frustrated, versus 16 per cent of those who married during college or seminary years, and 13 per cent who married when their husbands were in another vocation.

3. Of all respondents, 49 per cent reported both their parents and themselves to have participated regularly in the same denomination of which their husbands are now ministers. Of those from this type of background, about 11 per cent reported themselves as so-so-frustrated, versus 14 per cent of those who had been regular participants though their parents had not, and 21 per cent of those who had been irregular participants in local church life prior to marriage.

4. Under 10 per cent of MWs born third or later in their families reported themselves as so-so-frustrated, versus 15 per cent of both first and second-born. Under 10 per cent of daughters of farmers reported themselves as so-so-frustrated, versus 13 per cent of daughters of laborers and 16 per cent of daughters of business and professional men. There are no significant differences across educational levels with regard to reported satisfaction on item 46 of the MW-5 questionnaire. However, data from other questionnaires and interviews indicate a tendency for those who have attended college but not graduated to be less fulfilled and satisfied than other MWs.

5. The more than one-third of the so-so-frustrated who reported themselves to have felt positively toward church activities, and who were also quite active in their local congregations, presumably were frustrated with the particular situation in which they were then involved, or with their husbands, rather than with being a MW in general. There appear to be different kinds of frustration: situational, marital, and chronic.

6. Fifty-three per cent of teamworkers, 37 per cent of background supporters, and 18 per cent of the detached reported themselves as very satisfied.

7. Being a paid staff member of one's husband's church was very unusual: less than 2 per cent of MWs worked as paid church staff, and practically no other MWs reported desiring such a position.

8. Robert Blood and Donald Wolfe discuss social status (class) in *Husbands and Wives, op. cit.*, especially p. 32. Gerhard Lenski analyzes class structure in relation to *The Religious Factor* (Garden City, N. Y.: Doubleday and Co., 1961) on pp. 73-74. Data gathered in the Church Ministry Studies of the National Council of Churches of Christ in the U. S. A. (see *Information Service* [December 5, 1964], pp. 1-8) indicate that the value of housing provided (in a parsonage) more typically approximates 25 per cent of cash salary, rather than the 15 per cent figure generally used by church pension boards.

CHAPTER 5

1. Since MWs tended to marry after 20 and to be three or more years younger than their husbands (and therefore to "retire" prior to 65) the slight underrepresentation of the younger and older groups, and corresponding overrepresentation of the middle group, is easily explained. As discussed in Chap. 1, n. 32, underrepresentation of woman 50 years of age or older may have operated. And the women over 50 who did participate may have been the most alert, interested, and active of their age group. This is indicated, also, by the fact that of the approximately 450 respondents to the MW-7 questionnaire (women who had already completed the MW-5 and MW-6 questionnaires, and thus indicated high involvement in the purposes of the study) only 14.9 per cent were 50 or more years of age, versus 32.1 under 35 and 53.0 per cent 35-49 years of age. Differences between MWs over 50 and other groups would probably have been greater, therefore, had *all* MWs over 50 completed the questionnaire. Though nonrespondent bias probably operated, it does not seem to invalidate conclusions drawn from age-group comparisons.

2. The trend may have begun to reverse. For some seminaries report 25 per cent or more of their students over 40 years of age. For those moving into the ministry in mid-life, there has often been a previous sense of "call," which was not responded to at the time, but now the individual feels "I can delay no longer," or in the case of retired military officers this is seen as a "second vocation."

3. The following material comes from the May, 1963 *Monthly Staff Report* (Vol. VII, No. 5) of the American Association of Theological Schools in the United States and Canada (934 Third National Bank Building, Dayton 2, Ohio) as prepared by William Douglas and Robert Ayling. Other results of research included in the Lilly Pilot Program for Theology Couples are reported in Robert Ayling's 1964 Boston University doctoral dissertation. See Chap. 3, n. 13.

4. It is hard to know how representative the women involved in the pilot program are of *all* wives of theological students in these four seminaries, much less of those in *all* Protestant theological seminaries. They are probably reasonably representative of wives who would *volunteer* to take part in such a program: Chap. 3, n. 14. Percentiles

for seminarians' wives on the Edwards Personal Preference Schedule are available on request.

5. In Robert Ayling's dissertation, *op. cit.*, there is a detailed analysis of differences among seminaries.

6. Some of this material appeared in an article by the author entitled "Ministers' Wives: A Tentative Typology," in *Pastoral Psychology*, Vol. 12, No. 119 (December, 1961), pp. 10-16. The same issue contains another article by the author on "Minister and Wife: Growth in Relationship," based on a Weyerhaeuser Lecture delivered at McCormick Theological Seminary, October 1960.

CHAPTER 6

1. See Chap. 3, n. 10. Erikson considers intimacy to be possible only on the basis of secure identity, just as identity presupposes autonomy, trust, etc. This corresponds to Maslow's conception of "self-actualization" depending on the fulfillment of more basic needs.

2. See Chap. 3, n. 15.

3. Marthas are less often daughters of business and professional men (26 per cent) and more often daughters of laborers (38 per cent) than are other MWs. In contrast, Marys tend to be daughters of either farmers or business and professional men, but less often (22 per cent) daughters of laborers. Indeed, of the eight "purest-type" Marthas, five are daughters of laborers and three of farmers, while of the eleven "purest-type" Marys, six are daughters of business and professional men, four of farmers, and only one of a laborer.

4. Blood and Wolfe, *op. cit.*, p. 110. This passage considers satisfaction with standard of living, but age difference (as well as difference in education, social status, religion, etc.) was found to affect all types of satisfaction. Blood and Wolfe conclude (p. 257) that "homogamy provides the foundation on which a strong marriage can be built. What the couple does with their potentialities determines how satisfactory the marriage really is. . . . Compatible individuals must go beyond choosing one another to loving each other and . . . serving the partner in ways which satisfy his basic needs."

5. Source is the 1962 edition of the *Yearbook of American Churches*, published in November, 1961 and containing the most recent data available in 1961.

6. See Chap. 1, n. 30 and Chap. 3, n. 4.

7. These figures are for *full*-time clergy of *one* church as *the* minister of that church—i.e., not part-time, multiple-charge, or multiple-staff. Considering *all* respondents from the 14 denominations involved in these three groupings, median ministerial incomes are as follows: Bap-Evan—$4,793; Dis-Meth-UCC—$5,788; and Epis-Luth-Pres—$5,813. Most recent comparable data appear in *Information Service* (National Council of Churches, Department of Research), Vol. XLIII, No. 19 (December 5, 1964), pp. 1-8. These data relate to clergy compensa-

tion earned in 1963, and cash salary figures are close to those reported above. The National Council study, directed by Ross P. Scherer, included all of the denominations in our three basic groupings, except for Church of the Nazarene, and two others as well: Reformed Church in America and Church of the Brethren. Averaging figures for denominations in a particular grouping (and this is not really accurate, since different numbers of clergy are involved) median cash salaries in the National Council study would be: Bap-Evan—$4,528; Dis-Meth-UCC—$5,308; and Epis-Luth-Pres—$5,327. In the National Council study, the average supplementary income for utilities and fees, beyond cash salary, was $548, and seminary graduates received an average of $200 more. If the $748 adjustment is made, median ministerial incomes (not including housing) for the three groups in 1963 become: $5,276, $6,056, and $6,075. And if $1,300 is added for the average value of housing reported in the National Council study, figures become $6,576, $7,356, and $7,375. Data from the MW-5 questionnaire (on ministerial incomes of 4,777 Protestant ministers in 1960) and from the National Council study (on the compensation of 5,263 Protestant parish clergymen in 1963) are, then, generally supportive of one another. And they tend to indicate that salaries did not change a great deal from 1960 to 1963.

8. Median income of various categories of full-time male salaried workers in the U. S. A. in 1963 was as follows: engineers and technical workers—$9,512; professional social workers—$8,820; college professors—$8,163; managers and officials—$8,115; foremen—$7,038; Protestant clergy (15 denominations)—$7,006; elementary and secondary schoolteachers—$6,950; and sales workers—$6,537. From *Information Service, op. cit.*, based on Current Population Reports, September 29, 1964 of the U. S. Census and other sources for social workers, professors, and clergy. As Dr. Ross P. Scherer, director of Church Ministry Studies of the National Council of Churches, points out: "relatively few parish ministers on the average can expect to receive *supplementary* types of income"; "important in determining size of salary is congregational membership"; "one important economic frontier which probably needs to be remedied first is inadequate provision for professional allowances, or inadequate reimbursement for expenses incurred in the conduct of the ministry"; there is a "need for more regular salary increases"; and "71 per cent of the clergy report a median debt of $1,596 in summer, 1964." From Ross P. Scherer, "Compensation of the Protestant Clergy in 1963," *Seminary Quarterly*, Vol. 6, No. 3 (Spring, 1965). Data in this article come from *Information Service, loc. cit.*

CHAPTER 7

1. Wallace Denton, "Role Attitudes of the Minister's Wife" (unpublished Ph.D. dissertation, Teachers' College, Columbia University, 1958); Beverly Kaiser, "The Role of the Minister's Wife in the Local

Church . . ." (unpublished Master's thesis, School of Education, Boston University, 1958); and Mary G. H. Suput, "A Study of the Emotional Conflicts of Student Ministers' Wives" (unpublished Master's thesis, Northwestern University, 1953). A number of other theses and course term projects have focused on ministers' wives and have been consulted, but the three listed above relate most directly to the problems under consideration.

2. For many MWs, writing appears to be a major outlet and source of fulfillment: "Now it's *my* chance to be heard." In a column entitled "For Mrs. Preacher" a writer with the nom de plume of "Martha" presented guidance for Methodist MWs in the *New Christian Advocate* in a series of issues beginning in October, 1956. Mary Cannon discussed "Being a Minister's Wife" in the *Chicago Theological Seminary Register* of January, 1950, while Anne Jordheim wrote "From a Country Parsonage," I and II, in the January 5 and 19, 1960 issues of *Lutheran Herald*. Mrs. Jordheim, who was born in Germany and lived in Norway for seven years as the wife of a Lutheran pastor before coming to Wisconsin in 1958, has also written for *Die Pfarrfrau*, a quarterly publication by and for German pastors' wives which began regular publication in 1960 with Ruth Schleiermacher (in Darmstadt, West Germany), as editor. When the first trial issue of this journal appeared in the fall of 1959, its stated purpose was that of giving help to everyday life (*Lebenshilfe*) in "mutua consolatio sororum." The journal generally has seven parts: articles on the situation, problems, and resources of MWs (51 per cent of the pages of the first 6 issues of 32 pages each); devotional writings, poems, and so forth (16 per cent); information— as on the church year and liturgical colors, and practical skills and "how-to's" (10 per cent); book reviews (5 per cent); personal sharing of experiences and readers' responses to topics raised in previous issues as solicited in questionnaires included in the journal (18 per cent). The problem discussed most frequently in articles is the responsibility of MWs in relation to their husband's ministry. In particular, there is concern about the traditional concept of "mother of the parish" and a protest against evaluating MWs in terms of the quantity of their activities rather than the quality of their lives. Like American MWs, these German pastors' wives worry about whether they can measure up to the expectations held of them. An issue which became acute earlier in Germany than in America (cf. the "religionless Christianity" of Bonhoeffer) is uncertainty about the relevance of religion in the industrial society of "grown-up persons" of objectivity (Sachlichkeit) and scientific proof. In this connection, some of the articles emphasize the distinctiveness of *die Pfarrfrau* as one who operates in terms of a personal approach, an *I-Thou* relationship, in the midst of the "objectivity" and impersonality of industrial society. Content analysis of three years' issues reveals that the major themes are very parallel to those discussed in this book; it is tempting to quote from the articles themselves, but space does not permit this!

3. Kaiser, *op. cit.*

4. Denton, *op. cit.*, pp. 200 ff.

5. Suput, *op. cit.*, pp. 163-73.

6. See the discussion of "Some Historical Perspectives" and corresponding notes—especially 1 and 2—in Chap. 1, which include extensive quotations from the 1832 *Hints from a Clergyman's Wife.* . . .

7. Reuel L. Howe, *The Miracle of Dialogue* (Greenwich, Conn.: Seabury Press, 1963), pp. 69-71, 82.

8. This is a major conclusion of Keith R. Bridston and Dwight W. Culver, in *Pre-Seminary Education* (Minneapolis: Augsbury Publishing House, 1965). See pp. 55-87 on "Secular Cultivation," and pp. 50 ff. of the "Portrait of the Pre-Seminarian," who is described as "church-bound."

Technical Appendix

I. THE MW-5 QUESTIONNAIRE
(Inventory for Ministers' Wives)

IN FORMAT, the MW-5 questionnaire is a twelve-page printed booklet, approximately 3¾ by 8½ inches in size. Page 1 contains a "covering letter" encouraging participation and giving instructions: "Please *circle* the number of the answer *closest* to your situation, experience, or opinion, though none may fit *exactly*. Since this will be machine-tabulated, it is important that you complete each question, and circle *one* answer only for each question." At the bottom of page 1, a six-digit identifying number was stamped, the first two digits representing the denomination and the other four digits representing the individual. Pages 2-5 contain items 11-39 on "Present Situation," pages 6-9 contain items 40-65 on "Attitudes and Activities," pages 10-11 contain items 66-80 on "Personal Data," and page 12 provides space for "additional comments or suggestions you would like to make."

Research assistants coded fourteen items which required summary codes—such as number of church activities, enjoyment of church activities, number of "semi-pro" activities, religious affiliation background of self and parents, etc. IBM cards were then "key-punched" and "verified" directly from the questionnaires, without use of intermediate data sheets. For reasons of space, the complete questionnaire is not reproduced here, but it may be obtained by sending a self-addressed, stamped envelope to the author. Wording of questions has been abbreviated for questions 8-37, and response categories "collapsed" from the original five or more to the summary three or four used in all cross-tabulations.

Data are summarized here for five groups of respondents: (1) 4,777 MWs who returned the questionnaire 90 per cent or more complete, in time for data processing; (2) 2,000 "FTMOC" MWs, selected from the "Total" 4,777 on the basis of being wives of *full*-time ministers of *one* church as *the* minister of that church (i.e., not part-time, or in a "multiple charge" or "multiple staff") from the denominations included in the three subgroups that follow; (3) 700 "EB" (Evangelical and Baptist) MWs from the Church of God—Anderson, Church of the Nazarene, Evangelical United Brethren, American Baptist Convention, and Southern Baptist Convention; (4) 700 "DMU" MWs from the Disciples of Christ, Methodist Church, and United Church of Christ; and (5) 600 "LP" MWs from the American Lutheran Church, Lutheran Church in America, Lutheran Church—Missouri Synod, U. S. Presbyterian ("Southern"), and United Presbyterian in the U. S. A. ("Northern"). The rationale for these groupings is found in Chapter 6. In general, responses of Episcopal MWs follow the pattern for LP MWs. Group 2 = the sum of subgroups 3+4+5. Data summaries are available for each of the thirty-seven participating denominations, and for "part-time," "multiple-charge," and "multiple-staff" MWs.

Numbers listed are the *percentages* of respondents from a group who give particular responses. "No response"—which averages less than 5 per cent for all items—has been eliminated and numbers rounded, so that percentages total 100 per cent. Thus, of those for whom information is available regarding "8. Geographic region," respondents from the South are 38 per cent of "Total," 39 per cent of "FTMOC," 53 per cent of "EB," 35 per cent of "DMU," and 27 per cent of "LP" MWs. In comparing subgroups 3, 4, and 5 of "FTMOC" MWs, percentage differences of 6 per cent or more would occur less than five times out of a hundred on the basis of chance.

SUMMARY OF MW-5 RESPONSES: FIVE GROUPS OF RESPONDENTS

Present Situation	1. Total N = 4,777 Per cent	2. FTMOC N = 2,000 Per cent	3. EB N = 700 Per cent	4. DMU N = 700 Per cent	5. LP N = 600 Per cent
8. Geographic region					
Northeast (New Eng., Mid. Atl.)	17	17	10	19	22
Midwest (E. & W. No. Cen.)	33	32	28	31	39
South (So. Atl, E. & W. So. Cen.)	38	39	53	35	27
Far West (Mtn., Pacific)	12	12	09	15	12
14. Size of community					
Under 2,500	30	27	36	23	22
2,500–9,999	20	24	21	26	25
10,000–49,999	24	24	22	26	24
50,000 or more	26	25	21	25	29
15. Church's adult membership					
Under 200	34	28	46	15	22
200–399	28	33	27	35	36
400–699	19	25	15	31	29
700 or more	19	14	12	19	13
18. Type of housing ("residence") now have					
Furnished parsonage	19	16	07	39	02
Unfurnished parsonage	66	76	81	55	92
Own home—housing allowance	10	07	09	05	06
Other	05	01	03	01	00

	1. Total N=4,777 Per cent	2. FTMOC N=2,000 Per cent	3. EB N=700 Per cent	4. DMU N=700 Per cent	5. LP N=600 Per cent
19. Location of residence					
Next door to church	38	41	42	42	38
Less than ½ mile (not next door)	32	34	32	36	36
½ to 2 miles away	17	17	17	15	18
More than 2 miles away	13	08	09	07	08
23. Type of housing would *prefer*					
Furnished parsonage	16	14	06	32	02
Unfurnished parsonage	47	51	59	41	55
Own home—housing allowance	34	33	34	25	41
Other	03	02	01	02	02
25. Husband's ministerial income (1960)—excluding housing allowance, but including utilities, car allowance, pension & insurance, fees, etc.					
Under $4,000	19	14	31	05	03
$4,000–6,999	61	70	59	77	79
$7,000 or more	20	16	10	18	18
26. Sufficiency of ministerial income for family needs, as judged by MW					
Sufficient—no "scrimping" required	31	29	22	31	35
Barely sufficient	37	41	37	43	41
Insufficient—hard to make ends meet	32	30	41	26	24
29. Wife's employment					
Full-time	10	10	13	08	07
Part-time	19	19	20	20	15
Does not work	71	71	85		

33. MW's judgment of her *present* economic status, relative to *childhood*					
"Better off" now	64	64	71	61	61
About the same	25	23	19	25	25
"Worse off" now	11	13	10	14	14
36. Age of MW's *youngest* child					
No children	07	07	07	08	06
Under 6	39	41	41	36	46
6–16	32	32	32	32	31
Over 16	22	20	20	24	17
37. What she most admires about her husband as a minister					
Professional *skills* (preaching, counseling, success, etc.)	28	29	28	29	30
Social relationships (love for people, likeableness, etc.)	23	22	23	24	20
Sincere *faith* and dedication	49	49	49	47	50
40. In relation to your husband's ministry, how would you describe your degree of involvement?					
Very involved, as a *teamworker* sharing in his ministry	21	20	30	18	11
Very involved, but in a *background, supportive* way	64	66	61	67	69
Involved, but no more than if he were in another vocation	15	13	08	14	19
Not too interested, or rather antagonistic	00	01	01	01	01

Attitudes and Activities	1. Total N = 4,777 Per cent	2. FTMOC N = 2,000 Per cent	3. EB N = 700 Per cent	4. DMU N = 700 Per cent	5. LP N = 600 Per cent
41. To the degree that you are involved, which of the following (there may be other reasons) *most* motivates you to take part in your husband's ministry?					
Desire to contribute through useful work	27	26	26	29	23
Belief in the purposes of the Church	33	36	28	39	43
A call to be a minister's wife, or to full-time Christian service	27	26	38	20	20
Desire to be close to your husband, or because it's expected of you	13	12	08	12	14
42. Which of the following best describes your feeling about being a MW?					
An individual, for whom others cannot legislate	03	02	01	02	03
A Christian, with the same responsibilities as any other church member	75	77	66	81	83
Set apart, to witness for Christ	20	19	30	15	11
Other	02	02	03	02	03
43. In addition to being a good wife and mother, which of the following would you consider your *major* responsibility, if you had to choose among them?					
Promoting world peace and brotherhood, or improving local community conditions	11	11	08	14	09

Making the church what it should be	48	49	52	47	50
Fulfilling your own potential as a person	36	37	37	38	37
Other	05	03	03	01	04
46. In general, how have you found being a MW?					
Very satisfying and fulfilling	36	37	40	36	33
Satisfying and fulfilling	50	49	49	49	51
So-so, or frustrating and confining	14	14	11	15	16
47. The joy or opportunity which has meant the most to you, in addition to sharing in your husband's work [question reworded] is					
Having a place of respect in church and community, or knowing a wide range of people, or personal growth and fulfilment	26	26	21	35	24
Showing people a better way of life	19	19	37	13	09
Learning more about the Christian faith	31	33	23	31	48
Being of service to your fellow men	17	18	17	20	17
Other	07	04	02	01	02
48. The problem or conflict which has been most real for you [question reworded]					
Your inadequacy as a leader	19	20	21	18	20
Few close personal friends, or goldfish-bowl living, with little privacy	30	33	35	34	35
Husband's irregular work schedule, or inadequate finances, or not enough time for self and family	36	35	36	38	35
Other	15	12	08	10	10

	1. Total N = 4,777 Per cent	2. FTMOC N = 2,000 Per cent	3. EB N = 700 Per cent	4. DMU N = 700 Per cent	5. LP N = 600 Per cent
49. Most important suggestion you would give to a young MW [question reworded]					
Face problems with your husband, or be your own best self—don't worry about the expectations of others, or have a genuine interest in people, or become emotionally mature with sense of humor	27	26	26	28	24
Your first responsibility is to be a good wife and mother	33	33	30	34	36
Deepen your personal commitment to Christ and the Church	30	32	35	26	34
Be in full sympathy with your husband's work, or become adequately trained and educated for your work as a MW	10	09	09	12	06
50. What would be the major change in your life if you were *not* a MW?					
More time for own interests, or higher family income	24	25	25	26	23
Freer to "be yourself"	12	13	13	12	14
Fewer opportunities for service and growth	17	17	14	20	16
No real change	47	45	48	42	47
52. Number of activities performed with some regularity in present church: 16 are listed [teaching a SS class, choir, women's groups, etc.] with space for writing in others					

11 or more	19	21	32	17	14
5 to 10	68	70	63	74	72
Less than 5	13	09	05	09	14

53. Relative enjoyment of local church activities [number of those MW reports enjoying, versus those she reports not enjoying]

Generally enjoy	43	47	61	41	37
Enjoy some but not others	29	29	26	33	30
Generally do not enjoy	28	24	13	26	33

54. Number of "semi-pro" activities performed in local church [calling on sick and shut-ins, counseling, leading devotional services, leadership training, on staff of church, etc.]

4 or more	25	27	41	23	15
2 or 3	45	47	42	51	48
None or one	30	26	17	26	37

55. Number of nonchurch community activities performed [YWCA, PTA, scouting, women's clubs, etc.—10 listed, with space for write-ins]

4 or more	15	13	08	18	14
2 or 3	35	38	33	41	40
None or one	50	49	59	41	46

56. Relative enjoyment of nonchurch community activities

Generally enjoy	12	12	10	15	09
Enjoy some, but not others	30	30	23	34	29
Generally do not enjoy	58	58	67	51	62

Percentage agreeing to "Some Statements Which MWs Have Made." (Original responses were on a scale of Strongly Agree–Agree–Disagree–Strongly Disagree.) Items 57, 58, 60, 61, 62, and 63 deal with set-apartness from laity, and 59, 64, and 65 with felt deprivation (though set-apartness may be deprivation, too). Note that the scale on items 57, 59, and 62 runs in the opposite direction from the other items. Thus, on item 57, 35 per cent feel set apart versus 34 per cent on item 60, while on item 59, 44 per cent feel deprived versus 86 per cent on item 64.

	1. Total N = 4,777 Per cent	2. FTMOC N = 2,000 Per cent	3. EB N = 700 Per cent	4. DMU N = 700 Per cent	5. LP N = 600 Per cent
57. The MW's responsibilities are those of any laywoman.	65	65	57	67	64
58. The MW has many acquaintances but few friends.	88	89	91	89	89
59. In general, ministers spend as much time with their families as do other professional men.	56	57	57	56	57
60. It's hard to "be yourself" as a MW.	34	36	37	34	36
61. MWs should be trained for their special responsibilities.	70	72	85	69	61
62. One's closest friends, as a MW, come from her husband's congregation.	40	40	37	44	40
63. Always being an example is a strain.	43	45	50	44	43
64. Ministers are generally underpaid.	86	87	90	85	80
65. It's hard, as a MW, to have regular family					

Personal Data	1. Total N=4,777 Per cent	2. FTMOC N=2,000 Per cent	3. EB N=700 Per cent	4. DMU N=700 Per cent	5. LP N=600 Per cent
66. How old are you?					
Under 35 years of age	31	32	32	32	34
35–49 years	45	46	48	42	45
50 years or older	24	22	20	26	21
67. Is your husband older or younger than you?					
He is 5 or more years *older*	22	22	21	24	20
Same age to 4 years older	64	64	64	65	65
He is *younger* than I	14	14	15	11	15
68. How long have you been a MW?					
Less than 5 years	09	08	06	05	12
5–9 years	22	22	21	21	24
10 or more years	69	70	73	74	64
70. At what point in your husband's preparation for the ministry were you married?					
After his seminary training	38	35	22	34	51
He was in college or seminary	37	42	41	48	38
He was in another vocation	19	17	29	13	08
Other	06	06	08	05	03
72. Before marriage, what was your, and your parents', general level of church participation?					
Both regular participants—self and parents	49	49	49	42	55
Self regular participant, but parents not	39	40	39	46	34
Self irregular, or nonparticipant	10	10	10	10	09
Other	02	01	02	02	02

	1. Total N = 4,777 Per cent	2. FTMOC N = 2,000 Per cent	3. EB N = 700 Per cent	4. DMU N = 700 Per cent	5. LP N = 600 Per cent
73. What was your father's (or other major wage earner's) primary occupation?					
Business or professional	38	38	28	41	46
Farming	26	25	34	21	18
Labor, skilled or unskilled	31	32	34	32	28
Other, or unclassifiable	05	05	04	06	08
74. In order of birth, were you the first child, second, . . . in your family?					
First-born	36	38	33	41	41
Second-born	23	23	21	22	25
Third-born or later	41	39	46	37	34
76. In what size community did you spend most of your "growing up" (grade school) years?					
Under 2,500 population	43	43	49	42	36
2,500–9,999	17	17	18	18	13
10,000–49,999	18	18	18	18	21
50,000 or more	22	22	15	22	30
77. What size church did you attend during most of your "growing up" years?					
Under 200 members	41	39	52	35	27
200–399	26	27	25	25	29
400–699	18	18	13	22	22
700 members or more	15	16	10	18	22

78. How important in general would you say that religion was in your home when you were growing up?

Very important	60	61	61	56	65
Somewhat important	33	33	31	38	31
Not important at all	07	06	08	06	04

79. What was the highest year of school that you completed?

College graduate or more	37	39	30	44	44
Beyond high school, but not college graduate	34	34	34	35	33
High-school graduate or less	29	27	36	21	23

80. What was your husband's education?

Seminary graduate or more	75	82	67	85	94
More than 2 years of college, but not seminary graduate	17	13	21	14	05
2 years of college or less	08	05	12	01	01

II. THE MW-6 QUESTIONNAIRE
(Attitude and Experience Survey)

In format, the MW-6 Questionnaire consists of six multilithed pages, 11 inches wide by 8 inches long. After each of the following open-ended questions there was space for response.

Thank you so much for completing the Inventory of Ministers' Wives (MW-5) so carefully and promptly. And thank you, too, for being willing to share with us, in greater depth than that form allowed, your feelings, insights, and experiences. You have been selected as part of a small, select group (about 10 per cent of those receiving the MW-5 Inventory) to take part in this next stage of research.

I hope that this questionnaire will be helpful to you, as well as to us, as you "look whole" at your situation. Such opportunities for analysis and reflection are all too rare in our rushed, crowded lives. And if the space provided for an answer is insufficient, please feel free to attach additional sheets of paper. (Even diaries would be gladly accepted—as perhaps the best source of information of "what it is like to be a minister's wife"!) As in the earlier questionnaire, please be assured that ALL INFORMATION SUPPLIED WILL BE HELD IN THE STRICTEST CONFIDENCE, and recorded under code numbers only. Realize, too, that unless you are honest in your responses the study will have been in vain.

(Page 1) A. *Sentence Completions.* Please complete the following sentences, writing down "what first comes to you." Your feelings are more important than the way in which you express them. Be as brief and spontaneous as possible; we are not looking for carefully considered essays, but rather for feelingful responses.

1. Being a minister's wife has meant for me . . . . . .
2. If I were not a minister's wife, my life would be different in that . . . . . .
3. When I was younger, I . . . . . .
4. My husband . . . . . .
5. What is most important to me is . . . . . .

6. The hardest thing . . . . . .

7. The congregation . . . . . .

8. In the future, I . . . . . .

9. Always being an example . . . . . .

10. My closest friends . . . . . .

11. A minister's children . . . . . .

12. My husband's denomination . . . . . .

(Page 2) B. *Home and Family*

1. How would you compare your own present *home and family* life to that of your childhood? (E.g., how do the "roles" you and your husband play—in decision-making, discipline, finances, etc.—compare with those of your mother and father? How do you feel about the similarities and differences?)

2. How would you, in a few phrases, describe your *husband*? (Include in your description what you *admire* about him, as well as what "*gets on your nerves*" at times.)

3. How would you, in a few phrases, describe *yourself* as a person? (Include in your description those aspects of your personality with which you are dissatisfied.)

4. In what ways, if any, are your *husband's expectations* of you influenced by the fact that he is a minister?

5. When things are "getting you down," *with whom* and *how* do you "blow off steam?" (To what extent can you use your husband as listener and "sounding board?" In addition to your husband do you have any real "confidantes"?)

6. Suppose that you were advising the wife of a ministerial student, and that she was expecting her first baby. How would you seek to guide her concerning situations she may encounter in "raising the minister's children?" (Did anyone guide you at this point? Was the guidance of help?)

7. Have you ever found yourself regarding the *church as a rival* for your husband's affections? (If so, in what sorts of situations does this tend to occur?)

8. Some ministers' wives report problems in the *sexual love* aspects of their marriage—in terms of their husbands' physical and emotional exhaustion at the end of a long day, with "not much left over for me." Has this ever occurred for you? (If

so, how do you respond to it? If not, are there other problems for you in the sexual love aspects of marriage?)

(Page 3) C. *Personal Growth and Fulfillment*

1. Do you have any *hobbies*, or things you do "just for fun?" (If so, what are they? And *with whom*, if anyone, do you usually do them?)

2. Does your husband's church offer *activities* with real *satisfaction* for you as an individual? (If so, what are they? If not, where do you turn for such activities?)

3. What talents, interests, or aspects of your *personality* do you find it most difficult to express and/or develop as a minister's wife?

4. Describe a minister's wife whom you particularly admire(d); she may be fictitious or "real life." (In what ways are you like her? In what ways are you different from her?)

5. Of your "daily round of activities," what parts are most *satisfying?*—most frustrating?

6. Looking over your life, before marriage as well as after it, which "*phases*," times, or periods have been most *satisfying* and fulfilling?—which most *frustrating*, discouraging, or disillusioning? Why?

7. How would you describe your personal and/or family *devotional life*? (What role does this, or has this, play(ed) in your personal growth?)

8. What about your present situation (including your husband) most supports, or encourages your *personal growth* and fulfillment? What most frustrates it?

(Page 4) D. *Critical Incidents.* For each of the following incidents, which are apt to occur in the life of a minister's wife, indicate what you probably *would* do under the given circumstances, and what you think you *should* do.

1. You move to a new (to you!) parsonage, which has just been redecorated in a style which you "can't stand."

2. You are leaving for a family outing, planned and looked forward to for several weeks, when the phone rings. It's Mrs.

Jones, a chronic complainer and self-pitier, who "must see your husband right away."

3. It's 10 A.M. and you'd like to get at the housecleaning, but your husband (no study or office at the church) is still "underfoot."

4. Your 10-year-old son (imagine you have one, if you don't) is criticized by a schoolteacher for "not acting as a minister's son should."

5. You have come two months ago to the pastorate of a small church. The Sunday-School superintendent resigns a month before fall classes are to begin. Your husband asks you to serve, until a replacement can be found.

(Page 5) E. *Values and Goals.* Realizing that all of the following "goals of life" are important and desirable, please *rank* them, from 1 (most important) to 10 (least important) for you—whether or not you are able to attain them. Mark 1 next to the most important, 2 next to the next most important, etc.

[See Chapter 3 for description of values ranked. Items derive from the "General Goals of Life Inventory" (published by the Cooperative Test Division of the Educational Testing Service) as adapted by Frederick R. Kling. These "goals" come, in turn, from the data and theory of Charles Morris.]

Realizing that words can never adequately express our faith, please write a brief "creed"—a statement of your theological position. ("Labels," such as evangelical, fundamentalist, liberal, etc. are not necessary, but you may use them if they help to identify your position.)

F. *Art—Just for Fun.* Moving from the sublime to the (almost) ridiculous, we'd like to know what "picture" comes into your mind when you think of "*a minister's wife.*" And, we'd like to know, too, the "picture" you have of yourself as a person. You may either paste on a cartoon or photograph from a newspaper or magazine, or draw it yourself, in whatever "art form" you desire. As in the Sentence Completions, feelings are more important here than technique!

(Page 6) G. FOR EMPLOYED MINISTERS' WIVES ONLY
(If you are not employed full time, you are through with the
questionnaire. Thank you so much for your assistance.)

1. What is your present position or job?
2. How long have you been employed in this position or job?
3. Had you held other positions or jobs before this one? If so,
   what were they?
4. Why did you go to work, or go back to work?
5. As best you can assess it, what is the effect on your home and
   family life of your being employed?
6. As best you can assess it, what is the effect on your involvement in your husband's work and/or in church life of your
   being employed?
7. What is the response of your husband's congregation to your
   being employed? And of your husband himself?
8. If your husband's ministerial income were more than sufficient
   to meet your family's needs, would you still work? If so, why?
   If not, why not?
9. If you were single or a widow, would you hold the same job
   as now, or a different one? Why?
10. To what extent have there been, or will there be, family cir-
    cumstances that would prevent your working?
11. What personal fulfillment(s) do you find through your job—
    or lose through your job—that would not be true if you were
    "just a MW" or "just a wife and mother?"

THANK YOU so much for your help, as together we seek to be
of assistance in the future guidance and orientation of ministers'
wives. Return the questionnaire in the envelope provided—to
Box 55, 745 Commonwealth Ave., Boston 15, Mass.

III. THE MW-7 QUESTIONNAIRE
(Roles and Relationships)

[In format, this questionnaire consists of separate forms for
husband and wife, with page 2 of both forms the same. Each

form consists of two multilithed pages, on one sheet of paper 8 inches wide by 11 inches long, with most items open-ended.]

Wife's Form Even after 4,800 MW-5s and 600 MW-6s, questions remain! Particular issues concern us, as we plan for the pilot program for seminary student couples, to be conducted next year. So, once again—for the last time!—a questionnaire comes to you. This time, in addition, we are asking that husbands complete a parallel form, so that we may have their perspectives as well.

As you complete these forms, please *do not discuss them with one another* before or after completing them. We want individual honest perspectives and perceptions, not joint presentations, or responses affected by what husband or wife will think of them.

Be assured again that no individual information, or questionnaires, will *ever* be released to *anyone*. All processing takes place on IBM cards, with code numbers representing individuals.

A. *Statistical Data Revisited.* To answer the following, you will need to use the enclosed MW-5 Questionnaire (which you may keep, incidentally—*do not* return it). Item numbers given are those in MW-5. Do *not* try to remember what you said then; we are evaluating change over time, *not* your consistency or memory. [Questions follow on items 11, 12, 14, 15, 18, 19, 25, 29, 30, 32, 40, 41, 46, and 60 of MW-5, and exact dates are requested for birth, marriage, joining church, becoming a MW, and children's births, plus indication of children's sex and whether or not any were adopted or died.]

B. *Things Other MWs Have Said.* Indicate your degree of agreement by marking SA (Strongly Agree), A (Agree), D (Disagree), or SD (Strongly Disagree).

1. ——The MW's key problem is her husband's attitude and expectations.
2. ——Different congregations require you to play different roles.
3. ——I'm sorry that people *don't* bother me. I get lonely.
4. ——The young minister's family should have a baby-sitting fund provided by the church.
5. ——The unhappy MW would be unhappy, as a person, in any other situation.

6. ——People are a constant delight—not critical or hard, but wonderful.

7. ——I feel that my own life was dedicated, to do my part.

8. ——It's harder to grow as a good Christian in the parsonage.

9. ——There is no one I can bare my real self to, as a person to go to.

10. ——As a MW, you have to make up for your husband's weaknesses and limitations.

C. *Personal and Family Devotional Life.* For the following, mark 1 for always, 2 for often, 3 for usually, 4 for seldom, and 5 for never. The scale, for frequency, is 1 to 5. [In recording data, 2 and 3 were not distinguished, since "usually" and "often" were reversed by error. The scale used in tabulations: always—usually or often—seldom—never.]

1. ——My husband and I hold family devotions together, on a daily basis.

2. ——Church services act to deepen my personal devotional life.

3. ——At a time of personal crisis or tragedy, I turn to Bible reading and prayer.

4. ——Rather than "set devotions," I "intersperse" reminders of God's presence through the day.

5. ——My husband takes the leadership in our family devotional life.

6. ——My husband and I discuss his sermons before he delivers them.

7. ——As a MW, "professionalized religion" makes personal religious life more difficult.

8. ——The fact that my husband is leader of worship detracts from my own worship, somehow.

9. ——I agree with the doctrinal emphases of my husband's sermons.

10. ——I agree with the social and political emphases of my husband's sermons.

(Page 2: the same on both Wife's Form and Husband's Form)

D. *Values and Goals.* Rank the following "goals of life." [Cf. Section C of MW-6. The order in which values are presented is

changed, two values are omitted ("peace of mind . . ." and
". . . personal immortality"), and two other values added ("enjoying life . . ." and "promoting . . . happiness . . ."]

E. *Self and Mate Description.* Next to all those which apply to
you mark S for Self; next to all those which apply to husband
mark H, or to wife mark W. Circle the *three* S's and the *three* H's
or W's next to those which seem to you *most* descriptive. You
may mark the same adjective both S and H or W, if it seems to
apply to both of you. . . .

—— 1. Happiest when active.
—— 2. Prefers being quiet and alone.
—— 3. Puts ideals before people.
—— 4. Willing to sacrifice for others.
—— 5. Carefree and easy-going.
—— 6. Judged energetic by others.
—— 7. Lonesome even when with others.
—— 8. Rather slow and deliberate.
—— 9. Seeks to avoid trouble.
——10. L i k e s to a n a l y z e others' motives.

——11. Too sensitive for own good.
——12. Thinks little of others' opinions.
——13. Trouble relating to children.
——14. Dislikes taking a firm stand.
——15. Dedication to church work, at family's expense.
——16. Tends to be messy, sloppy, careless.
——17. Rather shy and timid.
——18. Procrastinates and puts off when possible.
——19. Too rigid and/or perfectionist.
——20. Not sensitive to mate's feelings.

F. *Critical Incidents.* Indicate, for each of these situations, what
you think your *husband's* or *wife's* response would be—in *actions*,
not ideals.

    1. When there is a conflict between home and church responsibilities, choose: . . . . . .
    2. When one or more of the children require discipline: . . . . . .

3. Assuming that you live in a parsonage, when repairs are required: . . . . . .
4. When a call to a new church comes, evaluate it in terms of: . . . . . .
5. When criticized by members of the congregation: . . . . . .
6. Indicate ways in which your response would be different from your husband's or wife's, to the incidents listed above: . . . . . .

G. *Ages and Stages.* Of the total time in which you have been involved in the married ministry, which was the hardest?
1. Hardest age or stage: . . . . . .
2. What in the *situation*, including husband or wife, made the age or stage difficult?
3. What in *yourself*—the way you behaved, responded to things, etc.—contributed?
4. What led to, or may lead to, resolution of the problem(s) and/or conflict(s)?

THANK YOU for your co-operation. RETURN BOTH HUSBAND'S AND WIFE'S FORMS in the envelope provided, to . . . . . . We respect your privacy so much that we would suggest that you *not* read one another's forms.

[Page 1 of *Husband's Form* has questions on personal data, ranking of ministerial responsibilities—on dimensions of importance, effectiveness, enjoyment, and time spent, emphases and goals of ministry, comparison of his denomination with others, role figures, and description of "ideal parish and community." These data will be reported in another volume.]

IV. PARTICIPATING DENOMINATIONS AND RESPONSE RATES

	(a)* Gross & (Net) No. MW-5s Sent	(b) Net No. MW-5s Ret.	(c) Gross & (Net) Response Rate	(d) Gross No. MW-6s Sent	(e) MW-6s Ret. Gross & Resp. Rate
1. Advent Christian Church	22 (22)	15	68.2 (68.2)	5	4 (80.0)
2. Seventh Day Adventists	141 (119)	47	33.3 (39.5)	9	5 (55.6)
3. Assemblies of God	437 (389)	164	37.5 (42.2)	19	11 (57.9)
**4. American Baptist Convention	247 (193)	156	63.2 (80.8)	32	20 (64.5)
**5. Southern Baptist Convention	1,330 (1,171)	559	42.0 (47.7)	135	88 (65.2)
6. National Baptist Convention, U.S.A., Inc.	193 (163)	17	8.8 (10.4)	11	4 (36.4)
7. American Baptist Association	61 (46)	14	23.0 (30.4)	3	2 (66.7)
8. Free Will Baptists	91 (85)	29	31.9 (34.1)	4	1 (25.0)
9. North American Baptist General Conference	22 (19)	16	72.7 (84.2)	2	1 (50.0)
10. Church of the Brethren	101 (87)	65	64.4 (74.7)	12	11 (91.7)
**11. Christian Churches (Disciples of Christ)	354 (298)	248	70.1 (83.2)	37	28 (75.7)
**12. Church of God, Anderson, Ind.	142 (126)	93	65.5 (73.8)	17	12 (70.6)
13. Church of God, Cleveland, Tenn.	259 (252)	84	32.4 (33.3)	10	4 (40.0)
**14. Church of the Nazarene	239 (236)	164	68.6 (69.4)	30	24 (80.0)
**15. Congregational Christian Churches	264 (227)	189	71.6 (83.3)	38	26 (68.4)
**16. Evangelical and Reformed Church	118 (105)	81	68.6 (77.1)	13	9 (69.2)
**17. Evangelical United Brethren	210 (185)	178	84.8 (96.2)	35	23 (64.7)
18. International Church of the Foursquare Gospel	31 (25)	25	80.6 (100)	4	3 (75.0)

	(a)* Gross & (Net) No. MW-5s Sent	(b) Net No. MW-5s Ret.	(c) Gross & (Net) Response Rate	(d) Gross No. MW-6s Sent	(e) MW-6s Ret. & Resp. Rate
**19. Lutheran Church—Missouri Synod	266 (230)	208	78.2 (90.4)	27	21 (77.8)
**20. American Lutheran Church	101 (88)	85	84.2 (96.6)	13	7 (53.8)
**21. Augustana Evangelical Lutheran Church	59 (51)	51	86.4 (100)	6	6 (100)
**22. Evangelical Lutheran Church	106 (97)	75	70.8 (77.3)	5	5 (100)
**23. United Evangelical Lutheran Church	10 (10)	9	90.0 (90.0)	1	1 (100)
**24. United Lutheran Church in America	222 (193)	174	78.4 (90.1)	42	33 (78.6)
25. General Conference Mennonite Church	9 (8)	8	88.9 (100)	1	1 (100)
26. Mennonite Church	83 (79)	55	66.3 (69.6)	5	5 (100)
27. African Methodist Episcopal Church	172 (119)	14	08.1 (11.8)	2	2 (100)
28. African Methodist Episcopal Church Zion	77 (63)	10	13.0 (15.9)	4	3 (75.0)
29. Christian Methodist Episcopal Church	81 (70)	8	09.9 (11.4)	5	1 (20.0)
**30. Methodist Church	1,296 (1,247)	1,006	77.6 (80.7)	162	111 (68.5)
31. Cumberland Presbyterian Church	43 (36)	27	62.8 (75.0)	5	5 (100)
**32. Presbyterian Church in the U.S.	160 (141)	128	80.0 (90.8)	27	22 (81.5)
**33. United Presbyterian Church in the U.S.A.	535 (448)	435	81.3 (97.1)	90	80 (88.9)
**34. Protestant Episcopal Church	421 (362)	274	65.1 (75.7)	56	35 (62.5)
35. Christian Reformed Church	32 (32)	30	93.8 (93.8)	3	2 (66.7)

36. Unitarian Churches	25 (25)	23	92.0 (92.0)	5	4 (80.0)
37. Universalist Church of America	15 (13)	13	86.7 (100)	4	3 (75.0)
TOTALS:	7,975 (7,062)	4,777	59.9 (67.6)	879	623 (70.9)

*(a) "Gross" refers to the total number of MW-5 questionnaires mailed in the spring of 1961, while "Net" is "Gross" minus those returned for insufficient or incorrect addresses, or because inapplicable to the persons to whom they were mailed. "Net" is the *maximum* number of MWs who could have returned the questionnaire.

(b) "Net" refers to the number of MW-5 questionnaires returned 90 per cent or more complete, in time for machine tabulation. Several hundred more were returned less than 90 per cent complete, and 24 were returned too late for machine tabulation.

(c) "Gross" response rate, expressed in percentage, is (b) divided by Gross (a), and "Net" response rate is (b) divided by (Net) (a). However, if "Gross" return figures (including MW-5s returned less than 90 per cent complete, or too late for machine tabulation) were used, there would be a higher response rate.

(d) Number of MW-6 open-ended questionnaires mailed in the summer of 1961 to a random subsample of MW-5 respondents (those whose code number ended in 8) plus selected subsamples of those who reported themselves as employed full-time, or dissatisfied as MWs. Data analysis focused on 300 questionnaires selected for equal representation of denominational and regional groupings, as well as bases of selection (random, employed, dissatisfied).

(e) Number of MW-6 questionnaires returned 90 per cent or more complete, in time for coding and machine tabulation.

**Research results are particularly relevant to these denominations, with sufficiently high response rates and numbers of respondents for extensive data analysis. During the course of the research project, which began in 1959, denominations 15 and 16 became part of the United Church of Christ; 20, 22, and 23 part of the American Lutheran Church; 21 and 24 part of the Lutheran Church in America; and 36 and 37 part of the Unitarian Universalist Association.

Bibliography

The preliminary form of this bibliography, which aims at representativeness, not inclusiveness, was constructed in the summer of 1960 and distributed to 120 theological school and Bible college libraries for suggested revisions. The original, much more extensive, form contained sections on dissertations and articles in religious and secular periodicals, as well as material on women, the family, church women, wives of professional men, and missionary wives, in addition to the sections included in this much more selective listing. Libraries may obtain copies of the original bibliography on request.

Many books referred to in the text or notes are not listed here. This is but a sampling of books by and about MWs, to give something of the flavor and tone of the literature.

A. "Self-Help" Literature (General Surveys)

1. GOLDA E. BADER (ed.), *I Married a Minister* (Nashville: Abingdon-Cokesbury, 1942). Considers aspects of a MW's life such as home, children, appearance, friends, hobbies, spiritual life, opportunities, and privileges. General consensus that the MW's home should come before all else, but that she should also share in the ministry of her husband.

2. CAROLYN P. BLACKWOOD, *The Pastor's Wife* (Philadelphia: Westminster Press, 1951). Probably the best known in its field and covers many important situations. Traits desired in MWs by laywomen include consecrated Christian character, sincerity, friendliness, a gracious personality. Traits criticized are bossiness, lack of interest in church work, forming cliques, "holier-than-thou" attitude, and desiring the limelight. A great trial for the MW is not being able to have close friends.

3. WALLACE DENTON, *The Role of the Minister's Wife* (Philadelphia: Westminster Press, 1962). A revision of Denton's 1958 Columbia University doctoral dissertation. Some of Denton's findings are discussed in the "Other Studies: Confirmations and Qualifications" section of Chap. 7. Contains particularly good summaries of the literature on MWs.

4. WELTHY H. FISHER, *Handbook for Ministers' Wives* (New York: Women's Press, 1950). Practical hints on household organization and hostess etiquette. But the many examples of situations which the MW might face and the ways in which they may be handled are a little overwhelming. The professionalized picture of the MW presented would intimidate many young wives.

5. ALICE REYNOLDS FLOWER, *Building Her House Well* (Springfield, Mass.: Gospel Publishing House, 1949). Emphasizes what qualities a MW should have instead of how she should act in given situations. The spiritual side of the MW is stressed and biblical references are used.

6. ARTHUR W. HEWITT, *The Shepherdess* (New York: Harper & Brothers, 1943). The earliest contemporary, single-author handbook. Stresses the husband-wife relationship, which is overlooked by nearly all other of the self-help books. If the reader is not bothered by the self-consciously folksy style of writing, there is some basically practical advice contained in the book.

7. *Hints for a Clergyman's Wife; or, Female Parochial Duties* (London: Holdworth & Ball, 1832). (May be found in Harvard Divinity School Library.) Historical perspective on the issues discussed in the contemporary MW handbooks. See particularly "Some Historical Perspectives" (and corresponding notes) in Chap. 1, which contain many other nineteenth-century sources.

8. ANNA F. JOHNSON, *The Making of a Minister's Wife* (New York: Appleton Century Co., 1939). "Ministers' wives have never been officially recognized as a part of church leadership, yet the Lord has always seemed to have a role for them to play." Mrs. Johnson goes on to say that the making of a MW is a long, slow molding by friends, family, and parish. She thinks the smaller the parish, the more duties the MW has. Her account of the routine of being a good mother, wife, and MW is especially helpful.

9. DOUGLASS S. MCDANIEL, *The Pastor's Helpmate* (Nashville: Broadman Press, 1942). Particularly helpful for Southern MWs.

10. KATHLEEN N. NYBERG, *The Care and Feeding of Ministers* (New York: Abingdon Press, 1961). Sound insights of a midwestern Methodist MW with a light touch. Discusses subjects other books miss, such as "pruning and grooming" your husband, "how to unbend without falling on your face," and your husband's "ego problems." Considers "being an involved and responsible minister's wife a marvelous mixture of the sublime and the ridiculous, the solemn and the silly."

11. FREDA S. O'NEALL, *The Better Half of the Ministry* (Boston: Christopher Publishing House, 1963). Discussion of practical problems faced by a MW, by one who considers her life as that of a "worthy partner in a worthy cause" and who drives her point home (on public relations, children, culture, retirement, etc.) with concrete illustrations and extensive use of historical and literary allusions—all in 83 small pages.

12. Lora L. Parrott, *How To Be a Preacher's Wife and Like It* (Grand Rapids, Mich.: Zondervan, 1956). This book covers the same ground as the other self-help books, but deals with a more limited range of situations.

13. Helen Raley, *As the Years Go By* (Standard Printing Company, 1958). Mrs. Raley, wife of the president of Oklahoma Baptist University for twenty-five years, emphasizes the partnership inherent in the ministerial profession.

14. Gustine C. Weaver, *The Minister's Wife*, collected by the Council of Ministers' Wives of the Disciples of Christ (Cincinnati: Powell & White, 1928). Essays, poems, prayers, and so forth, including "I Am the Minister's Wife" and the "Minister's Wife Creed," which begins, "I believe in my Husband and his high calling apart. . . ."

15. Lloyd E. Williams, *Queen Without a Crown* (San Antonio, Tex.: Naylor Co., 1952). The description on the jacket says that although it follows to a degree the life of the author's wife, it is not her strict biography. The tendency is to melodrama and advice contrary to most other handbooks, but many of the happenings are typical.

A summary of the major emphases of these books concerning "the ideal MW" is found in Chap. 1 of the present volume. These handbooks codify a set of cultural expectations which it would be hard for any mortal, finite woman to match. The key of the ideal is background support—active, but not dominant—plus setting an example for congregation and community. However, more recent books such as those by Denton and Nyberg encourage much more realism and freedom. For the best general survey of the history of the "child of the Reformation" who has "had very little thanks for all the unpaid work she has done through the course of five centuries," consult the final item under this head:

16. Margaret H. Watt, *The History of the Parson's Wife* (London: Faber & Faber, 1943).

B. *Autobiographies and Biographies*

1. [Eunice W. Beecher (Mrs. Henry Ward)], *From Dawn to Daylight* (New York: Derby and Jackson, 1859). Financial hardships plus the many duties of a MW made life in the nineteenth century very trying for a MW, but the woman described seemed to accept it all with good grace. Anecdotes of daily living give a good insight into her life. The book was first published anonymously.

2. Thyra F. Bjorn, *Papa's Wife* (New York: Rinehart and Co., 1955). Deals with bringing up a family of eight children in Sweden, then moving to America. Father is a minister. Sequels include *Papa's Daughter* (1958) and *Mama's Way* (1959).

3. Grace N. Fletcher, *In My Father's House* (New York: McGraw-Hill Book Co., 1955). Life in a New England parsonage as related by a daughter. Helpful book for the spiritual guidance of

student ministers and their wives. Mrs. Fletcher is also the author of
Preacher's Kids (New York: Dutton, 1958), in which a mother-MW
is an ideal of stability to her children.

4. BETTY FRIST, *No Wings in the Manse* (New York: Fleming
Revell, 1956). A daughter of a minister marries a minister. The story
of the fun she knew in her childhood parsonage, and a testimony to
the Christian living of the family, their prayers and day-by-day ac-
quaintance with the Bible.

5. ANNA L. GEBHARD, *Parsonage Doorway* (New York: Abingdon-
Cokesbury, 1950). This tells of a minister and his family. It indicates
the part of each youngster in planning family activities—worship,
work, play, etc. The minister's wife's role is one of "simple purity."
Mrs. Gebhard is also the author of *Guideposts to Creative Family
Worship* (New York: Abingdon-Cokesbury, 1953) and *Rural Parish*
(New York: Abingdon-Cokesbury, 1947), which discusses the adjustments, trials, and achievements of a young bride and her minister-
husband in the rural Minnesota territory.

6. CORRA HARRIS, *A Circuit Rider's Wife* (Boston-New York:
Houghton Mifflin Co., 1933). (First published in serial form in *The
Saturday Evening Post* in 1910.) A fun-loving Episcopalian before
marriage to a "shouting Methodist" circuit rider, Mrs. Harris gives an
excellent account of her experiences among people of the Southern
mountains. She indicates the problems of the MW in adjusting to
religious viewpoints and practices different from those in which she
has been reared.

7. KATHLEEN JARVIS, *Diary of a Parson's Wife* (London: A. R.
Mowbray, 1958). Easy diary style captures rush and humor of vicarage
life with three lively children and a pet menagerie in London. Pano-
ramic, with little detail, but occasional searching questions and insights
within an appreciative presentation of life as a MW.

8. MARIA W. SHEERIN, *The Parson Takes a Wife* (New York:
McGraw-Hill Book Co., 1940). When Maria Williams decided to
marry an Episcopal minister, her uncle warned her: "You will look
like a parson's wife. . . ." However, life in the rectory was a happy
experience for this former Richmond, Virginia debutante. Mrs. Sheerin
exhibits a fine sense of humor throughout the book, and her interpretation of a comfortable, cheerful existence as MW is a welcome relief
from many of the depressing accounts given by others.

9. HARTZELL SPENCE, *One Foot in Heaven* (New York: McGraw-
Hill Book Co., 1940). This is the story of the author's father, a
Methodist minister in Iowa. His wife was active in the church, teaching Sunday School, training a youth choir, and doing unofficial counseling. She gave her husband confidence in his work and often had
to take full care of the family due to her husband's involvement in
church work. In general, she had a liberalizing influence on her husband. In *Get Thee Behind Me* (New York: Whittlesey House, 1942)
Spence continues his story of an upbringing in a parsonage family

which gave him "perspective . . . , tolerance . . . , and unwavering conviction that man and God are good."

10. PHYLLIS STARK, *I Chose a Parson* (New York: Oxford University Press, 1956). This is a story of a happy wife in the parsonage. It reflects a positive attitude toward the church. It is written by the wife of an Episcopal clergyman in the Midwest, who later became a bishop.

C. *Fiction*

1. GLADYS CARROL, *One White Star* (New York: The Macmillan Co., 1954). Laura resigned herself to the role ascribed to her by a much older minister-husband whose strict morals were imposed upon her. She longed for children which she was unable to have and threw herself into church work out of her loneliness. After her husband's death, she remarried—a Roman Catholic.

2. ALICE R. COLVER, *The Parson* (Philadelphia: Macrae Smith Co., 1951). The parson causes controversy within the congregation by associating with nonchurchgoers, supporting a radical new teacher, and condoning his daughter's "emancipated" behavior. The parson's wife throughout all the difficulty supports her husband's progressive ideas and acts as a buffer between him and the community.

3. KENNETH S. DAVIS, *The Years of the Pilgrimage* (New York: Doubleday & Co., 1948). An extremely sensitive, scholarly minister has personal problems working out his faith. He also finds himself inadequate in many pastoral relationships. Eventually, the congregation asks for his resignation, and he founds an interfaith social service agency. Throughout these vicissitudes, his wife gives him encouragement and strength to work through hardship and failure.

4. MARGARET ECHARD, *The Return of Christopher* (New York: Doubleday & Company, 1951). Christopher, a psychology professor who is the son of a minister, is encouraged to enter the ministry, but his wife objects violently. She cannot see herself as a MW. "She had no virtue for display." She considers divorce as an escape from being a MW. Only slowly does Christopher win her over. A similar theme is presented in Mrs. Echard's *The Unbelieving Wife* in which Bruce's fiancée breaks the engagement when he announces that he is changing from law to theology. However, after an emotional struggle and a religious conversion, Vicki marries Bruce and becomes a MW, a big adjustment for a society girl with a playwright mother.

5. SHEILA KAY-SMITH, *The View from the Parsonage* (New York: Harper & Brothers, 1954). A renegade Anglican priest leaves the church in order to save his personal integrity. His wife remains quietly in the background, trying to understand her husband's search for faith. Although a practicing Christian, she does not try to change her husband's belief system.

6. ROBERT NATHAN, *The Bishop's Wife* (New York: Grosset & Dunlap, 1947). An Anglican bishop devotes himself to his administrative

tasks and plans for a new cathedral, to the neglect of his family. His puritanical attitude toward sex further alienates his wife, who lavishes her love on their daughter. The rest of the story is a fable of the wife's love affair with a rather earthy "angel," who comes to serve as her husband's Archdeacon. After the "angel" returns to heaven, the bishop resolves to spend more time with his family.

7. ANNA CORA RITCHIE, *The Clergyman's Wife and Other Sketches* (New York: Charleton & Co., 1867). An idealized short story of a wealthy young girl who marries a minister despite admonitions that it will be a hard life. The parishioners are completely won over by her "prompt sympathy, quick appreciation, cheerful looks, winning manners . . . and . . . the penetrating melody of her voice."

8. JAMES STREET, *The Gauntlet* (New York: Doubleday & Co., 1945). A young minister and his wife, Kathie, go to a church in Missouri during the depression. There is an intensely unhappy relationship between the wife and the church members in their competition for the time and affections of the minister. *The High Calling* (New York: Doubleday & Co., 1951) is the sequel to *The Gauntlet,* telling of the marriage of the minister's daughter, after his wife's death, to a young man preparing for the ministry. Her father opposes the marriage.

9. AGNES S. TURNBULL, *The Bishop's Mantle* (New York: The Macmillan Co., 1947). Alexa Laurens finds difficulty adjusting from a life of social prominence to becoming the wife of an Episcopal clergyman in an inner-city area. She learns kindness and service through many tragic misadventures, and by the end of the book has found fulfillment and happiness through her place in her husband's ministry. By the same author: *The Gown of Glory* (Boston: Houghton Mifflin Co., 1952), which tells of the trials and tribulations of the family of a Presbyterian minister in a small town in Pennsylvania. She is disappointed in her husband's slow professional advancement, and driven by her own ideals.

10. EMILY H. YOUNG, *The Vicar's Daughter* (New York: Harcourt, Brace & Co., 1928). The vicar is suspected of having fathered a girl, now a maid in his church warden's home. The story concerns his wife's struggle to discover the truth and her return to a renewed love of her husband.

In general these novels, and many others like them during the past century, stress the negative aspects of a MW's situation: the rigidity and criticalness of members of the congregation, and their competition with her for her husband's time and affections. Several stories focus on the struggle toward a faith of integrity and intellectual adequacy on the part of the minister and/or his wife. "Good" wives tend to be patient, supportive, adaptive, sacrificial. "Bad" wives are flashy, immature, self-seeking. The stories tend toward superficiality, contrived plots and falsely dramatic and idealized portrayals of parsonage life.

D. *Books on the Ministry*

1. CHARLES BRIDGES, *The Christian Ministry* (New York: Jonathan Levett, 1831), pp. 219-30. The effect of family religion and ways in which the pastor's wife can be of help—the author considers her place in his ministry very important.

2. J. OSWALD DYKES, *The Christian Minister and His Duties* (Edinburgh: T. & T. Clark, 1909). Chap. VIII deals with "The Home." It is important for the minister to be married so that he can better understand and counsel others. However, his family needs to be in sympathy with his calling. His wife should be a good companion and good housewife.

3. DANIEL P. KIDDER, *The Christian Pastorate* (Cincinnati: Hitchcock Walden, 1871). Qualifications of a MW should correspond in all important respects with those demanded in the minister because of her peculiar responsibilities and duties. She should be a model Christian woman, maintain a model home, be a true helpmeet and never be forward. If she lacks these qualifications she should make every effort to attain them.

4. C. B. MCAFEE, *Ministerial Practices* (New York: Harper & Brothers, 1928). See Chap. 26, pp. 168-75. The wife is very important in the minister's effectiveness. Mr. McAfee gives helpful and still very relevant suggestions for MWs.

5. H. C. G. MOULE, *To My Younger Brethren* (London: Hodder & Stoughton, 1842), pp. 112-14. Moule considers it better for the clergy not to be married, to enable them to be free for their work.

6. *A Pastor's Jottings*, (American Tract Society, 1864). See especially pp. 147-53. The author's description of a "model pastor's wife" embodies good Christian home background, simple unassuming piety, good example, being an officer of no society, industry, economy, kindness, and cheerfulness.

7. CHARLES MERRILL SMITH, *How To Become a Bishop Without Being Religious* (Garden City, N.Y.: Doubleday & Co., 1965), pp. 19-28. Tongue-in-cheek wisdom regarding factors the aspiring clergyman should consider before selecting what will be the "most important one piece of equipment" he will have in his ecclesiastical career, namely, his wife.

8. DANIEL D. WALKER, *The Human Problems of the Minister* (New York: Harper & Brothers, 1960). Walker suggests that a good MW should seek to understand her husband, accept responsibilities as a mother, and maintain a positive attitude about her own job. The work of a MW is a profession in its own right (p. 108).

9. J. C. WYNN, *Pastoral Ministry to Families* (Philadelphia: Westminster Press, 1957). Excellent book. See Chap. 8, "The Pastor as a Family Man," pp. 181-201.

Despite the references listed, it is striking how seldom books on the Protestant ministry take account of the fact that most ministers are married, with responsibilities as husbands and fathers. The guiding image, after the Protestant Reformation as well as before it, appears to be a celibate priesthood, in which the clergyman gives his undivided loyalty and time to the Church. Few authors meet realistically and constructively the conflicts faced by a minister who seeks to balance the competing demands and responsibilities of his family and his congregation.

Index

Format by Ronald Farber
Set in Linotype Caledonia
Composed, printed and bound by The Haddon Craftsmen, Inc.
HARPER & ROW, PUBLISHERS, INCORPORATED